The Norman Conquest of
Southern Italy and Sicily

The Norman Conquest of Southern Italy and Sicily

GORDON S. BROWN

McFarland & Company, Inc., Publishers
Jefferson, North Carolina, and London

Library of Congress Cataloguing-in-Publication Data

Brown, Gordon S., 1936–
    The Norman conquest of Southern Italy and Sicily / Gordon S.
Brown.
      p.   cm.
    Includes bibliographical references and index.

    ISBN-13: 978-0-7864-1472-7
    softcover : 50# alkaline paper ∞

    1. Italy, Southern — History — 535–1268. 2. Sicily (Italy) —
History — 1016–1194. 3. Normans — Italy, Southern — History —
To 1500. 4. Normans — Italy — Sicily — History — To 1500.
I. Title.
DG867.2.B76   2003
945'.703 — dc21   2002153822

British Library cataloguing data are available

On the cover: Foreground: Robert Guiscard and Pope Gregory VII during the siege of Rome *(Art Today)*. Background map: ©2002 Art Today

Manufactured in the United States of America

*McFarland & Company, Inc., Publishers
  Box 611, Jefferson, North Carolina 28640
  www.mcfarlandpub.com*

To Olivia

Table of Contents

Preface   1

Introduction   3

    I. Civitate   7

    II. The Adventurers   16

    III. Tancred of Hauteville   24

    IV. Mercenaries for the Basileus   33

    V. Rebels   40

    VI. Warlords in Apulia   49

    VII. Count of Apulia   56

    VIII. The Pope's Wrath   65

    IX. Consolidation   76

    X. Guiscard   85

    XI. Calabria   95

    XII. Sicily   103

    XIII. Cerami   114

    XIV. Rebellion   122

    XV. Victory   129

    XVI. The Duke and the Pope   139

    XVII. Salerno   149

    XVIII. Carrying War to the Enemy   159

    XIX. The Pope's Savior   168

XX. Terror of the World   174
XXI. The Quest for Glory   184
XXII. The End of the Beginning   191

Chronology   201
Genealogical Table — Sons and Grandsons of Tancred
    of Hauteville   205
Bibliography   207
Index   211

Preface

The story of the Normans in Southern Italy and Sicily is much better known in Europe than in the United States. Most American readers have at least some familiarity with one Norman conquest, namely that by William of Normandy, who invaded England in 1066 to assert his claim to the throne. But the same readers are often surprised to learn that other Normans were successfully engaged in Italy, even before William's great enterprise, in wresting a kingdom of their own from the Byzantine Empire, the local princes, and the Arab rulers of Sicily.

Yet this other conquest by the warrior knights from Normandy, descendants of the Vikings, had great importance in its time, and even long afterwards. No more at the beginning than a disorganized movement by young, ambitious, and land hungry knights, it turned into a historical creation. The southern Italian state founded by the Norman knights soon became one of the richest, most cosmopolitan and most powerful states of the late medieval period, one which contributed greatly to the opening up of the Mediterranean and the crusading movement. In the great struggle between pope and emperor of the period, Norman power and wealth at first offered the reforming popes their most muscular support, but later provided emperors with the wealth to confront the papacy. Even though the Normans ruled as kings for only a hundred years, the state they had founded lasted for another six hundred and fifty, unfortunately growing weaker and more backward with time.

This book is not an effort to tell the whole story of the Normans in Italy. It attempts, instead, to follow the main threads of the early period: how these interlopers from northern Europe managed to find their historical role in the Italian provinces of the Byzantine Empire, how they succeeded in replacing the Byzantine and local rulers, and then how they drove the Arab rulers out of Sicily. In focusing on the protracted period of the conquest, that is, the second half of the eleventh century, this book sets out in particular an account of the achievements of that remarkable set of brothers, the sons of Tancred of Hauteville, who spearheaded the effort.

The story of the Normans' historical role in the south came alive for me as I discovered lingering traces of their presence in a variety of Mediterranean countries that I had the pleasure to live in or visit during an earlier career. In trying to bring that story alive to an American audience, I have drawn on my previous diplomatic experience to try to explain the political acts of the eleventh century protagonists in ways that make sense to a modern reader. While this approach has undoubtedly shortchanged the elements of faith and superstition that were such an important part of medieval thought and action, I would contend that the Normans were, above all, a practical and pragmatic people driven by a kind of self-interest that is fully understandable in today's times.

I can claim no major research breakthroughs in this presentation. The all but definitive research and analysis performed many years ago by the noted French scholars Chalandon and Gay has served as the basis of my analysis—as indeed it has for modern scholars much more deeply grounded in the period than I. I am indebted to their work, as I am to the more contemporary books of Lord Norwich, whose witty and colorful rendition of Norman and Byzantine history cannot but influence other writers—*vide* the use of the phrase "this other conquest" above. I can only regret that the meticulous scholarship of G.A. Loud's book was available in print only after I had finished most of the research for this work. Finally, I am grateful to Professors Barbara Kreutz and Joanna Drell for encouraging me, an outsider to the medievalist profession, to try my hand at making this fascinating history more accessible.

Introduction

They did not, at first, intend to conquer. The young Norman knights who went south to Italy in the first half of the eleventh century did so simply to earn a living, to find adventure, or even to escape the confines of their own society and justice. Daring, ambitious, and hardy, those young men embodied the nascent energy of a northern Europe that was poised for growth and progress. Over the coming centuries, that energy would bring about great economic and commercial expansion, inspire a great surge of cathedral building, spawn the *reconquista* in Spain and the Crusades, and lead to the flowering of the high medieval period.

Those Norman adventurers found in southern Italy not only possibilities for employment, but opportunities for maneuver and personal advancement. The region, even more than usual for Europe at the time, lacked strong central authority, harbored competition between the major powers, and was the scene of continual conflict among the minor local states. It was a situation full of possibilities for observant and opportunistic adventurers.

The Norman knights, trained in warfare and accustomed to interpreting the law imaginatively to their own ends, were ready to take advantage. In Italy, they soon learned that they might do better than simply make their living. The lucky ones might well earn, or steal (the two were often synonymous), that greatest prize: a fiefdom for themselves. The military prowess of these knights, their audacity, persistence and lack of scruples fueled their initial successes. A few leaders soon became significant actors in the local military balance. Soon, constantly reinforced by new recruits from their homeland, they began to be brokers of power as well. They had become a permanent part of the political and military landscape of the region, but their efforts remained individual and uncoordinated.

Gradually, the Normans gained their own lands and vigorously, even ruthlessly, expanded their power. Inevitably, they also increased the number of their enemies and the threats against them. Their own political leadership evolved in response, and eventually coalesced around two poles: a group at Aversa, north of Naples, and a group centered at Melfi, in northern Apulia. Just before mid-century, two remarkable young leaders came to Italy, where their family connections eventually allowed them to become leaders of the two groups: Richard Dregnot at Aversa, and Robert Guiscard in Apulia. Robert was one of the many sons of Tancred of Hauteville, and his brothers had already opened the way for him by their election as counts of Apulia. He and Richard would lead the Normans into a new phase in their occupation of the area.

Eventually, conquest became an option. Unlike the Norman conquest of England, deliberately planned by the Duke of Normandy with the resources of his state behind him, the Norman conquest of southern Italy grew out of incremental opportunities. Robert and Richard may have had the vision, but they had to wait for the opportune moments, the mistakes of their opponents, or the weaknesses of their enemies to make the vision a reality. They both had ambition in surplus, but it was Robert, at first launched by his elder brothers and then assisted by his younger ones, who wound up more powerful.

With increased power came a greatly enlarged role in the politics, not just of the immediate region, but Europe. The lawless freebooters of the early days gradually were obliged to become adept at statecraft, and in so doing they changed their role in history. The adventurers matured; they laid the foundations of a great and prosperous state, and established a lasting and historically significant alliance with the papacy.

The disorganized plunder of the early years was gradually surpassed by a planned program of expansion, led by the sons of Tancred. Robert Guiscard's often conflictual partnership with his youngest brother Roger provided the leadership as well as the necessary force. Eventually, they subdued the previous occupiers, Byzantines and Muslims, as well as their own fractious fellow Normans. The Byzantine empire, heir to Rome, was driven out of its lands in Italy, while the Arabs who had occupied Sicily for over two centuries were expelled soon afterwards. The sons of Tancred had founded a state that, with changes of dynasties, would last over seven hundred years.

The life of these amazing military adventurers has come down to us through contemporary records and, most importantly, the vivid accounts of the chroniclers. Key research done by French scholars in the early years of the last century has gone a long way to reconcile the differing versions of events put forth in the chronicles, and the broad outlines and even most specifics of the story are by now unmistakable. But a key gap remains:

what we have is largely stereotyped images of the major actors, who emerge from the chronicles as either paragons of virtue or objects of hatred. The often intriguing female protagonists, alas, get even more incomplete treatment. Reconstruction of personalities, motivations, and interactions can only be informed guesswork. We will always want to know more.

These men and women shaped the history of their times, and left a lasting imprint on the future. But they themselves could afford no such long view of their achievements. Their progress was piecemeal and their frustrations continuous, yet in the end their success was enduring. That they succeeded was due to audacity, luck, and great personal qualities, demonstrating once again that exceptional individuals can change the course of history.

Civitate

The pope's army was destroyed, the terrible Normans victorious. The devastating charge of Richard of Aversa's Norman knights had routed the pope's Italian foot soldiers. They had fled ignominiously, that morning's boasts about their numerical superiority and holy cause forgotten in the rout. Even the seemingly invincible German swordsmen had been slaughtered to the last man by Norman horsemen led by Humphrey and Robert, two sons of Tancred of Hauteville. The field of battle theirs, moreover, the Normans had pressed their advantage relentlessly. Pillaging and burning the outbuildings, they had brought their troops up to the very walls of the town from which the pope had watched the battle.

The pope was left with neither army nor allies. The town elders, not wanting to suffer a crippling attack in defense of a lord who was theirs only in his spiritual capacity, pleaded with him to depart and leave them in peace. He had little choice. Reluctantly, he recognized that he would have to put himself in the hands of the very Normans whom he had determined to bring to heel.

For four years since his elevation to the papacy, Pope Leo had tried to bring the unruly and avaricious Normans under control, to stop their depredations and exactions against the population, and particularly against the properties of the Church. He had tried at first to reason and treat with them. But, he had found, the promises made by the nominal Norman leaders were of little use; they couldn't in truth control the many independent knight-freebooters who terrorized the region. The complaints against Norman acts of plunder, exaction, rape and murder flowing to Rome had, in fact, only increased.

The pope's frustration was immense. His priority upon ascending reluctantly to the papacy had been to reform the Church, beset as it was by so many weaknesses. Yet he had been obliged to spend too much of his time in office dealing with problems created in southern Italy by the Normans. He had, perhaps unwisely, even compounded his problems by agreeing to be lord and protector of Benevento, one of the areas most directly harassed by those troublesome knights. Having added this new secular obligation to his existing spiritual duty to defend the rights of the Church, Pope Leo's indignation and frustration over the Normans' behavior had grown still greater. He had some time previously concluded that the Normans would not change their expansionist ways as a result of peaceful persuasion. He needed to subdue them. First, he had tried to form a coalition of local and regional rulers against them, only to see it fall apart when the Normans' few but important local allies stood firmly at their side.

Pope Leo, still, was a determined man. Unexpectedly, he had been given a new opportunity. The Norman leader was assassinated in an uprising of his resentful and rebellious new subjects, and shortly afterwards a similar fate befell the Normans' chief regional ally, who was struck down by his own fractious family. Then the Byzantine emperor in Constantinople had offered to send an army to help crush their common Norman enemy. The pope had jumped at the chance. He had personally led his army into battle. Perhaps, in retrospect, he had been too rash, too confident.

Certainly, nothing had worked out. The Normans had quickly elected a new leader and rallied their forces, while the Byzantine army had shown little backbone and had allowed itself to be outmaneuvered. Now, the army that the pope had brought to battle had been humiliated by Norman determination and valor. The pope would have to swallow his anger, even his desire for revenge, and submit — or at least make pretence of submission. Resignedly, he prepared to leave the protection of the town walls and put himself into the hands of those he had made his enemies.

Pope Leo and his retinue emerged from the town gate, resplendent in their best robes, displaying the full panoply of his high office, but ready for their dose of humility. They were not, however, met by a spiteful and triumphant army. The Normans, showing for once the softer side of a nature that combined ruthlessness and piety, received Leo as their spiritual lord, not as the defeated leader of a punitive expedition. The very knights who had been cursed by the pope just yesterday as little better than infidels, who had been taunted by his (now dead) German allies as puny and insignificant warriors, and who had in effect been given an ultimatum of expulsion or death, now submitted themselves to the man whom they had just defeated. The blood-stained Normans even prostrated themselves before the pope, vowed their loyalty to the Church, and begged his pardon for their sins.

This astonishing submission — even if much of it was feigned —could not of course hide the facts of the situation, which remained embarrassingly clear. The pope, defeated even if honored by the victors, had become a virtual prisoner of the Normans. They would escort him in honor to his own city of Benevento— but they would not ease up their pressure until he met their terms.

This dramatic scene of victory and statesmanship took place in June of 1053, on the road outside a small town in southern Italy called Civitate. The medieval town, which no longer exists, lay within sight of the River Fortore and near the modern town of San Severo, in the north of the province of Apulia. The pope was Leo IX, the first of those great reform popes of the eleventh century who would bring the Church to the pinnacle of its power. His opponents, the Normans, had established themselves in southern Italy only relatively recently, but had, within the previous ten years, begun to expand their landholdings so dramatically as to present a real threat to the existing order in the area. What was at stake in this struggle between the papacy and the Normans was not just the present behavior and misdeeds of these land-hungry knights, but the future of the entire region and the awkward balance of power which existed there.

Southern Italy and Sicily at the time presented a rich but jumbled mosaic of political entities and cultures. Successive waves of conquerors and settlers— Greeks, Romans, Lombards, Byzantines, Arabs— had, over the centuries, added their blood, their customs, laws, and religions to the mix. The diversity was political as well, with the result that the region was indifferently governed. The claimants to ancient Rome's authority vied for position and dominance, but neither the Basileus (who still used the title Emperor of the Romans, but ruled over the Byzantine state from Constantinople), nor the self-styled Roman emperors, the heirs of Charlemagne, exercised continuous or consistent control over those lands they claimed. Their power in this, to them, peripherally important area was generally delegated to local officials or vassal princes, who took advantage of the situation to squabble endlessly amongst themselves. The popes, in Rome, had a greater degree of interest in the stability of the region because of their position as neighbors, but exercised little authority unless they could enlist the force of their allies, the Holy Roman emperors.[1]

Only Sicily, early in the eleventh century, enjoyed a degree of political unity under its Muslim rulers. In southern Italy, real central authority had died out with the Roman Empire many centuries earlier. Borders were not fixed and fringe areas changed hands frequently; the rulers often controlling little beyond the areas around the major towns, and exerting their rights in the often mountainous hinterland largely through periodic tax gathering. In this situation, local governors, landholders, or nobles had succeeded in carving out a goodly measure of autonomy, even as communal movements were nurturing a spirit of independence in the major towns.

The political reality was the mosaic, but a shifting and unstable one. Three rival Lombard principalities, the remnants of a Germanic Lombard kingdom that had had its heyday in the eighth century, ruled in the rich farming area around Naples now known as the Campania. Those states —Benevento, Capua, and Salerno— acknowledged allegiance, as circumstances made convenient, to emperor, pope, or Basileus. Three other entities, the rich trading city-states of Naples, Amalfi, and Gaeta, acknowledged ties to Constantinople but acted with virtual independence. Sicily had been lost to the Arabs over two centuries earlier. In the remainder of southern Italy — essentially the modern provinces of Apulia, Basilicata, and Calabria — the major political power was Byzantium, which possessed the territory as a direct legacy from the old Roman Empire, but ruled it indifferently.

In the early eleventh century, Byzantium was ascendant in the region. Under the strong leadership of the Macedonian dynasty and particularly Emperor Basil the Bulgar Slayer, Constantinople had reestablished its authority in Italy, driven out the remaining Lombard and Arab forces, established new garrison colonies, and seemed poised to dominate the region. Unfortunately, Basil's death in 1025 ushered in a period of weak and rapidly changing rulers, under which the empire's hold gradually collapsed.[2] Over the next decades, periodic efforts were made to reassert Byzantine power in Italy, most notably in an effort to regain the long-lost territory of Sicily. But, by mid-century, imperial attention increasingly was directed toward its own appallingly degenerate internal political struggles, as well as toward a crucial strategic threat in the east, posed by invading Pechnegs and Turks. Left increasingly to their own resources, Byzantine administrators in southern Italy had neither the power nor the autonomy — being constantly second-guessed by Constantinople and at the mercy of court intrigue — to maintain the steady dominion that would fend off either internal or external challenges. There would be both.

Against Byzantium's claims and actual possession of southern Italy, the Holy Roman emperor and his spiritual ally the pope advanced their own separate claims. Emperor and pope, locked in an uncomfortable relationship as the temporal and spiritual guardians, respectively, of the west, had overlapping claims. The popes, by virtue of an eighth century docu-

SOUTHERN ITALY in 1025
Approximate Political Boundaries

KINGDOM OF ITALY
(HOLY ROMAN EMPIRE)

Rome

ADRIATIC SEA

ILLYRIA

LANGOBARDIA

Gaeta Capua
Benevento   Bari   Durazzo

BYZANTINE EMPIRE

Naples
Amalfi Salerno   (APULIA)

CALABRIA

IONIAN
SEA

TYRRHENIAN SEA

Palermo

Legend:

Lombard Principalities

City-states allied with Byzantium

Papal Patrimony

Muslim Sicily

ment called the Donation of Constantine — known now to have been a forgery, but generally accepted at the time — claimed overlordship of southern Italy and the Mediterranean islands for the papacy. The emperors, on the other hand, asserted rights over southern Italy as a legacy from Charlemagne, who had conquered the Lombard Kingdom of Italy and acquired its claims to rule the entire southern part of the peninsula.

The claims of pope and emperor were not necessarily mutually exclusive, and like much else in their very complicated relationship, were subject to interpretation and compromise as well as to their mutual dependence. That dependence was real: the popes needed the power of the emperors to give authority to papal decrees, for a pope's temporal power was virtually nonexistent outside of Rome and a limited band of land in the center of Italy that he controlled as a lay ruler. Equally, every emperor needed to make himself acceptable to the current pope, because without a papal coronation as emperor, he was no more than the elected king of Germany and of Italy. This mutual dependence led to an uneasy cooperation, but by no means to harmony. Pope and emperor had different requirements, and often very different political constituencies. When a pope was selected by the Germans (as Leo had been), any differences were generally manageable, but when the powerful Roman aristocratic families or other groups succeeded in having their own candidate chosen bishop of Rome and pope, conflicts could and often did arise. The papacy, moreover, had become spectacularly corrupt in the first half of the eleventh century. The office had degenerated into a political prize, with rival Roman families fighting each other to obtain the benefit; sale of Church offices was widespread, vows of clerical celibacy not enforced.

Nonetheless, as far as overall strategy toward southern Italy and Sicily went, pope and emperor were generally in agreement. Both wanted to see the Arabs driven out of previously Christian lands, and to reduce the power and influence of the rival Byzantine empire. Each, however, saw his own institution as the lead instrument by which to achieve those common aspirations. Their rivalry, with each other and with the Basileus, allowed the small states of the region to play them off against each other in seemingly endless rounds of intrigue and petty warfare.

In this kaleidoscope of strategic conflicts and tactical opportunities, the recently arrived Normans had become the unpredictable new factor. Their decade-long campaign of expansion and plunder in Apulia had not only made them feared, it had upset the fragile status quo in ways which the major regional actors chose, each in his own way, to deflect or turn to their own advantage. Pope Leo had tried to crush them, and had failed. After his defeat in battle at Civitate, the question for him became what to do next.

For the Normans, united in victory if not generally in action, the question was how to turn their astounding victory to their long-term advantage.

Pope Leo would have a goodly amount of time to ponder his choices. Even though the Normans, after their victory at Civitate, accompanied him in honor to Benevento and allowed him freedom in his city, they were camped around the gates. Their glowering presence there made it quite clear that, however free the pope might be in his chambers, he would not be at liberty until he gave them satisfaction. The contemporary chroniclers tell us virtually nothing of the negotiations that must have taken place between the two parties, but the fact that they lasted for nine months before Leo was allowed to continue his journey indicates that they were certainly protracted, if not necessarily intense.

In captivity, the pope continued to conduct the Holy See's business without apparent interference. He made it clear by his actions, however, that he had in no way dropped his hostility to his captors or to their aspirations. Nor, after the promises of good behavior which he had wrung from the Normans two years earlier had been so openly flouted, did he have any reason to trust their word with respect to the future. He tried to buy time, to seek another opportunity to deal with his infuriating opponents.

All the same, the pope's political options were limited, his supporters few. It appears that there was subtle but pointed criticism from his own supporters about his role in the recent debacle; hints were made that he had overstepped his role as leader of the Church by captaining a punitive army for worldly purposes. His relative and main supporter, Emperor Henry III, was preoccupied with other matters closer to home in Germany, where he had just put down a rebellion of the Saxons and Bavarians and was dealing with a breakaway Hungary. The emperor's only contribution to the papal army had been the contingent of Swabian swordsmen (now embarrassingly slaughtered), and his current difficulties made it unlikely that he would provide any new aid.

The Byzantines, too, had proven uncertain allies. They had been better at stirring up an anti–Norman uprising in Apulia the year before than they had been as military allies when actually needed. Some in the papal party thought, in fact, that the Greeks had played a treacherous game. Be that as it may, Byzantine cooperation would still be essential to any effective anti–Norman strategy: not only was it their territory in Apulia that the Normans had been arrogating to themselves, but they were the only local power that could raise enough troops to oppose the Normans. So Leo tried to renew his alliance with Byzantium, this time by sending a high-ranking delegation directly to Constantinople to negotiate with the Basileus. Unfortunately, whatever hopes he had for that negotiation soon paled, as both his own negotiators and those of the Basileus proved to be remarkably inept — the latter allowing themselves to be completely outmaneuvered by the anti-Roman party in the Byzantine capital. The denouement of those negotiations, however, came in July, months after the pope's release from his virtual captivity.

The constant pressure of the Normans outside the walls eventually had had its effect, and in March Leo agreed to terms that would permit his departure. Agreement finally having been reached, the Normans, headed by Humphrey Hauteville, accompanied Pope Leo and his party in state to Capua.

The terms of the pope's release were not made known, and appear to have been ambiguous. Papal historians of the time described the act as a victory for Leo: he had secured the submission of the Normans, they claimed. That may have been true after a fashion; the Normans did indeed submit to the pope in matters spiritual, and as his vassals for the Italian lands that they had recently conquered. But the cold fact was that the Normans had gotten the most they could reasonably expect. Instead of being outlaws, holding uncertain title to their recent acquisitions, reviled by the Church and the target of a concerted effort aimed at their elimination, the Normans had now been invested in their conquests by the head of the Church himself. In return, they had made certain –also unpublished— promises of good behavior and loyalty to the Church.

Ever realistic and opportunistic, the Normans had reason to be satisfied. They were now recognized as major players in the future of the region that they had decided to settle, and had achieved a major step up the ladder to legitimate control of the territories they had seized. As to their promises, well, they would see what the limits to their action were by testing them.

The Normans' satisfaction was bitter to Leo. Their earlier successes in grasping and extending their territory had, after all, motivated his drive to crush them. Perversely, his campaign had only resulted in giving the upstarts a greater success, and greater legitimacy to boot.

The pope would not have time to ponder his revenge, for he fell ill in Capua and died shortly thereafter, in April 1054, in Rome. He left the prospect of retribution against these unwelcome and dangerous Norman invaders of southern Italy to his eventual successors in the chair of Saint Peter.

Notes

1. The term Holy Roman Empire did not actually gain usage until subsequent centuries, but will be used here to distinguish the western emperor (who was also king of the Germans and king of the Italians) from the eastern emperor, or Basileus.

2. Basil's name survives in southern Italy, since the province of Basilicata, created in recent times, was named after him. (The area of the new province is also known by its ancient name of Lucania.) In Byzantine times, its territory was split administratively between Apulia — then called Langobardia in recognition of the Lombard nature of much of its population — and Calabria.

The *Adventurers*

W ho, then, were these Normans whose successes and excesses had so angered Pope Leo that he had personally gone to war against them? What, moreover, were they doing in southern Italy, and why had they become such thorns in the sides of the imperial and papal powers there? How had they gained such a position in this new land, and could they continue to expand their lands and power?

The Normans, the men of the North, were a relatively new and still expanding presence in eleventh century Europe. Their forefathers had cut and thrust their way into the area less than two centuries earlier as part of the great Viking expansion. Dreaded and effective both as raiders and settlers, the Vikings had ravaged the coasts and penetrated up the rivers of present day Great Britain, Ireland, France, the Low Countries, and even Russia — wherever they and their versatile longboats could reach from their homelands in the Scandinavian peninsula. In France, a band of Vikings under the exiled Norwegian chieftain Hrolf had wrested control of the lower Seine River valley from the resident West Franks so effectively that the Frankish king, Charles the Simple, was obliged in 911 to grant them a small fiefdom. That fertile land formed the nucleus of what later became the Norman Duchy of Normandy, and there the Vikings soon enough settled down, began to intermarry, lose their Viking ways, and assimilate. When Hrolf died twenty year later, his funeral rites exemplified the state of the assimilation as of that date: as a convert, Rollo (his Christian name) provided substantial gifts to monasteries, and was buried with Christian ceremonies. But, just to be on the safe side with respect to his pagan Viking roots, a hundred captives were also sacrificed in his honor!

The pagan ways did not last long. Within two generations, the ex–Vikings had converted to Christianity and absorbed much of the language and culture, as well as the feudal political and military organization, of their Frank neighbors. The Norman region evolved rapidly into a prosperous and well-governed state, under powerful dukes who could keep law and justice among their energetic, ambitious, and often turbulent subjects. The Normans had, perhaps surprisingly, readily adopted two pillars of the local civilization: the law, and the Christian faith, and although they could be accused of using both for their own purposes when it suited them, they professed a pragmatic devotion to both.

What did remain of the old Viking character was a good measure of that thirst for adventure or battle, a search for glory mixed with fatalism, and that readiness to travel and take chances that had propelled the Normans' forefathers across the hemisphere. Those traits, added to their valor, talent for political organization, and group cohesiveness in times of need, would fuel the great Norman successes of the eleventh and twelfth centuries.

The adoption of Frankish feudalism gave the Normans a much more structured political system than their Viking forefathers had experienced, and one that they eventually took with them into southern Italy. At a time when central government was weak and landed estates were the principal source of wealth for the ruling class, the feudal system provided an effective way to tie the responsibilities of governance directly to landholding. A noble could only hold land (and, consequently, wealth) legally through a fief granted by his superior lord in the feudal hierarchy. In return, he became that lord's vassal, and pledged to him both loyalty and military service. In Normandy, the ruling duke granted major fiefdoms or holdings to his counts, who in turn granted estates within their counties to their barons, and each member of that hierarchy in turn owed loyalty and specified military obligations to his lord. In practice, of course, the chain of mutual responsibilities was much more complicated. As land and its obligations could also be obtained (through inheritance, marriage, purchase, or seizure) in differing counties— or even duchies or kingdoms— the result was often, for a knight with multiple properties, a complex skein of responsibilities and potential loyalties rather than a simple hierarchy. In Normandy as elsewhere, disputes about landholding were both common, and inseparable from questions of loyalty and obligation.

Land, as the principal source of wealth, was inevitably the main source of social promotion, and hence competition, among the secular aristocracy in Europe. Normandy was no exception. In fact, because of its small size and growing population, eleventh century Normandy was rife with competition for land. And, not unexpectedly in view of the fact that the major part of the lay aristocracy at that time constituted a professional military class, many of those disputes were resolved by force.

Warfare, in the eleventh century, was the normal business of this armed, ruling aristocracy. Small-scale warfare for private purposes was endemic, as normal to the knights as peace; it was indeed their occupation. Since the feudal system provided each landholder with some of the attributes of sovereignty in his own territory, he was to a large degree free to compete militarily with his peers—to extend his landholdings, pursue a family feud, or simply to enrich himself by plundering his neighbor's lands, or by seizing and ransoming unwary merchants or other travelers. This warfare involved few battles, but was rather a process of raids, sieges, and pillage in which the main victims were often the poor peasants whose crops were despoiled. While the Church tried to limit the damages of this constant state of war by instituting a truce of God, which enjoined war against Church properties, women, or the poor, it had little capability to force the knights to respect such a truce. In Normandy, the powerful dukes had more authority to limit the private, proprietal warfare of their barons, but were still not able to end it. Nor perhaps did they entirely wish to; after all, the competition assured that the most able barons would keep the warrior traditions of the duchy fresh, and moreover the requirement that the most recent winners be confirmed in their new landholdings gave the dukes grounds to demand periodic oaths of fealty and submission.

To be a landholder or an aspiring landholder, then, was to be a knight, since only the Church could hold lands without the attendant military obligations. And to be a knight was to be a warrior, trained in arms and in the uses of power. A Norman knight was trained from childhood in horsemanship, hunting and outdoor survival skills, and learned at least a smattering of literacy, etiquette and the practical skills of command. At adolescence, his long and arduous military training began: still more horsemanship, physical conditioning, and the use of arms. By the time he reached manhood, a young Norman knight was strong enough to wear over 50 pounds of armor for extended periods, adept at controlling his warhorse, or destrier, in a charge or a melee, proficient in protecting himself with his kite-shaped shield, and effective in the use of his lance, sword and dagger. Individually excellent fighters, with much of the courage and hardiness of their Viking ancestors, the Norman horsemen had also learned to train and fight in group formations, and the cavalry charge had become their prime offensive weapon.

The Norman knight's armament was not markedly different from that of the other fighters they would meet, but it was particularly well-adapted to their preferred cavalry tactics. The helmet was conical in shape, and over time added a long nose guard designed to deflect blows. The straight sword was descended from the Viking great-sword, but less than three feet long for effective use on horseback. The Norman chain mail shirt, or hauberk, was generally longer than that of other soldiers of the time; it could protect the knight's legs while he was in the saddle, while his shield with its long tail also served the same purpose. The saddle was deep and equipped with long stirrups, giving the knight an exceptionally firm seat in battle. Thus equipped and trained, the Norman knights became renowned fighters. In addition, during their days in southern Italy they mastered a technique that made their charges virtually irresistible. This technique, which they probably adapted from a little used Byzantine practice, consisted in charging with their lances held in a couched position, that is, secured between the arm and the body. This allowed them effectively to add the horse's weight and momentum to the force of the blow, and made a rapid and focused cavalry charge their weapon of choice to turn the tide of battles.

A knight's equipment was expensive. A set of armor, a destrier for battle and one or several palfreys for travel, plus the other kit for a life in the field, could cost as much as a small farm and represented a major investment by a young knight's family in his future. In peacetime, that investment was wasted unless the knight could find rare employment in a lord's retinue. No wonder that warfare was attractive, as it provided possibilities for employment, booty, ransom of captured knights, or even seizure of land. Of course, going to war had its costs, too; a knight was responsible for the squires, other attendants, or infantry who accompanied him on campaign. Often, in addition, an experienced knight would have in his troop, and be responsible for, a number of other knights as well as sergeants (trained fighters who could not afford a horse, but aspired to knighthood in a warrior class that at the time provided reasonable social mobility). The costs of such a retinue also had to be borne. Warfare, in the circumstances, was the principal avenue for advancement available to the Norman knight, the means through which he could earn a return on his investment, profit through a share of any spoils, or even gain land or honor — the latter two often being synonymous.

These, then, were the men who traveled to southern Italy, and who would in time upset the balance of power there. An energetic and warlike people, they seemed to have excess energy to burn, and ambition to expand. The chroniclers of the time, whether friendly or hostile, are all but unanimous in characterizing the Normans as bold, desirous for domination and riches, and cunning. None of these were attributes that had unfavorable connotations at the time. Indeed, the description of a friendly chronicler — in terms which seem somewhat unflattering to our modern sensibilities — was intended as praise[1]:

> They are a shrewd people indeed, quick to avenge injury, scorn-
> ing the fields of their homeland in hopes of acquiring something more,
> avid for profit and domination, ready to feign or conceal anything,
> achieving a certain balance between largess and avarice.... Unless
> checked by the yoke of justice, they can be most unrestrained. They
> are ready to endure great effort, hunger and cold when fortune
> requires it. They devote themselves to hunting and falconry. They
> delight in luxury when it comes to horses and to the rest of the tools
> and costumes of war.

Another contemporary, a Lombard friendly to the Normans, was still more frank. The Normans, he said, were "avid for rapine and insatiably anxious to seize the property of others."[2]

To see why and how these Normans got to Italy, it will be useful to look at the reasons for their leaving Normandy in the first place, and the specific events that drew them to the south.

Normandy in the early eleventh century, according to most calcula-tions, was beginning to suffer from overpopulation — particularly among the aristocracy, which had grown in over a century of relative peace. Since inheritance by primogeniture was not yet the custom, existing fiefs or landholdings had become smaller and increasingly fractured as the num-ber of young knights seeking land increased. Few new fiefdoms were avail-able; Norman territorial expansion had for some time been blocked by the duchy's powerful neighbors in Anjou, France, and Brittany. As a result, opportunities in Normandy for young knights were increasingly limited, the competition for advancement difficult. At the same time, the strong rule of successive dukes kept lawbreakers and would-be predatory knights in check; troublemakers were regularly exiled and their goods confiscated, forcing them to find something to do abroad. Even the period of instabil-ity during the minority of Duke William the Bastard (later to be known as the Conqueror) had the ironic result of creating more Norman exiles, for once William had succeeded in defeating the rebellion of his vassals in 1047, the resultant redistribution of fiefdoms left many knightly families seeking to recover their fortunes abroad.

Because of the lack of opportunity in Normandy, many footloose, land-hungry or exiled knights chose to find their living outside of the duchy as mercenaries. The possibilities for such employment in southern Italy were beginning to be understood as the century opened. Other knights chose to go on pilgrimage, which had the double advantage of being encouraged by the Church and a kind of adventure travel. Three pil-grimage destinations in particular drew such travelers from France to southern Italy. The first was the pilgrimage to Rome, an almost routine trip for spirited men in the expanding world of the early eleventh century. The second pilgrimage route was to a more ambitious destination, the Holy Land. One of the most traveled routes, using the remains of the great Roman roads, passed along the east coast of southern Italy to Bari, in Byzantine territory, where the pilgrims embarked for the trip through what is now Albania, to the great capital of the Christian east, Constantinople, and then on to the Muslim Levant. That route also made possible a stop at a place which was a pilgrimage destination of particular interest to Normans— the shrine of their militant patron, Saint Michael, at Monte Sant'-Angelo on the Gargano peninsula — the spur on the boot of southern Italy's shape.

The shrine at Monte Sant'Angelo provided the connection that resulted in bringing the Normans to southern Italy in substantial numbers. The grotto-shrine had been visited by pilgrims since the day, in the late fifth century, when Saint Michael was said to have miraculously appeared there. (The site, indeed, was venerated even in antiquity, and the shrine to Saint Michael had been built over an earlier pagan shrine.) For the Normans, this shrine to their warlike patron saint had a particular significance. A part of the saint's cloak, which the legends said he had left behind in Gargano, had been spirited off by a French monk in the ninth century, where it provided the impetus for building the great abbey of Mont Saint Michel on the border of Normandy.

According to the chronicles, a group of Norman pilgrims who were visiting the shrine in the early years of the eleventh century were approached by a man, dressed in Byzantine fashion, who requested their help.[3] He explained that he was Melo, a Lombard from the province of Apulia, and that he represented a rebel movement among the citizens of that Byzantine-ruled province (which the Byzantines called Langobardia). The mostly Lombard population of the province were resentful, he told them, over the recently reimposed Byzantine central rule and the resultant heavy taxation. The province, he said, was ready for rebellion, but the leaders needed outside help after having failed in a previous attempt several years earlier. Melo appealed to the Normans to come back to help renew the rebellion, and to bring more warriors like themselves. What he promised them in return is not that clear, but it must have been more than enough to excite their enthusiasm. The Normans, it would appear, needed little persuasion to seize this opportunity for gain, fame, or just plain adventure, that even came with a conveniently worthy objective — helping free a Latin community from its Orthodox oppressors. In any event, their recruitment drive, supported by the nearby Prince of Salerno and other Lombard princes (who were anxious to create trouble for their

Byzantine neighbors as much as to help their Lombard brethren), was successful. Within a year's time, in 1017, Melo had obtained enough outside help to begin his rebellion. His Lombard bands and the new arrivals from the north joined forces in Capua, and fell upon the surprised Byzantine military garrisons in Apulia.

The revolt against Byzantine rule, given surprise and the additional power provided by the several hundred Norman and other adventurer knights, was at first successful. The rebels won several preliminary battles, while the cities along the Apulian coast sought to throw off rule from Constantinople and reestablish their autonomy. Unfortunately for the rebels and their aspirations, however, Byzantium was still too strong; it had more resources and no lack of will. In the summer of 1018, the newly assigned Byzantine military governor (or *katapan*) of Langobardia, Basil Bojoannes, moved to crush the rebellion at the head of a powerful imperial army incorporating elements of the famed Varangian and Bucellarion guards. The two armies met the following year at the historic battlefield of Cannae in northern Apulia — the site at which Hannibal, badly outnumbered, had crushed an army of the Roman republic over twelve hundred years previously. But this time the more numerous imperial troops roundly defeated their opponents, and the rebel army, including its Norman mercenaries, suffered heavy losses.

The Lombard rebellion was over, along with any hopes the Norman recruits may have had of winning quick fortunes. Melo himself went off to northern Europe to try to seek help from the western emperor for a new effort to wrest control of the region from the Byzantines. He died on the trip but left a son, called Argyros, about whom we will hear again.

The victorious Katapan Bojoannes ruled competently and wisely until 1027 — a long period in the rapidly churning world of the Byzantine bureaucracy — during which period the Lombard princes trimmed their sails to the eastern empire's dominance in the region, and there was no more talk of revolt. To the contrary, the Byzantines were ready to go on the offensive; they took punitive action against some of the rebels, and were preparing a major expedition to solidify their new dominance of southern Italy, even to invade Arab Sicily, when Basil, the last great emperor whom Constantinople would see for sixty years, died. The expedition died with him, even though the high tide of Byzantine predominance in southern Italy persisted for well over a decade.

In Apulia, Bojoannes had consolidated his position. He had the vision to see that his recent foes, the Normans, could be put to good use. On a strategic hill near the border of Lombard Benevento, the site of ancient Aecae, he had built a fortress town called Troia, and now he garrisoned it substantially with hired Norman knights whose job would be to guard the border. The first foe against whom they would have to defend the fortress was no less than the Holy Roman Emperor Henry II, come to southern Italy in 1022 in a show of force to reassert imperial and papal claims in the face of the Byzantine resurgence. The Normans and their colleagues in arms prevailed, withstanding a three month siege by the emperor's army and holding the border secure for the very Byzantine *katapan* who had defeated them at Cannae just four years before. Not for the last time, Norman knights had found that self-interest allowed them to change their military alliances to meet new demands, or satisfy new paymasters.

Notes

1. Malaterra I, C.3, p.8, as cited in Wolf, p. 149. The principal contemporary sources for details of the history of the Normans in southern Italy are friendly chroniclers, who wrote shortly after the events they described, and had the victorious Normans as their sponsors. The Normans of Italy were conscious that history is most often written by the winners, and were careful to see that their exploits were entered favorably into the record. Often short of manpower in the initial phases of their epic, moreover, they encouraged favorable propaganda, since it was useful in recruiting new fighters. Later, the favorable chronicles would help to legitimize the state that they had seized by the sword.

2. Desiderius of Monte Cassino, I.II, p. 1124, as cited in Wolf, p. 76.

3. The chronicles are not in full agreement as to the date or the exact process by which the first Norman knights were recruited to take up arms in Italy. What is clear is that a good number were recruited to assist in the Lombard rebellion of 1017, and that it marked a watershed in their infiltration into Italy.

Tancred *of* Hauteville

After the defeat of the rebellion, many of the knights who had traveled to Italy were once again adrift. Some returned to northern Europe, but others had begun to see that southern Italy, with its many disputes, weak central rule, and generally unwarlike population, might be a land of opportunity. Many turned for employment or adventure toward the Lombard principalities and the city-states along the western coast. The opportunities were there. The rulers of those states were a quarrelsome and fratricidal lot, rich economically but weak militarily, who were ready to hire the newly arrived Norman warriors to fight their feuds.

The three Lombard principalities of Benevento, Capua, and Salerno had many internal weaknesses. Over the years, they had lost power and capability as a result of their own internal divisions, through periodic efforts by Holy Roman emperors to assert their authority, and because of the resurgence of Byzantine power to their south and east. The princes competed ceaselessly against each other, against a background of internal faction and intrigue that was often encouraged by their neighbors. Brother plotted against brother, cousin against cousin, in a seemingly endless cycle of coups and struggles for dominance among the intricately interrelated princely families. The princes, moreover, no longer ruled unified or militarily powerful states. Over the years, their power had eroded to the benefit of a class of landholding but militarily feckless counts, or *gastaldts*, who often lived not on their lands but in the towns, and who did not owe their prince any military duty or, it appears, much loyalty. The princes were weakened still further by the fact that many Church enclaves in their territory were not only free of taxation by the princes, but enjoyed virtual independence as a result of papal or imperial protection. As a result of all these factors, the princes were often unsure on their thrones, had little control over much of their territories, and commanded only token armies.

The Lombard princes also had discordant relations with their coastal neighbors, the duchies of Naples, Gaeta and Amalfi. Though small, those city-states were inordinately rich; through their ports flowed the luxury goods of the East, not only from Constantinople but also from Arab capitals in Sicily, Egypt, Tunisia, and the Levant.[1] The profits of this commerce benefited the Lombard states, which provided capital and the channels by which the goods found their way into northern Europe. But the princes were constantly at odds with the polyglot merchant oligarchies of those city-states and their elected dukes. Not satisfied in enjoying the silks, spices, perfumes, and jewels of the east, or their share in the benefits of the trade, the Lombard princes lusted to take over their smaller but temptingly rich neighbors, and maneuvered endlessly to do so.

Complicating the picture still further was an element of local competition between the two emperors and the popes. The popes had a particularly close interest in the affairs of the principalities, as they bordered the papal territories and contained important Church properties. The most important of those was the vital abbey of Monte Cassino in Capua, home to the Benedictine order of monks which was active at the time in promoting Church reform. But the emperors, too, had interest in Church properties, many of which over the years had been put under imperial protection. Popes and emperors clashed regularly over appointments, grants and rights of the southern Italian religious establishments, their mutual dependence at the strategic level put aside when it came down to specific issues of patronage or revenue. Similarly, the popes in Rome and the patriarchs in Constantinople fought over organization of the Church in southern Italy which, nominally united, was increasingly divided between Greek rite and Latin rite congregations. This competition between the major powers gave the local rulers some room to maneuver and to play the powers against each other, but it by no means improved their long-term security. In sum, the political situation in the region as well as inside each state, if not already unstable, was ripe for destabilization.

The Normans provided a new element in this witch's brew of conflicts and weaknesses. In a practice that would in the end prove self-defeating, the local rulers each tried to gain advantage over his rivals by hiring these proven mercenaries. The suddenly footloose Norman knights found it relatively easy to find employment. Ever alert to the chances for self-advancement, they then found themselves in good vantage points from which to observe the problems and weaknesses of the Lombard states.

The Norman mercenaries found that the central issue of the moment in Lombard politics was the effort by the spectacularly predatory and unscrupulous ruler of Capua, Pandulf—called the Wolf of the Abruzzi—to dominate his neighbors. Pandulf, who had so preyed on his neighbors that he had been deposed and imprisoned for four years by Emperor Henry, had been released in 1027 by the successor emperor, Conrad, in a mistaken gesture of clemency. Seizing the opportunity, Pandulf immediately returned to the south, where he hired the most important of the Norman bands to help him reclaim his principality. He soon had regained Capua, dominated Salerno, and seized the Duchy of Naples, whose Byzantine protectors had been unable to defend it because of the recall of Katapan Bojoannes. Pandulf, much to the dread of his remaining neighbors, had rapidly become the dominant leader of the region. Emboldened but not sated, he also began a campaign of harassment and pillage of Church properties, including those of the imperially protected abbey of Monte Cassino. While these depredations further enriched him, they cost Pandulf in the long run, as they both infuriated the pope and made Emperor Conrad regret his decision to release him from his captivity.

Norman mercenaries had provided the muscle for Pandulf's remarkable resurgence; he needed them if he was to continue to pursue his quest for domination. As a result, they suddenly found themselves in a position of some potential leverage. Their leader was a knight called Rainulf Dregnot, brother of a knight who had fought at Cannae. Rainulf had been elected leader by his fellows, under the old Norman custom, and had subsequently, through generous and competent leadership, attracted the largest and most loyal following of any Norman leader in the area. Rainulf was also the first of the Norman leaders to take a long-range view of his prospects, and to study how to position himself and his knights to best advantage.[2] By 1029, Rainulf saw that it might not be in the long-run Norman interest to continue to help the unloved and unscrupulous Pandulf gain a commanding position in the region.

Other offers, as it happened, were available. The ex-ruler of Naples, Sergius, who was seeking help to recover his rights in that city, sent messengers to Rainulf suggesting that they make common cause. Negotiations led to an alliance, and Rainulf and his men changed sides. In short order, Pandulf had been expelled as lord of Naples, Sergius was back in his palace, and Rainulf was ready to accept the prize that presumably had been promised in the negotiations.

As a reward for the Normans' services, Sergius granted Rainulf a newly created fiefdom at Aversa, a hamlet only eleven miles north of Naples but strategically located near the border with Capua. There, his mission would be to build a fortress to defend Neapolitan territory, as well as to raid into

Pandulf's lands and harass him militarily and economically. Sergius, overoptimistically as it turned out, also attempted to reinforce the tie with his new vassal both by raising him to count, and giving him the hand of his sister in marriage.

The County of Aversa thus became the first land directly controlled by a Norman in southern Italy. The place seems insignificant today, swallowed up as it is in the metropolis of Naples. But it was both strategically important in the struggle between Naples and Capua, and a key breakthrough in the Normans' story in Italy. The status of Rainulf, now a landed man with ties to the ruling family of one of the Italian states, had changed entirely; he had joined the local power structure and was no longer merely an instrument of others' power. Establishment of a Norman polity in southern Italy also marked a major turning point for the other Norman knights there. No longer were they required to dine at other lords' tables as hired hands. They now had a foothold of their own and a rallying point, as well as a leader who had a sense of long-range mission, and was able to attract new recruits by his fair and resolute leadership. From his new fortress, Rainulf could build up his influence and wealth by raiding into Capua, and could strengthen his forces by attracting additional knights from the North. (The two elements indeed were inseparable, as it was the promise of booty from raiding that attracted new recruits.) The word was passed back to Normandy that these new opportunities existed. The response was rapid. In just a few years, the number of Rainulf's knights had increased remarkably.

Rainulf's new status as landholder and leader of a powerful band of armed men gave him increased bargaining power vis-à-vis the princes who wanted his services, or needed his neutrality. Profiting from his enhanced position, Rainulf embarked on a series of moves that, however perfidious they might seem to modern readers, succeeded in expanding his power and aligning him with the ascending power in each turn of fortune. His first move came after only five years' service to Naples and followed, if it did not result from, the death of his Neapolitan wife. He deserted his sponsor Sergius to go back into alliance with Pandulf. This crassly opportunistic act, which led to the ruin of Sergius, can be explained in part by a prize which Pandulf dangled before the new widower's eyes: another advantageous marriage, this time to Pandulf's niece, daughter of the ruler of Amalfi. By this marriage, Rainulf created still another claim to respectability within the kinship-oriented Lombard ruling class. But Rainulf and his men in turn soon deserted the Capuan ruler. Perhaps disturbed by Pandulf's gratuitous cruelty, tyrannous behavior and arrogance, or perhaps just looking to join forces with the ascending power of the region, they left Pandulf to take up alliance with the increasingly powerful Prince of Salerno, Guaimar IV. That young prince had taken up arms against Pandulf — his uncle — when the latter had tried to rape one of Guaimar's nieces.[3]

Through each of his changes of loyalty, Rainulf managed to hold onto his fief of Aversa, and in fact to expand it. In this rank opportunism Rainulf, like many of the Normans in Italy, was not deterred by petty matters of loyalty in deciding where his self-interest lay. The general objective for those soldiers of fortune seems to have been to take sides when it benefited them to do so, but mostly to maintain some sort of balance of power between the rival states, so that there should always be a market for their services, and an opening for their advancement.[4]

Among the knights who came to Italy around 1035 were two brothers from a knightly family in western Normandy, William and Drogo. From the small town of Hauteville near Coutances, on the Cotentin peninsula, the two were the elder sons of a minor knight by the name of Tancred. Tancred, a second-generation Norman whose grandfather had come at the time of Rollo, had little to distinguish himself other than a remarkable virility. Indeed Tancred succeeded, over the years, in fathering no fewer than twelve grown sons and an unknown number of girls. His first wife, Muriella, bore William, Drogo, Humphrey, Geoffrey, and Serlo before she died, while the second wife, Fressenda, gave birth to Robert, Mauger, another William, Aubrey, Humbert, Tancred, and Roger. Of the boys' family life, or of their mothers', we know little. According to the later chroniclers, Fressenda raised all the sons in a spirit of even-handedness, but it must have been a difficult job to retain harmony amongst such a crowd of young men, trained for combat and assertiveness. Subsequent events, indeed, would point to a certain amount of friction between the sons of the first and second marriages, as well as the brothers as individuals.

To produce and raise a family of such a size was a rarity even in those days. The effort to train and equip twelve sons for a knightly career was a major one, and we do not know how Tancred managed it. His could not have been a wealthy family, so there must have been a good deal of scrimping as well as pooling of family resources to outfit the sons as new knights. Probably, the boys were sent, as was a normal custom, to the households of wealthier lords, where they served their apprenticeships in the bearing of arms and courtly behavior. Here also they would eventually have earned their knighthoods in a simple ceremony — the passage to knight was not yet as freighted with chivalric symbolism as it was in later centuries. They also learned the basic set of political skills necessary for success in the competitive atmosphere of large feudal households. Wherever and however Tancred's sons were trained, they apparently developed few if any lasting ties from their early days, retaining their loyalty, once embarked on their knightly careers, primarily for their family and their own self interest.

What was even rarer was that so many of the sons distinguished themselves in life. Through good genes, good training, or a happy combination, they succeeded. Not the least striking element of their success was the fact that most of Tancred's sons who went to Italy managed to remain, by and large, in robust good health in a time of appalling disease and disastrous healthcare practices. But their military, and later political, achievements set this large group of brothers apart from their contemporaries. The history of Norman successes in Italy and Sicily is in many ways the story of this family of Tancred's, and the remarkable relations that united and at times estranged the brothers.

The dilemma of Tancred's family was simple: not enough land, not even for half the number of sons who passed to adulthood. Tancred had at one time performed a feat of arms that had drawn him to the duke's notice and provided a livelihood in the duke's household for some time. It had not, however, gained him more land, the necessary key to his sons' future. They would have to become household knights, earning their living at another lord's table if they could even find such work, or else strike out to find opportunities on their own. According to the chronicles,[5] they were all too aware that other Norman families in similar circumstances had either divided the land among the sons in holdings so small as to be incapable of supporting a knightly household, or had been torn apart by family feuds after one son had been chosen to inherit the family land. Accordingly, they reached a family decision: each son, on reaching his maturity, would go off and seek his living as he could. To the great good fortune of the Hautevilles, the successes of the first Normans in Italy opened up attractive possibilities for employment in the south, and an uncle who had recently returned from pilgrimage in Italy advised the young Hautevilles to take their chances there.

William and Drogo, the elder two sons, were the first to leave for Italy, followed not long afterwards by a third brother, Humphrey. In the end, eight of the twelve sons of Tancred would find their fortunes — and fame for their family — in Italy. Only Serlo of the first set of brothers stayed on in Normandy, where he served in the household of Duke Robert — but only after having spent a three years' exile in England as punishment for some infraction against the duke's peace. Still, as we shall see, even his son Serlo eventually traveled to join his increasingly successful uncles in Italy, lured by prospects much brighter than trying to make a living in Normandy.

Three of the second set of brothers—Aubrey, Humbert, and Tancred, it appears—stayed in Normandy but left no mark on history. At least two of the daughters married knights who also went to Italy. Indeed, the family's line in Normandy eventually disappeared, even Fressenda having gone to join her sons and grandsons in Italy after the death of the senior Tancred. Today, nothing in the little Norman village of Hauteville la Guichard would remind a visitor that it was the place of origin of the kings of Sicily, were it not for a small plaque erected in recent times.

In Italy, however, the newly arrived knights from Hauteville did not sign up with Rainulf of Aversa. At first they hired to Pandulf of Capua. But, like Rainulf and many other Norman knights, they eventually gravitated to the service of Guaimar of Salerno and in opposition to the prince of Capua. The move was fortuitous, because Pandulf was about to suffer another turn in his fortune. His attacks on Church property, added to Guaimar's newly declared opposition, had contributed to another of those climactic descents into Italy of a Holy Roman emperor, this time Conrad II. Conrad, acting to restore order in his southern realm and to protect the property of the Church against Capua's depredations, deposed Pandulf once again during a lightning trip south in the summer of 1038. Pandulf, beaten but scarcely vanquished, fled to Constantinople where he began plotting still another comeback, this time with Byzantine support.

Before returning to Germany, Emperor Conrad placed Guaimar of Salerno on the princely seat of Capua. Backed with this imperial authority and the force of his new Norman auxiliaries, Guaimar moved rapidly. He helped the newly installed abbot of Monte Cassino begin a long effort to drive out Pandulf's appointees and restore the Church's authority over its usurped or occupied lands. Guaimar also reestablished Salerno's overlordship over Sorrento, and succeeded as well in getting the Amalfitans to elect him as their ruler.

Soon, Guaimar had become the leading Lombard ruler, and he would lead Salerno into its coming golden age. In this popular and gifted leader, the Normans had found a sponsor who was prepared to enter with them into a long-term and mutually enriching alliance. His first step had been to assure that the emperor, before his return to Germany, confirmed Rainulf as Count of Aversa. There was, however, one important change in that confirmation: the fief was to be held as a dependency of Guaimar's Salerno, rather than of Naples. Thus Rainulf, linked to his new sponsor and now an imperial vassal, rose still another step up the ladder of respectability. The Normans were in southern Italy to stay.

For Tancred of Hauteville's sons William and Drogo, service with Prince Guaimar would soon provide the opportunities by which they would come to distinguish themselves, and to begin the remarkable success story of the Hauteville clan.

Notes

1. These cosmopolitan and rich towns were still tiny by modern standards. Naples in the eleventh century held less than 10,000 inhabitants thinly spread within its old Roman walls; its growth would not resume until the late twelfth century. Trade with the East was a low-volume, high-value business, and, sadly, not all of it was in luxury goods. The city states also served as significant channels for the export from Europe of a more sinister commodity, that is, captives from the Slavic lands of eastern Europe, sold into slavery in the Muslim world.

2. Chalandon, p. 76. Chalandon's work in reconciling the accounts of the various chroniclers is irreplaceable and, in the main, unchallenged by later scholars.

It will be useful at this point to introduce the major chroniclers, those near-contemporaries who wrote excellent descriptions of the Normans in action in southern Italy. Their books were, directly or indirectly, sponsored by the Norman rulers, and as a result are almost uniformly favorable, yet they are generally corroborated in their facts by other contemporary records. They are:

> — Amatus of Monte Cassino, who wrote his *Historia Normanorum* toward the end of the century under the sponsorship of the abbot of Monte Cassino, an ally and sponsor of the Normans.
> — William of Apulia, who began *Gesta Roberti Wiscardi* about 1085 under the sponsorship of Robert's son and successor Roger Borsa, largely as an effort to provide an aura of greater legitimacy to Robert Guiscard and the Hauteville regime.
> — Geoffrey Malaterra, who began his encomium *De rebus gestis Rogeri Calabriae et Siciliae, et Roberti Guiscardi ducis fratis euis* in 1090, and was commissioned to do the work by Roger himself.

Other important contemporary sources are:

> — Desiderius of Monte Cassino, abbot of that monastery and subsequently Pope Victor III, whose *Dialogi de Miraculis sancti Benedicti* was written 1076–79 and reflects his pro–Norman stance.
> — Princess Anna Comnena, who wrote the *Alexiad* some fifty years after the events described as a eulogy to her father, Basileus Alexius. By alternating praise and scorn for Alexius' major Norman adversaries, she both validates her father's victories and shows grudging admiration for Robert and Bohemund of Hauteville.

3. This, at least, is what the chronicler Amatus of Cassino would have us believe. But since Amatus consistently denigrated Pandulf, the story may be suspect. Loud, p. 47.

4. According to William of Apulia (I, lines 156–61, p. 106, as cited in Loud, p. 75):

> "The Normans never desired any of the Lombards to win a decisive victory, in case this should be to their disadvantage. By now supporting the one,

and then aiding the other, they prevented anyone from being completely ruined. Gallic cunning deceived the Italians, for they allowed no one to be at the mercy of a triumphant enemy." It is doubtful, however, if the Normans collectively — a notoriously independent lot — could have followed such a deliberate and sophisticated policy. With each leader acting opportunistically, however, the effect may have been the same.

5. Geoffrey Malaterra I, C.5, p. 9.

Mercenaries for the Basileus

Opportunity came soon, and opportunity for these professional soldiers meant war. This time, however, the war was not to be another of the incessant squabbles between the Lombard states. Their employer was to be the Byzantine emperor, and the objective strategic: control of the eastern Mediterranean. The empire's objective was no less than the reconquest of Sicily from the Muslims.

The balance of power in the central and eastern Mediterranean had been slowly shifting. The outposts and colonies in Italy that the Arabs had established during their earlier heyday had been gradually eliminated during the tenth century, while raids from Arab corsairs based in Sicily and Spain had been countered by stronger Italian defenses and even counteroffensives by Genoa, Pisa and Byzantium. Sporadic and even devastating corsair raids still occurred, but the Muslim states themselves were increasingly on the defensive, in North Africa, Sicily, as well as in Spain. In Sicily, a civil war had begun which absorbed the attention of the island's leaders, while their overlords in Tunisia were equally preoccupied with a chaotic internal situation there. Sicily had ceased, in short, to be a major strategic threat to the Christian powers in south Italy, and was beginning to look like a strategic opportunity.

Constantinople had not yet lost the military strength and momentum that had been built up by the great line of Macedonian emperors, even though its increasingly feckless rulers were leading it into a period of corruption and decline. Aggravated into action by Arab corsair raids on coastal cities and shipping, which had sprung up again in Italy following Katapan Bojoannes' departure, Constantinople had decided to move onto the offensive against the Muslim world around it. The power of the empire was committed to a campaign aimed at clearing the eastern Mediterranean of Muslim pirates. Victory followed victory, and in a series of highly successful campaigns by the army in Syria, and the navy along the Anatolian and North African coasts, the Byzantines succeeded in driving many of the pirates from the sea. But the pirate raids would only resume, Constantinople figured, if their home bases were not crippled as well.

The time was right, it was decided, to dust off Emperor Basil's plan to attack the corsair ports in Sicily. Doing so could break the pirate threat, and also protect Byzantine power and sovereignty in southern Italy. Basil's project, which had been abandoned on his untimely death, was thus revived some thirteen years later, in 1038. By late spring a great army had been raised to ravage Muslim Sicily and, if possible, bring it back under Christian rule.

Constantinople had reason to be optimistic. Sicily had been racked for several years by a major civil war, pitting one prince, or emir, Ahmad al Akhal, against his brother al Hafs. The conflict had divided the powerful local aristocracy, creating factions that struggled for power while the central administration gradually fell apart. The loss of central control in turn had allowed the Christian communities in the northeast of the island (the Val Demone), who had held to their faith during over two centuries of Muslim rule, to exercise greater freedom and seek support from potential Christian protectors in Italy and Constantinople. The Byzantines, indeed, were already taking advantage of the chaos afflicting their old enemies, and were preparing the ground for intervention through their superb intelligence systems, subtle diplomacy, and a lavish hand for buying off opponents and securing adherents. Now, secure for the moment on its eastern borders, the court at Constantinople saw that an intervention in Sicily might be successful.

Suddenly, Byzantium was presented with the ultimate tool — potential treason in the Muslim camp. No less than Emir Ahmad had invited them to invade his country. The emir had turned to Constantinople in desperation, after his army had been defeated by al Hafs. The latter's forces had been reinforced by troops sent from the North African Zirid Emirate, who were the sovereign protectors of Sicily. Ahmad now hoped that, with the help of a Byzantine army, he could turn the tables on al Hafs and the Zirids — who were, themselves, under severe pressure from their superiors in Cairo and probably unable to send further reinforcements. But then, too late, Ahmad began to recognize the implications of his act, and realized that the Byzantines might have bigger designs than merely to help him regain his position. Dropping his planned treason, he quickly, probably desperately, tried to patch up a common Muslim front against the coming invasion. But he had miscalculated again. Al Hafs accepted the principle of a reconciliation, but not the reality, and before long had Emir Ahmad was assassinated.

Even though deprived of their traitor, the Byzantines were not deterred. Preparations for the invasion continued, and the army that was raised for the invasion of Sicily was a truly imperial enterprise. The Eastern Empire had long since abandoned the Roman concept of a citizen army, even in its Greek and Anatolian heartland, and relied instead on a professional army of trained, seasoned, and disciplined troops. But the cost of maintaining a standing army, large enough to defend the empire's long borders against its many enemies, had become a major political issue in Constantinople—compounded by legitimate fear of the military aristocracy's political aspirations. This meant, in practice, that an army for a distant campaign—as was the one for Sicily—was composed of a minimal core of professional soldiers, supported by more numerous local levies, mercenaries, and contingents from allies.

The core of the invasion force was composed of Greek and Bulgar soldiers from the heart of the empire, supported by the imperial navy. But the Byzantine provinces of Italy, which presumably would be the first beneficiaries of an end to Sicilian pirate activity, were heavily assessed to support the invasion force. The militias of the major southern Italian towns, which originally had been organized to defend their homes against Arab raids, were now mobilized into the invasion force. Additional troops were levied and conscripted, the local citizens were taxed to cover expenses, and the Byzantine force was further strengthened by a large and motley body of mercenaries. Most interesting of those mercenaries, perhaps, was a contingent of Scandinavians headed by Harald Sigurdson, or Harald Hardrada, a magnificent warrior who figures as one of the last great Vikings. For the previous eight years, while suffering political exile from Norway, Hardrada had employed his energy and skill in the service of the rulers of Kiev as well as of the Byzantines. His Varangian, or Russian, contingent was one of the key infantry units of the invasion force.[1] Whether Hardrada and his Scandinavians found any particular affinities with their frenchified Norman cousins, also members of the invasion army, is open to conjecture.

Up to 500 Norman knights, including the Hauteville brothers William and Drogo, had joined the invasion force. When the Basileus had called upon his Lombard allies in Italy to support the invasion, Guaimar and the other princes had found it politic to agree. Guaimar, in fact, had very good reason to please Constantinople: his rival Pandulf was in the imperial capital scheming to get Byzantine support for regaining his old principality of Capua. Guaimar, by pleasing the Byzantines, could hope to neutralize Pandulf, and might even get the Basileus to recognize his own title to Capua. Moreover, with no wars with his neighbors looming, contracting out his Norman mercenaries would relieve Guaimar and his citizens of their dangerous presence — the Norman tendency to freelance raiding when not otherwise engaged having made them exasperating, expensive, even dangerous allies. On these considerations, Guaimar provided a contingent of about 300 knights to the Byzantine army.

Accompanying the Normans was a Lombard mercenary from Milan called Ardouin. Ardouin, who spoke fluent Greek, initially served in the role of intermediary or interpreter between the Greek army commanders and the Norman contingent. As the Normans apparently had no single leader of their own, however, Ardouin was able to use his position to emerge as effective spokesman for the Normans in the polyglot army.

The invasion army was led by Byzantium's greatest living general, a character of epic proportions called George Maniakes. From Asia, possibly of Mongol origin, he was a great bear of a man: strong, ugly, thoroughly intimidating. His victories in Syria some years earlier had rescued the regime at a time of great danger, and his military prowess was much respected in the capital, but he was a blunt man who had to survive under a regime increasingly given to palace intrigue and treachery. His opposite number as commander of the Byzantine fleet was a nobody called Stephen, who unfortunately for Maniakes was — whatever the chain of command may have said — better connected to the real power behind the Byzantine throne. Stephen's main qualification, in fact, was that he was brother-in-law to the eunuch John Orphanotrophus, who dominated both the vacillating Empress Zoe and the man she had raised to the throne with her, Emperor Michael. Stephen the plotter and Maniakes the fighter were a bad match, but not necessarily a fatal one; the Byzantines had had much experience in handling mixed-force armies and divided commands such as the one about to invade Sicily. Indeed, the first operations went exceptionally well. After picking up the Lombard, Norman, and other Italian contingents in Salerno, the fleet carried the army across the strait from Italy to Sicily, without incident and with every hope of victory.

The invasion, even without Emir Ahmad's assistance, was an initial success. Messina was stormed, major battles were won at Rametta and Troina, and within two years over a dozen major fortresses in the east of the island, plus the key city of Syracuse, had been subdued.[2] Byzantium held the initiative and was stronger on the ground and sea. Reestablishment of Constantinople's rule over this richest prize of the Mediterranean, with its huge grain surpluses, cotton, sugar, fruits, silks, and other luxury manufactures, was conceivable and could have changed the regional balance of power definitively.

Throughout the early victories, the Normans had distinguished themselves as useful allies and valorous warriors; according to their friendly chroniclers, they had often made a crucial difference. The Normans appeared to be part, albeit a small part, of a winning effort that might reestablish Byzantium's preeminence in the region. Among those Normans, William of Hauteville in particular began to stand out. A competent, unassuming soldiers' soldier, he apparently had a knack for attracting people's trust while not making enemies. But it was as a fighter that he made his name amongst the hard men of the invading army. When he dispatched the Emir of Syracuse in single combat outside that city, he was awarded the nickname of "Ironarm" by which he would thereafter be called, in tribute to the strength of his sword hand. It was the first step in developing the leadership role from which his family would launch itself to royalty.

Great as William Hauteville's personal successes were, the expedition itself began to lose momentum and eventually to fall apart. Pay for the auxiliaries began to slow down and even suffer major interruptions. Disputes arose over the sharing of booty, disputes serious enough, according to the chroniclers, to cause Norman disenchantment with the whole enterprise. Ardouin, according to those accounts, protested the niggardly share awarded to the valorous Normans, and the dispute reached kindling point over a horse which Ardouin had won in battle but which Maniakes had confiscated. Maniakes flew into one of his rages when his act was challenged by Ardouin, and publicly disgraced the proud Lombard by having him whipped throughout the camp. Given Maniakes' character, the story may indeed be true, even if it is self-serving for the Normans. Whatever the reasons, the fact is that both the Norman and Scandinavian contingents, as well as Ardouin, left the army before the end of 1040. The Normans returned to Salerno and Aversa, angry, bitter, and dangerous.

The Normans emerged from the experience, not as a valued part of a victorious Byzantine army, but as resentful and mistreated employees, fully ready to even the score at some later date with the Greeks, whom they had learned to despise as treacherous and effeminate. But in addition to developing a disdain for the Greeks, the Normans had learned valuable lessons in Sicily: the land was rich, the resident Christians were potential allies, the Muslim inhabitants were divided, and both the Greeks and the Muslims could be beaten in battle. All points that could be useful, at some later date, to those ready to capitalize on them.

The expedition lost all hopes of final victory in 1041, partly because of an argument between Maniakes and Stephen. The admiral had allowed an Arab fleet to escape through the Byzantine blockade; Maniakes had publicly upbraided the admiral, even assaulted him physically. Stephen, not one to take such an insult lightly when he had important patrons in the capital, complained to his relative the eunuch John. In the plot-ridden and suspicious atmosphere of Constantinople, Maniakes' successes counted for little, and in short order he was recalled in disgrace and imprisoned. Without his energy and skill, and without the Norman and Scandinavian mercenaries, the once glorious invasion force was left to a strategy of consolidating its gains and waiting for better days. But they never came. As it was, developments in southern Italy demanded more urgent attention.

The Sicilian expedition had backfired, as far as Byzantine rule of their Italian provinces was concerned. The heavy taxes and levies that had been necessary to raise the army, and the almost two years' absence of the militias, had fanned the ever-present spirit of anti–Byzantine separatism among the largely Lombard-Italian populations, particularly in the coastal towns of Apulia. Several Byzantine officials had been assassinated as early as 1038, and the tension ratcheted up throughout the next year. In 1040, open revolt broke out. The *katapan* was assassinated, and local militias took over control of most major cities in Apulia. The leader of the Lombard insurrection, it turned out, was Marianus Argyrus, none other than the son of that Melo who had originally urged the Normans to come to Italy some twenty years earlier. His timing was good, it seemed. With much of their army off in Sicily, the Byzantines had been caught unprepared for so extensive a revolt. But an energetic and capable new *katapan* was quickly appointed, who was able to hold the line and even roll back some of the rebellion by the end of the year, while waiting for reinforcements from Sicily.

All this might have been a matter of indifference to the Normans in Salerno, including those just returned from Sicily, had it not been for the machinations of their old comrade in arms Ardouin. That crafty Lombard, in spite of his questionable departure from the Greek army, still had credibility with the local Byzantine authorities, and approached them upon his return to Italy for new employment. He succeeded in gaining the trust of the new *katapan*, and then obtaining a military command at Melfi, a small but strategically important town in Apulia, controlling a pass on the Byzantine-Beneventan frontier. Unfortunately for the Byzantines, the new job did not secure Ardouin's gratitude, and he would prove to be a most disloyal lieutenant. Apparently still smarting from his humiliation in Sicily, and perhaps motivated as well by a touch of Lombard patriotism, he wanted to get even with the Byzantines. He began subtly, but successfully, preaching rebellion to the citizens of Melfi. Moreover, once he felt that he had the citizens ready to act, he approached the Normans to be the instruments of his vengeance.

In early 1041, Ardouin went secretly to Aversa, where he met with a group of his old Norman comrades and made them a seminal proposition. Come with me to Apulia, he urged; I can assure you control and posses-sion of Melfi, and from there you and I can drive the Byzantines from the rich but poorly defended areas of northwestern Apulia, and even beyond. It is not hard to imagine the excitement which Ardouin's proposal offered; by all accounts his urgings found a ready audience among the once-again underemployed young, restless, and greedy Norman knights. Nor was Prince Guaimar inclined to stop the headstrong Normans from another adventure; they had once again become a potential problem in Salerno's lands, where their excess of energy could only result in trouble. He may have thought that the Byzantines, now having difficulties both in Sicily and Apulia, were unlikely to hold him responsible for the Normans' escapades.

Once Gauimar agreed to release a number of knights from his ser-vice, Ardouin had little trouble in recruiting a force of 300 knights, headed by twelve chiefs. The raid was plotted and agreement reached to split any gains from the adventure evenly, with half to be shared by the Normans and half for Ardouin.

Among the twelve chiefs who would lead parties of knights on the adventure were the two elder sons of Tancred, William Ironarm and Drogo. Once again, they were ready when opportunity beckoned. Even though full ramifications of the step they were taking would not be evident for years, it was from this thinly disguised raiding party that a great kingdom grew.

Notes

1. Three years after the Sicilian invasion, Hardrada would return to his native country and become king. He died in 1066 at Stamford Bridge, thwarted by King Harold of England, whose throne Hardrada was challenging. King Harold, in turn, was defeated several weeks later at Hastings by that most famous of Normans, Wil-liam the Bastard, more commonly known today as the Conqueror.

2. One reminder of Maniakes' campaign remains to this day. North of the town of Bronte, the twelfth century Abbey of Maniace marks the site of one of the general's major victories during the campaign. In the nineteenth century, the abbey was presented to the hero of that day, the English Admiral Horatio Nelson, for his role in saving the ruling family of the Kingdom of the Two Sicilies during the Napoleonic wars. Nelson never visited the property, which has since passed to the community of Bronte.

Rebels

In early March, the Norman raiders and their men slipped across the mountains into the Apulian foothills, where they approached Ardouin's town of Melfi. Ardouin had promised the citizens that the Normans were "not enemies, but friends.... God has sent these knights to liberate you."[1] Convinced or not of the Normans' good intentions, the citizens, like many Lombards of the region, were ready to revolt against rule from Constantinople. They opened their gates. In reality, they may have had little choice, given the size of the raiding party and the surprise of their arrival. Possession of Melfi gave the rebel party — still largely composed of Norman knights — a foothold in Byzantine territory, a fortified and well-situated hill town from which they could expand their influence and prey on Byzantine possessions throughout Apulia. Within weeks, they had obtained the submission of the surrounding towns of Venosa, Lavello, and Ascoli, and happily enjoyed their proclivity for pillaging the countryside. They were also successful in presenting themselves as part of the Lombard rebellion, and began to gather supporters among the Apulian population.

The province of Apulia was the richest in Byzantine Italy, and had been experiencing a period of growing prosperity. Along the coast lay a string of prosperous trading and fishing towns. Inland, a broad and fertile plain supported many small landowners who grew bountiful crops of grain, wine, olives, vegetables and fruits with the aid of irrigation and cistern systems: "Fat Apulia," it still is called. In the towns, prosperous merchants and landowners had developed a strong sense of local initiative during the long periods when Constantinople had left them on their own to fight off Arab pirates. The Byzantines, in fact, had relied on the towns' nascent communes to collect taxes and raise local self-defense militias. In doing so, however, they had inadvertently encouraged that spirit of Lombard

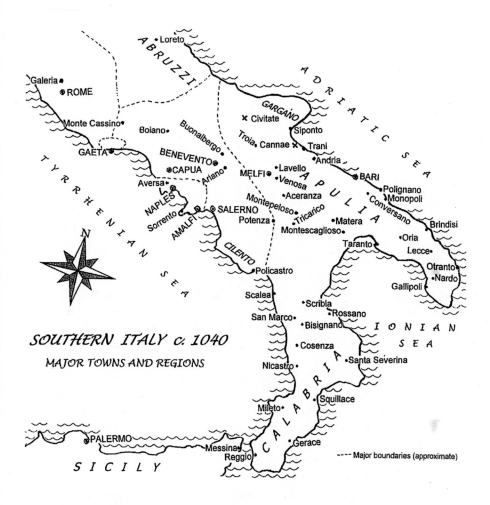

SOUTHERN ITALY c. 1040

MAJOR TOWNS AND REGIONS

nationalism to which Melo and then Argyrus had so successfully appealed in raising rebellion. The coastal towns were once again ready to rise up, but they were too large and strongly fortified by the Byzantines for the rebel bands to take on, as yet.

West of the plain, where the land rises toward the mountains of the interior, were the foothills, or "Stony Apulia." These lands were much more thinly populated than the plain, their towns located in the occasional arable valleys and providing a modest living from nut and fruit orchards, livestock raising, and small farms raising olives and grapes. The Byzantines had recently made efforts to repopulate these areas, particularly for strategic reasons, along the mountainous borders with the Lombard states. (Melfi itself had been fortified by the *katapans* for this reason, as had Troia.)

Even so, the hills remained lightly settled, and even more loosely controlled by the Byzantine authorities on the coast. It was ideal territory for land-hungry freebooters and raiders such as the Normans; a land where hills and still extensive forests could conceal their movements, where the towns were often lightly fortified, and where armed men could seize land with virtual impunity.

The Lombard rebels and their Norman allies had the advantages of surprise, momentum, and terrain, as well as the initial support of the population. The new *katapan*, however, was determined to stop the rebellion before it could grow. Showing commendable initiative and speed, he mustered all the local forces and tried to nip the movement in the bud, arriving before Venosa with a small army by mid March. He had, unfortunately for him, underestimated the Normans. This was no local insurrection he faced, but a group of professional warriors who were prepared to defend their existing gains and their prospects.

By the banks of the Olivento river, the two armies met. The Normans could only muster their 300 knights, plus maybe twice that number in foot soldiers, while the Byzantines had several thousand troops, including a number of their vaunted units of Varangians, or troops of Scandianavian-Russian origin. The *katapan* sent a herald to offer the Normans a stark choice: a safe return to Lombard territory, or a bloody battle. The Norman response, probably unplanned, was a stroke of psychological warfare — the kind of terror-provoking gesture that they would use regularly in the future to demoralize or disarm their enemies. When the messenger had finished, the Norman knight who had been holding his mount, one Hugh Touboeuf, simply raised his fist and, bringing down a huge blow on the poor horse's head, killed it on the spot. The herald, one can only imagine, was suitably impressed by the power and determination of the Normans. Once re-horsed and his ultimatum answered with words as well as gestures, the herald returned to the Byzantine camp to relay the Normans' emphatic refusal of the terms offered.

The next day, Normans and Byzantines fought for the first time since Cannae some twenty-four years earlier, but this time the outcome was reversed. The outnumbered Normans routed the Byzantines. Many of the latter, including the Varangians, were either slaughtered or drowned in the battle. The Normans retired in triumph to their hilltop stronghold of Melfi, sent out raiding parties to pillage Byzantine-held areas, and sought to expand the rebellion.

The *katapan*, as energetic as he proved to be luckless, did not allow the Normans much time to savor their victory. By early May, he had succeeded in raising a makeshift but still impressive army, including this time more regular troops from Asia as well as some units of the army that had returned from Sicily, supplemented with moral reinforcement provided by the two Greek rite bishops of Troia and Ofanto. Once again, he brought his army into the foothills, meeting with the Normans near Montemaggiore. The Normans and their allies had also reinforced their forces: newly recruited Lombard auxiliaries, and some additional Norman adventurers from Aversa and Salerno, had swollen their numbers. But they were still numerically inferior to the Byzantine army.

The Norman knights had elected as their commander William Ironarm, who fought in spite of a high fever. Once again, a Norman cavalry charge proved irresistible; the Byzantine army was crushed and many of the troops, including the two bishops, drowned in the nearby river. The poor *katapan* fell back on the port of Bari and called for reinforcements from Sicily, but soon was replaced.

The Normans had won their first substantial war booty: tents, silver and gold vessels, precious fabrics, arms and armor, horses and equipment. The fighters who had taken part were greatly enriched, and new knights were rapidly attracted to join the rebellion. More immediately important, the victory had won the rebel army a respite of a few more months to consolidate and expand their still precarious gains.

There remained one more pitched battle to be fought in Apulia, and it would be fought under new leadership on both sides. The Byzantines had appointed a certain Bojoannes as the new *katapan*, a son of the governor who had defeated the first Normans at Cannae in 1018; perhaps they hoped that he had inherited some of his father's skill and success. The leaders of the revolt, for their part, had pushed Ardouin out of his commanding role. The reasons for his loss of position are unclear, and perhaps he was even a battle casualty, but in any event he soon disappeared from history, deserted — or at a minimum not honored — by the Normans whose future he had made possible. The Normans and Lombards were able to agree for the moment on a new leader in Atenulf, a member of the ruling family of Benevento, who, some chroniclers imply, bribed his way in.[2] His election was, in a way, an affront to the Normans' sponsor, Prince Guaimar of Salerno, who could not have been happy that the Beneventans had gotten a handle on an adventure from which he had hoped to draw the profit. But Guaimar's allies the Normans were not yet calling the shots; their Lombard allies were too important to them for them to aspire to overall leadership of the revolt, and they would have to settle for the moment on being the military leaders.

The battle was fought near Montepeloso, today Irsina, in September. The rebel army had forced the Byzantine army out of this stronghold, in which they had established an impregnable position, by the expedient of stealing all their cattle and forcing them into a battle rather than having to face a debilitating siege. The battle was long and hard-fought, lasting most of the day, but in the end the heroics of the Norman cavalry, led once again by William Ironarm, turned the day for the rebels and the Normans. Katapan Bojoannes was captured and held for ransom.

The victory was decisive. After a summer of battles the Byzantine army was obliged to retreat to the coastal cities, leaving the hills to the rebels and the plain open to their raiding parties. The Normans and their Lombard allies found themselves suddenly virtual masters of the entire interior, reaching across the hills into Calabria, where the town of Matera declared itself for the revolt. Even the coastal cities of Bari, Monopoli, and Giovinazzo "abandoned their alliance with the Greeks,"[3] though this was more a payment of tribute to buy off Norman plundering expeditions, rather than an actual joining of the rebellion.

The victory at Montepeloso, in addition, spelled the end of Atenulf's leadership, for when the fighting men — Norman and Lombard — learned that Atenulf had kept the money from Bojoannes' ransom in his own purse, his position was no longer tenable. He was sent packing to Benevento. Selection of a successor, on the other hand, proved to be a bit more complicated. The Apulian Lombards wanted the new leader to be one of their own, not an imported Lombard as Ardouin and then Atenulf had been. They were supported in that demand by Prince Guaimar, who was glad to see the Beneventan gone and presumably believed he could influence a new Apulian leader. Interestingly, the detachment of Normans who had garrisoned Troia for the Byzantines all the years since the revolt of 1017 and who now were prepared to join the revolt, also wanted an Apulian leader in preference to one of the new, upstart Norman adventurers. The new Normans, for their part, argued that they had done the major part of the fighting over the year of successive victories, so should they not be rewarded with leadership of the enterprise?

The Norman knights were, in the end, outvoted and outpoliticked by their allies, and eventually had to acquiesce in the choice of Marianus Argyrus of Bari as their new leader. Argyrus would be a strong leader, they knew, and he would help solidify popular support since he had played a leadership role the anti–Byzantine revolt, as his father had before him. But the choice was primarily a tactical one. Argyrus was above all a Lombard patriot, a man who wanted neither Greeks nor Normans to rule in Apulia, but for the moment he was the man who could best provide leadership that could unite Normans and Lombards successfully.

These astounding battlefield victories against greater numbers changed the military equation in Apulia permanently. The *katapans* had underestimated Norman valor and determination, and never again would the Byzantines join in pitched battle with the Normans. The more cautious policy was, in fact, normal Byzantine practice. The empire had learned, over centuries of warfare on two continents, that it was cheaper and more effective in the long run to fight off its attackers with a defense in depth, neutralizing and seeking to control their enemies rather than risk the imperial armies, which were expensive to replace, in battles. Their previous experience with northern Europeans had in fact taught them that patience and wiliness were better tactics than audacity. In the previous century, Basileus Leo the Wise had described Frankish armies in terms that in many ways still applied to the Normans:

> The Franks and Lombards are bold and daring to excess ... they regard the smallest movement to the rear as a disgrace, and they will fight wherever you offer them battle. When their knights are hard put to in a cavalry fight, they will turn their horses loose, and stand back to back against very superior numbers rather than fly. So formidable is the charge of the Frankish cavalry with their sword, lance, and shield, that it is best to avoid a pitched battle with them until you have put all the chances on your own side. You should take advantage of their indiscipline and disorder; whether fighting on foot or on horseback, they charge in dense, unwieldy masses which cannot maneuver because they have neither organization nor drill.... They are destitute of all respect for their commanders; one noble thinks himself as good as another; and they will deliberately disobey orders when they grow discontented. Nor are their chiefs above the temptation of taking bribes; a moderate sum of money will frustrate one of their expeditions. On the whole, therefore, it is easier and less costly to wear out a Frankish army by skirmishes, protracted operations in desolate districts, and the cutting off of its supplies, than to attempt to destroy it at a single blow.[4]

Byzantine armies were by no means inferior. They were disciplined, had good logistics, and a superior infantry that was trained to maneuver in large units. They also had good heavy cavalry that could match the Norman knights, though it was not much used in Italy. In spite of their victories, the Normans in Italy still had many weaknesses. Their infantry was largely composed of untrained auxiliaries (many of them recently recruited Lombards), their logistics primitive, and their tactics almost entirely dependent on the shock value of their cavalry charges to turn the tide of battles. In this mounted warfare, however, they were probably unmatched in the contemporary world; they had increased their discipline and advanced the art greatly since the time of Leo the Wise. The Norman knights were violent in their charge, effective in the resulting melee, and disciplined enough to disengage and maneuver on command. Moreover, in Italy the Norman adventurers had the great advantage of what the chroniclers called their "energy"—that is, their sheer determination to succeed: their greed for victory, power and wealth. It was this quality in particular that set them apart from the often demoralized, time-serving troops of the empire, and justified the cautious Byzantine military strategy after the defeats of the first years. Constantinople would work, in preference, to defeat these troublesome invaders by attrition, the persuasion of money, or the tools of diplomacy and treason.

One of the first things the Byzantines did after their defeats, indeed, was to move on the political front. They released the still troublesome Pandulf from his confinement, knowing that he would stir up trouble for Guaimar and his Norman allies once he returned to Italy. From then on, the Normans would have to fight the Byzantines on two fronts: the military one and the internal one, with Constantinople's rulers using their immense wealth and influence to destabilize and undercut the invaders.

In spring, however, a turn of fate in Constantinople provided the Byzantine forces in Apulia with a renewed military option, and specifically a leader capable of checking and even rolling back the rebel gains. Still another change of emperors in Constantinople had resulted in the release and rehabilitation of the feared general Maniakes. Appointed as the new *katapan*, with orders to crush the rebellion, he landed in Taranto in April 1042, where an undermanned Norman effort to besiege him was soon abandoned. Once he had driven the Normans off, Maniakes had a free hand in the south. For the next four months, and avoiding battle with the Nomans, his army engaged in a savage campaign of terror and repression against those towns that had submitted to or even expressed sympathy with the rebels. In Matera, the atrocities he ordered included murders, crucifixions, rape, and even burying children alive up to their necks. Monopli also was made to pay in blood for its readiness to accept the rebellion's terms. Not surprisingly, local support for the rebellion dried up in the face of this campaign of terror.

The poor Apulians now found themselves pillaged and harassed by both sides. The rebel forces, rather than seeking to defeat Maniakes in the south of the province, had decided instead to consolidate their hold on the north and to carry the war to the remaining Byzantine-held cities of the coast. A large force under Argyrus settled in to besiege the important town of Trani (including with, for the first time in Italy, Norman use of siege engines and small naval units). At the same time, Norman bands, perhaps bored with the rigors of a siege or perhaps simply engaged in their favorite spare-time activity, busied themselves in pillaging whichever part of the countryside they could, with plausible reason, attack.

In the end, the two armies never came to a collision because of another astounding turn of the wheel of fate in Constantinople. Maniakes was once again recalled. His new recall was engineered not by John the Eunuch and Stephen, who had already lost power in a conspiracy that was salacious but, unfortunately, is irrelevant to our story. This time Maniakes was brought down by his enemies in the entourage around the man whom Empress Zoe had just chosen to be her third husband and fourth co-emperor, Constantine Monomachus.

Maniakes, able to guess what his fate would be in a corrupt court now controlled by his mortal foes, refused to accept the recall and instead raised his own revolt. His goal was not in Italy; it was rather to march on Constantinople and to rule there himself. Realizing that his army was not large enough to achieve that goal, and with necessity providing the motive, he even tried to recruit some of the Norman and Lombard rebels, yesterday his enemies, to his new cause. He was not successful. The Normans most likely took a careful look at Maniakes' prospects, and simply found them lacking. As indeed they were. He led his army from Italy in the fall, crossed victoriously through Illyria and Macedonia, but died in battle near Salonica. Thus the one general who might have saved Byzantium's position in Italy, and even regained Sicily for it, was done in by the intrigues and conspiracies of the increasingly ineffective and corrupt court in Constantinople.

Unable to defeat the Normans and the Lombard insurgents by war, Constantinople turned to its often more effective tools: diplomacy and money. In the late summer, with Maniakes as well as the Apulians engaged in separate revolts in southern Italy, the Byzantines needed to find a new *katapan* quickly. They made overtures to Argyrus, who, if he could be turned, would decapitate the revolt while at the same time denying any Lombard support to Maniakes. They may well have been in touch with him considerably earlier; he had been, after all, raised in Constantinople and had remained well connected there throughout the twists and turns of imperial palace politics. What they promised him, beyond a new title as Duke of Langobardia, is not clear, and he may have been playing a double game all along.[5] What is clear is that Argyrus had few qualms about breaking off from his new allies, the Normans. The latter, to this Lombard patriot, must have appeared on closer examination to represent a danger to the Lombard cause that they had been hired to support. Driven by their land hunger, greed, and general lack of scruple, they had already shown signs that they would not be easy allies, and rather aimed at being lords of Apulia.

Perhaps Agryrus believed he could serve Lombard interests best under the relatively easygoing rule of Byzantium rather than Norman domination. Perhaps he was simply won over by money and the promise of a title. In any event, he deserted the Norman cause at the end of summer, abandoned the siege of Trani, burned the valuable siege engines, and moved to the capital of Bari, from which he would prove to be a redoubtable opponent of the Normans and their ambitions in Apulia.

Notes

1. Amatus, C., 19, p. 77, as cited in Delogu, p. 41.
2. Taviani-Carozzi, p. 161.
3. William of Apulia, I, line 400, p. 120, as cited in Laud, p. 94.
4. Leo VI, *Tactica*, C. XVIII, lines 80–101, as cited in Oman, pp. 204–5.
5. Gay, p. 456.

Warlords in Apulia

O nce again the rebellion was without a leader. More fatally, it had also changed its character. The defection of Argyrus had crippled it as a joint venture between Lombard patriots and Norman mercenaries. For the Normans, Argyrus' treason was proof that they needed their own leader to succeed. This time, the Normans of Troia agreed with them. Guaimar, whose support of the rebellion had put him on the end of a limb as far as his relations with Constantinople were concerned, realized that only strong Norman leadership could keep the limb from breaking. And the poor Lombards, thrown on the defensive by the defection of Argyrus, had to go along.

For all these reasons, the choice fell on a Norman as the new leader of the insurgency. The consensus candidate, who was chosen at Matera in the autumn of 1042, was the military hero of the recent battles, a man known for his good sense, energy, and relative lack of enemies, "a man most valiant in arms, and endowed with all good manners; handsome, young and generous"[1]: William Ironarm, son of Tancred of Hauteville. He was given the rather ambitious title of Count of Apulia, even though, as yet, only a minor part of that province had fallen to the insurgents.

The movement that William had been chosen to lead was no longer the patriotic insurgency that had begun at Melfi. The Lombard patriots were beginning to desert, discouraged by a year of war, a growing distrust of their Norman allies, and the terror invoked by Maniakes' reprisals. Argyrus, who was now Byzantine governor of the province, promised a less burdensome rule and was effective in undercutting the remaining rebel leaders. With the flame of revolt sputtering, the patriots' alliance with the Normans came to a virtual end, even though young Lombard men continued to enlist as Normans auxiliaries out of greed for possible spoils.

William now led a venture that had taken on a much more Norman character. Though it still aimed at ending Byzantine rule in Italy, its leaders themselves now wanted to replace Constantinople's officials as rulers wherever possible, or at a minimum, to establish or seize comfortable fiefdoms for themselves.

To mark the new order of things and to arrange their new life in the land that they had chosen to make their own, the Normans held a council at Melfi in the early months of 1043. Beforehand, William had traveled to Salerno in order to regularize his new title. Count of Apulia only by virtue of his selection by his colleagues, William's title meant little until validated by a greater lord. History as well as political wisdom indicated that the Prince of Salerno, patron of the Normans in Italy, be the sponsor and legitimator of the newly captured county. Accordingly, William took an oath of fealty to Guaimar, and "...from that moment, recognized Guaimar as his prince, and Gauimar made him his governor, inviting him to divide the land — both that which was conquered and that which would be conquered."[2] In return for William's fealty, Guaimar offered him an important blood link into the Lombard aristocracy, that is, marriage to his niece Guida, daughter of Guy, Duke of Sorrento. For Guaimar, strengthening his links with the Normans of Apulia consolidated his power. The marriage alliance, not inconsequentially, would oblige William to defend his new lord against any threats from Rainulf of Aversa, whose growing strength and proximity Guaimar had reasons to distrust.[3]

Guaimar, then, was present at Melfi as the leader and nominal lord of the Normans in Apulia. Indeed, after Melfi he began to entitle himself as Duke of Apulia, hoping to gain, with Norman help, lands to which Salerno had long laid claim. The title, however, was probably more useful in trying to balance Argyrus' title as Byzantine Duke of Langobardia, or to fend off the continued pretensions of the ruling house of Benevento, than it was in establishing any real control over the Normans. Accompanying Guaimar came Rainulf of Aversa, previously not directly involved in the Melfi adventure, but who was too important to be left out of the success, and was now present to take a share of the spoils.

And dividing the spoils is exactly what the Normans present at Melfi did. Confident that they could continue to wrest land from the Byzantines, the twelve chiefs decided that the province could appropriately be apportioned out, even where it still remained in Byzantine hands. Rainulf was granted tile to Siponto and Gargano (still, incidentally, in Byzantine hands), including the shrine of St. Michael, while his brother Ascletin was granted Aceranza. William was given Ascoli, and Drogo Venosa, while another set of brothers (and distant cousins of the Hautevilles), Gauthier and Pierre, sons of Ami, were given the claims to Civitate and Trani respectively. And thus it went for the other chiefs: Tristan, Arnolin, Rainfroid, Rudolf, Hugh Falloc, Herve, and Hughes Touboeuf, each of whom got the right to hold a baronage of his own, or to conquer it if it was still in Byzantine hands.

Ardouin's promised share of fifty percent had apparently been totally forgotten, as was the man himself; the Norman war chiefs were not generous to the weak. Nor was much consideration given to the rights of those natives of Apulia who lived on the land or in the cities thus arrogated by the Norman chiefs; under the feudal fashion that the Normans brought with them from the North, it was assumed that the inhabitants would simply owe their allegiance and feudal service to the new owners of the land.

Melfi was not assigned to any single chief, but was to be held in common as a symbol of their joint enterprise. Each count would have a residence in the city, which was to provide the seat of their councils and armory for any joint efforts that they chose to undertake. This idea of condominium was an essential part of the division of Melfi. With each of the chiefs considering himself a peer of the others, William's title of Count, in the eyes of his colleagues, simply made him the first among equals, battle leader of the Norman forces and chairman of their joint councils, but not necessarily their feudal lord. Each of them was left free to carve out his own landholdings, within the general guidelines of the division at Melfi, and in cooperation with or independently of his peers. William, as Count of Apulia, could rally them to face common external enemies, but he could not control them on their own lands or on lands left unallocated in the division.

William did have a few but important privileges as Count that he could use to build up his own holdings beyond those agreed upon at Melfi. Having become related by marriage to one of the great Lombard ruling houses, William was able to establish a household, or *mesnil*, more prestigious than those of his Norman colleagues, and thus could attract the better qualified knights to its brighter prospects. Moreover, the division at Melfi had given him the right, as Count of all Apulia, to conquer new lands beyond the areas assigned at Melfi, and to build a network of patronage through naming new barons as his own vassals in such newly conquered territory. He and his brothers would, in time, use those aspects of the division to extend their family's holdings far beyond what the other barons had foreseen at Melfi.

But that was in the future. As yet, there was precious little substance to the grand vision of Melfi. For the Norman chiefs—now counts and barons, but still adventurers—the coming years would be ones of consolidating their initial gains and slowly realizing the vision. They were still weak in numbers in spite of growing success in recruiting new knights and sergeants from northern Europe, and moreover they had lost their Lombard allies — even if they could hire local adventurers and incorporate them into their own, French-speaking, units. Where they previously had enjoyed local support, they now faced increasing resistance from a sullen and even hostile population. In this last respect, the Normans had created their own problem, being insensitive to local conditions and all too often driven by short-term ambition or tactical expedience.

In spite of their weaknesses, the Norman knights were effective in expanding their territory. Their methods were as simple as they were brutal. First, small bands of horsemen would ravage the countryside, prey on trade, and deprive the population of the means of resistance. Their numerical weakness pushed them into tactics of terror — murder, rape, and arson each had a role in cowing the population and making their path to domination easier. Once they controlled the countryside, they would often settle for payments of tribute. But if they wanted to capture or subdue a large town or city, they avoided sieges, trying instead to have their way by blockading the environs and trying to starve the inhabitants into surrender. Once a town surrendered, it could be — and occasionally was — subject to brutal reprisals if it had resisted. Once again, this cultivated an image of savagery that was useful to the immediate purposes of the Normans. The subdued town usually entered into a treaty relationship with the Norman conquerors, agreeing to pay tribute, providing hostages as guarantees of behavior, and sometimes accepting a Norman garrison.

Almost always, a subjugated town saw a Norman castle raised in the immediate vicinity, and garrisoned adequately to put the town under constant surveillance and threat of reprisals. This castle building was in fact the major innovation in governance that the Normans brought to the region. Soon, each significant valley was dominated by a Norman castle and its garrison. Modeled on the tower and wall fortifications common in Normandy, the forts were originally simple and utilitarian: a rock and mud wall, a wooden tower. Later, they were stone-built, and still later some of them were enlarged into the large castles whose ruins we see today. From these new castles, the knights could control the neighboring towns as well as the surrounding countryside. Small wonder that the castles soon became the most hated symbols of what was seen by the population as a grasping and brutal military occupation.

The gradual occupation of inland Apulia — the major coastal cities remained in Byzantine hands—followed no pattern. With each chief and his followers working to forward his own interests above all, there was a sort of urgency to seize and subdue all one could as fast as one could. The pattern of landholding was chaotic as well, with barons holding lands in widely dispersed areas, and the rule of law unequally applied. What continuity of government did exist did so largely because of the barons' unreadiness to take up direct rule. Instead, they preferred to tax or levy tribute on the local communes, leaving most of the administration in place, and enforcing their rule through applications of brute power when necessary. The Norman knights and the local aristocracy mixed uneasily. The latter having been largely small landholders and merchants, they had little in common with the Norman military aristocracy. The Normans, in short, occupied and skimmed the wealth from much of Apulia over the years following their arrival, but were still, as the mid-century mark approached, an alien and unloved military occupation.

The Norman barons were able to establish their private fiefdoms in Byzantine Apulia with little interference from the rest of southern Italy's political players. The Lombard rulers' attention was riveted, instead, on dramatic events in Campania. Pandulf's return from Constantinople had begun a new phase in his struggle with Guaimar. Pandulf, with the Normans of Aversa once more in his employ, began to harass Guaimar and the lands of Salerno with armed incursions, and to make life miserable again for the monks of Monte Cassino. Pandulf in fact succeeded in creating so much trouble in Salerno's home territories that Guaimar and his new nephew William Ironarm had to cut short an expedition they had launched into Calabria in 1044.[4]

Unexpectedly, Rainulf of Aversa died. Although he had once again put his knights in Pandulf's service, he had concentrated on harassing Monte Cassino and had wisely avoided getting into direct combat with either Guaimar or the Normans of Apulia. Rainulf's first successor lived only a few months before also passing on. In the ensuing struggle to influence selection of a new Count, Guaimar made the mistake of backing the losing candidate. Not surprisingly therefore, the new count, Rainulf II, was hostile, and showed signs of being ready to move militarily against Salerno. Prince Guaimar found himself under pressure, and in danger of losing his hold on the leadership of southern Italy. He needed help from his Norman allies in Apulia.

But only six months after the death of Rainulf of Aversa, William Ironarm also passed away. In his last years of life, he had led the Norman barons to victories over Argyrus' forces twice, but the battles were neither as heroic nor as decisive as those of his first year in Apulia. He was mourned by his fellow barons, not the least because they were once again faced with the difficult task of choosing a new leader. William had preferred that

Drogo, his brother, succeed him. But the cousins of the Hauteville brothers proposed that the next count be Pierre of Trani, now solidly entrenched in the rich town he had seized since Melfi and on his way to becoming one of the largest Norman landowners in Apulia. They argued that the leadership should not pass down in the same family, and had solid support from many of the other barons.

The election was close, but was eventually decided by the pressure of Guaimar, whom all the knights respected as their liberal-handed sponsor, and who came down on the side of Drogo. Guaimar needed all the support he would get, and preferred a son of Tancred, with whom he had family ties. Once Drogo was elected, Guaimar reinforced those ties with still another marriage — this time the Prince's own daughter was betrothed to Drogo, the new Count. Drogo, in return, was able quickly to repay Guaimar, at least in part, by mediating his dispute with the new Rainulf of Aversa.

Drogo's election, however, sat badly with the two sons of Ami, who had not only been beaten in the political maneuvering, but had been humiliated when Drogo briefly imprisoned Pierre of Trani in the process. Their resultant hostility would bedevil the Hautevilles for another forty years.

Shortly after his election, Drogo began to play a role in broader Italian affairs. Unlike his elder bother, his talents were not in war but in politics, and indeed that skill — plus his solid and religious nature — were among the reasons for his selection as Count. Following his success in reconciling Rainulf of Aversa and Guaimar, he was faced with a still bigger political challenge: how to maintain his support for Guaimar and yet avoid the anger of the Holy Roman Emperor, Henry III, who was expected momentarily in southern Italy. Henry, a determined supporter of the growing movement for Church reform, had come to Italy primarily to straighten out the horrible mess into which the papacy had fallen — in Rome, he had to depose no fewer than three competing popes before he could install his own candidate, the German Clement II. But, it was well known, this powerful emperor (perhaps the most powerful the empire would ever see) also intended to cut back Prince Guaimar, and perhaps separate him from his powerful Norman allies. Guaimar, the emperor feared — with Pandulf leading him on — had grown too independent, whereas the empire's game in the region had always been to create a local balance of power that would keep these distant vassals dependent on imperial intervention.

Following his stop in Rome, Henry proceeded to Capua to organize and pacify the unruly south. He summoned Guaimar, Rainulf, Pandulf, Drogo, and other regional leaders to meet with him, and there he told them of his imperial decisions. Pandulf, once again, was to be reinstated as ruler of Capua, this time at Guaimar's expense. Pandulf was, at the same time, chastised for his attacks on the property of the abbey at Monte Cassino, and obliged to surrender some of his plundered gains. But Guaimar was the big loser. Not only was Capua taken away from him, he was also given another hard pill to swallow: his two Norman vassals, Rainulf of Aversa and Drogo of Apulia, were suddenly confirmed in their fiefdoms directly by the emperor. Admittedly, Guaimar's actual control over those two vassals had always been weak (and in the case of Rainulf entirely questionable), but nevertheless Emperor Henry's act in raising the Normans to the status of imperial vassals virtually negated Salerno's claims to their allegiance. Henry, it appears, had mistakenly thought he could set up the Normans as a balance against the two Lombard princes.

Notes

1. Amatus of Monte Cassino, II, C. 29, p. 93, as cited in Delogu, p. 45.
2. Amatus of Monte Cassino, II, C. 29, p. 93, as cited in Delogu, p. 45.
3. Chalandon, p. 105. Guaimar feared, justifiably, that Rainulf II would ally himself with Pandulf. Pandulf's return to Italy was already serving Byzantine aims, by destabilizing Gauimar and his Norman allies.
4. The expedition did, however, succeed in reinforcing Guaimar's claims in the area by building and manning a fortress at Scribla. It also whetted William's appetite for further campaigns in the thinly defended Byzantine province.

Count of Apulia

Emperor Henry, in his short stay in Capua in early 1047, had made momentous decisions, some of them misguided. He had tried to balance the various local powers, to check the power of Guaimar and weaken his alliance with the Normans. But, in the end, he set up a new imbalance because most of his decisions turned out to be favorable to the Normans of Apulia. In elevating Drogo to the status of imperial vassal, Henry gave him a prestige that his Norman colleagues in Apulia could not match; he was no longer first among equals in a common effort, but had clearly gained in stature relative to the other counts and barons. The emperor's decisions had also compromised Salerno's already questionable control over the Normans, without replacing it with meaningful imperial control. The Normans simply had been given a freer hand to act independently of any regional power — including, it turned out, both the empire and the papacy, which wanted to enforce its claims over the Church lands and dioceses of the south. Moreover, in reinstating Pandulf in Capua, the emperor had strengthened a dangerous vassal, and surely Pandulf would have created more havoc had he not had the bad luck to die only two short years later. But the emperor made still another bad decision. When faced with the hostility of Benevento, a city that he considered to be an imperial protectorate but which refused to receive him within its walls, Henry in a fit of pique not only saw to it that the town's leaders were excommunicated, but, more importantly, authorized the Normans of Apulia to discipline Benevento on his behalf. This was, indeed, putting the fox in charge of the hen house, and the Normans would in time take full advantage of this lapse of imperial judgment. Together, the emperor's decisions assured that the power of the Lombard princes would eventually be broken, and that the ascendant and growing population of Normans would be able to capitalize on the new situation.

The Normans' successes attracted a flow of new recruits, among whom were two newcomers who would in due course lead the next phase of Norman expansion. The first to arrive was Richard, son of that Ascletin who had been made Baron of Aceranza during the partition of Melfi, and who was thus nephew to the first Rainulf of Aversa. This gallant knight was, however, badly received at Aversa by the second Rainulf, who no doubt feared his talent and claims to the succession. Richard went to Apulia, where he was better received by Tancred's son Humphrey, who had arrived shortly beforehand from Normandy and been granted the barony of Lavello. However Humphrey was not yet well enough established to offer employment to Richard and his band, so Richard was obliged to take up a life of freebooting, including forays against his relatives in Aversa. Fortunately for Richard, he did not have to live the life of a brigand for long, as his distant cousin Rainulf II conveniently died within the year. Richard was soon selected as the new Count of Aversa.[1]

The other key newcomer was Robert of Hauteville, the fourth son of Tancred to come to Italy, and the one who would become the most famous as well as Richard's future rival. Robert's arrival in Melfi was as unpromising as Richard's had been in Aversa. Count Drogo, who apparently harbored some distaste for the sons of Tancred's second wife, already knew that his younger half-brother was both highly talented and ambitious: a dangerous combination, he thought. So he, too, turned his relative away.

Robert soon found employment with Pandulf of Capua, but two such strong personalities were bound to clash. A falling out over alleged promises of land and a bride caused Robert to leave, and try his chances once again with his brother. This time, Drogo had devised a role for Robert that could advance the family's fortunes, and yet keep him away from the seat of power. Robert was sent, along with his small band of followers, to man the frontier fortress of Scribla that had been built by William and Guaimar deep in Byzantine Calabria some three years earlier. In a miserable, malaria-ridden location, the fortress seemed scarcely a prize, even though it overlooked the coastal plain that in antiquity had supported the luxuriant life style of a Greek city called Sybaris. There was nothing sybaritic, however, in the living conditions that Robert and his men would have to endure, or in the standard of living of the poor Calabrians on whom they would prey.

Calabria represented an interesting opportunity for the Hauteville brothers. In Apulia, the brothers had been busy building up their personal holdings, like most of the other Norman barons created at Melfi.

Humphrey had been particularly active in accumulating lands for himself throughout the province, from his seat in Lavello to Troia in the north, and Tricarico on the southern border with Calabria. Count Drogo had also worked to solidify the general Norman presence, marshaling the forces of his Norman colleagues on several occasions in order to counter Byzantine counterattacks. The *katapans* were defeated twice in clashes, and Norman power gradually subdued local resistance. Many coastal cities were obliged to enter into treaty relationships and pay tribute, or suffer the customary and devastating Norman pillaging raids. As early as 1046, in fact, Humphrey of Hauteville had obliged the provincial capital of Bari to sign such a humiliating treaty.

Their piecemeal but expanding conquest of Apulia had begun to make many of the adventurer knights rich, with the Hautevilles and their cousins the sons of Ami leading the pack. The sons of Tancred, in addition, had begun to enjoy the prerogatives of their political leadership, and to enjoy the attention paid them by the other leaders of the region. Drogo's title of count brought with it implied and real responsibilities of governance, diplomacy and statesmanship, ones which Drogo and his brothers were only beginning to live up to. They had, it is true, begun to show a penchant for image building, combining public piety with largess. Rich grants to new Latin Church establishments began to alternate with the acts of despoliation which earlier had characterized the Norman expansion, and Drogo began as early as 1043 to rebuild a Lombard monastery in Venosa, the Santissima Trinita, which would later become the family mausoleum. The count's household even took on, as time progressed, more and more of the outward trappings of the Byzantines whom the Normans were dispossessing. Displays of eastern luxury, fine fabrics and foods began slowly to replace the hard kit of the traveling knight.

Growing wealth by no means dimmed the Norman appetite, however. "They wanted to have every people subject to them and under their lordship," a friendly chronicler admitted,[2] and the next frontier for conquest lay in the Byzantine province of Calabria. Norman expansion across the mountains from Apulia and into Calabria had not been foreseen in the division of Melfi, but simply resulted from the efforts of individual knights to seize land for themselves. Foremost of these were the members of the Hauteville family, who were particularly well placed to conduct the necessary campaigns. Drogo's situation as leader of the Norman effort gave him an advantage over the other Normans in mobilizing resources; he also had the authority, under the Melfi agreement, to seize lands in Calabria and enfeoff new vassals there. All the same, the brothers' advance into Calabria was small-scale and tentative at first. They wanted to learn the lay of the land and see what they could gain on their own, rather than enlist other barons who would have to be rewarded for their parts in a joint effort.

Calabria offered less rich pickings than Apulia. Most of the interior was mountainous, either heavily forested or badly eroded, and in both cases unsuitable for more than subsistence agriculture. The coastal plains were underdeveloped as a result of malaria and centuries of Arab pirate raids that had driven much of the population to inland mountain towns. Those towns were small, wretched, and all too often poor, their populations moreover extensively Hellenized since antiquity and thus more loyal to Byzantium than the Apulians had been. Still, it was worth an effort, and Robert was sent to develop the family claim that had been staked out by Drogo. The fort at Scribla had been strategically located for that purpose, along one of the ancient Roman roads that still served as the major arteries of the region. Its location at the edge of the Val de Crati, the only broad, or relatively broad, arable, and rich valley in the entire province, gave a potential point of control for that region. But Robert and his band were given few resources. They would have to live off the land.

The main step taken by Drogo to further the family's fortunes was to open the door to Calabria. First, he sent Robert to Scribla to establish a permanent Hauteville presence in the province. Then, in 1048, his forces defeated a Byzantine detachment at Tricarico. With this victory, he gained control of the mountain passes and easier access to Calabria from the Norman-held territories in Apulia. Following that victory, the Byzantines never again had a significant military presence in Calabria, and the way was open for the sons of Tancred.

For Robert and his band of brigand knights, the initial problem was simply survival. He found himself in a land of few rich prizes, with fewer than a hundred men in his band, some of them locally recruited bravos from Slavic settlements in the hills. Just to fill their stomachs, the band engaged in the crudest kinds of robbery, extortion, and oppression of the local peasants. Even the favorable chronicler Amatus had to be frank:

> His knights were few. He had no money in his purse. And since he lacked for everything except for meat, which he had in abundance, he lived as did the children of the desert.... He went wherever he could find bread. He plundered continually, as it pleased him. Where once he had done it in hiding, he came out to do it in the open.[3]

In spite of this hand-to-mouth existence, Robert was gradually softening up Calabria for its later seizure by the Hautevilles. He moved his base from the unhealthy location at Scribla to a new fortress he built nearby at San Marco Argentano, from which he could eventually dominate the entire Val de Crati. His raids on the surrounding towns, not always successful, nonetheless taught the local populations to fear the Normans and to prefer dealing with them to fighting them; in fact he consciously used terror as a weapon to compensate for the small number of fighting men he commanded. A favorite tactic was to set fire to the crops, then demand money to put out the fires. He also began to get a reputation for shrewdness and cunning, which he doubtless encouraged. "Whether he obtained the palm of victory for himself by craft or through the exercise of arms, Robert regarded it as the same, because what he was not always able to bring about through violence, he accomplished by means of the craftiness of his mind."[4]

Some of the stories recounted later by the Norman chroniclers were probably inventions, or even attributed to Robert in error, but taken together there emerges the portrait of a remarkable leader, one who could inspire his men by personal feats of bravery and leadership, yet who would also endure hardships with them, and the occasional good time. One story gives a sense of the conditions by which Robert and his men earned a living.

Robert's presence in the Val de Crati had given him opportunity to have a reasonably open relationship with Peter of Tyre, the Byzantine governor of the nearby town of Bisignano, and they met from time to time to resolve problems or disputes. Robert arranged one day to meet Peter privately, presumably to continue their normal dialogue. But this time, facing a particular shortage of funds, Robert took advantage of Peter's trusting nature, seized him by force, and held him for ransom. Once the handsome sum was paid, Peter was released and the relationship resumed on a more guarded, but still cordial, basis. Indeed, Robert, once he became rich, even rewarded Peter with a sum many times larger than the original ransom. The desperate nature of his ruse underlines the poverty of his options at the time.

Robert was gradually making a name for himself. He apparently had an instinctive understanding of leadership and how to project it through the techniques we now call public relations, and it was this quality as much as his actual achievements that paved his way to success in Calabria. While the Norman chroniclers have only praise for his human qualities, the personality that emerges from his actions is one of great ambition, ability, and considerable charm, underlain by a determined, calculating, and unscrupulous intellect. He knew that a great leader should be feared by his opponents but loved by his allies, and that is indeed how he appeared to his contemporaries. Even in the most desperate days of his brigand existence, he shared both the hardships and the scarce booty with his men, and was generous to others. His generosity was in keeping with the feudal spirit of largess, which dictated that a truly noble knight owed it to himself and his glory to keep nothing in his hands. But such generosity was also useful to Robert by increasing his renown. How else to explain his great generosity to Geoffrey, the Bishop of Coutances in Normandy, who during a trip to Italy in 1050 — even while Robert was suffering severe money problems— was loaded down with gifts of gold, jewels, and precious fabrics for the new cathedral he was building? At a time when he still needed to recruit good men in Calabria, Robert appears to have been intent on assuring that tales of his generosity would spread throughout the network of contacts that existed between the Normans in Italy and their compatriots at home. The image of a noble, and generous, knight was much more useful than the realities of his difficult existence in Calabria.

Robert, indeed, was suddenly lifted from his hard existence because of the favorable reputation he had developed. He was visited one day by a Norman knight called Girard, who had taken the name of Buonalbergo after a rich property in Beneventan land that he had succeeded in seizing. Girard had heard of Robert's rising star, and saw advantage in an alliance; he may even have been a distant relative.[5] His proposal was too good to resist for the perennially resource-poor Robert: marriage to Girard's aunt Alberada (who, despite the relationship, was still a young girl) and, instead of having to pay a dowry, the loan of 200 good Norman knights to pursue the looting of Calabria. Robert accepted, gained a lifetime ally in Buonalbergo, a saucy young wife and, with his new status as a married man, the beginning of his own *mesnil* or manorial establishment. Most important in the short run, he gained the military capability to push to success in Calabria. Last but not least, Robert gained from Buonalbergo the nickname by which he would be known to history: that of Guiscard, variously translated as cunning, sly, or clever. The marriage began an upward spiral for Robert Guiscard. His new strength enabled him to raid and extort more money from the unlucky Calabrians; a fair distribution of the spoils gained him reputation and more recruits, which in turn gave him still more power. Robert's exile to Scribla had, thanks to his own qualities and to Buonalbergo's shrewd investment, proven to be a success.

The Robert Guiscard who thus began to emerge on the world stage, and who would dominate southern Italian politics for over a quarter century, was loved by some of his allies, but feared by both his enemies and his allies. Some of the strength of his presence and character emerges from a description written a half century later by the Byzantine princess Anna Comnena, daughter of Robert's great antagonist Emperor Alexius. While not intended to be flattering, the description nonetheless exposes the admiration and fear which even his enemies held for him:

> This Robert was Norman by descent, of insignificant origin, in temper tyrannical, in mind most cunning, brave in action, very clever in attacking the wealth and substance of magnates, most obstinate in achievement, for he did not allow any obstacle to prevent his executing his desire. His stature was so lofty that he surpassed even the tallest, his complexion was ruddy, his hair flaxen, his shoulders were broad, his eyes all but emitted sparks of fire, and in frame he was well-built where nature requires breadth, and neatly and gracefully formed where less width was necessary. So from tip to toe this man was well-proportioned, as I have repeatedly heard many say.... Thus equipped by fortune, physique and character, he was naturally indomitable, and subordinate to nobody in the world.[6]

Fame, though, was in the future, and for the moment Robert was still a minor warlord in a distant province, the Normans not yet a serious threat to the Byzantine state. But they were a growing, and troublesome, presence in the region. Over a decade, the twelve Norman knight adventurers and their followers had succeeded in carving out for themselves a loosely knit aggregation of counties in Apulia and beyond. They had wrested land and cities from the Byzantine authorities, placed military settlements on unoccupied land to subdue their neighbors, intimidated communes to pay them protection money, and not hesitated to lay hands on Church properties when it suited them. Ambition drove them, in the form of greed for land and the wealth and respect that it brought, and in a hard an unsqueamish age they had proven to be highly successful. Their expansion had also made them significant factors in the local political balance, and actors, even if reluctant ones, on a lager stage.

But the Norman gains were not yet secure. Byzantine forces still held the major coastal cities, and could field substantial armies. The Greeks had experienced many ups and downs of empire in their long history, and saw no reason why they would not, in time, drive the Normans from their recent, loosely held, and still unconsolidated conquests. The Normans, moreover, had made many enemies. From liberators, they had in less than a decade become the oppressors of Apulia. Their erstwhile allies, the Lombard patriots, felt betrayed as the Normans first took over the insurrection, then turned it to their own ends. The general population, once supportive, had turned against the occupiers because of the harsh and greedy measures by which they were enriching themselves. Dispossessed landlords, uprooted peasants, ransacked religious establishments, plundered merchants, and intimidated municipalities all had intense grudges against the Normans and their tactics of seizure and pressure. In such a climate of anti–Norman passion, Byzantine diplomacy and money — so often preferred by Constantinople over direct recourse to warfare — had fertile ground in which to cultivate conspiracies against the men of the north. Constantinople's initial effort to undermine Guaimar and his Norman allies had fizzled out when Pandulf of Capua had died, but other conspiracies would prove more fruitful.

The Apulian population, split between its Greek and Latin components, was easier, however, to unite against the Normans than in favor of a return of Byzantine rule. Communities divided into rival political factions, some of them even pro–Norman, all of which augmented a climate of instability. In addition to pro–Byzantine factions, there were those who wanted to continue the struggle for Lombard autonomy. Still others looked to Rome or the Holy Roman Emperor, hoping either would act to marginalize both the Greeks and the Normans.

Luckily for the Normans, neither pope nor emperor was in any position to intervene in pursuit of their historical pretensions to rule southern Italy. Emperor Henry III was preoccupied with consolidating his rule in Germany, and had neither time nor army available to mount one of those massive (and usually ephemeral) expeditions that had marked past imperial interventions in the area. The papacy, for its part, was encumbered by a succession of weak and short-lived prelates who had few means or even desire to intervene in southern Italy. Inexorably, however, the rationale and the pressure for intervention grew. The flow of anti–Norman complaints from Church communities and religious establishments in Apulia was compelling; Norman exactions against even their own co-religionists in the area had become a scandal that the Holy See could not ignore.

The Normans in Apulia had only themselves to blame for their increasing isolation. In their single-minded drive to establish end enrich themselves, they had relied on military means almost to the exclusion of political ones. With no single leader, moreover, they had little coherent political strategy, unless strong-armed expropriation and intimidation counted. They had only one important ally, Guaimar of Salerno, who been weakened by the loss of Capua and was increasingly isolated. He was being undercut by Emperor Henry's effort to play off the southern rulers against each other, and held responsible by the papacy for the depredations of his Norman allies. Amalfi was in revolt against his rule, and even his nominal allies the Normans of Aversa were acting independently and threateningly. Guaimar and the Apulian Normans were locked in a relationship of mutual dependence, with few political options available for either. In addition, there was a growing threat that pope and emperor — perhaps even both emperors— would combine to bring them down.

Notes

    1. Not without controversy, however. Richard was not immediately selected count. Instead, he was named as regent to Rainulf's infant son Herman, who, however (and conveniently), disappeared from history shortly thereafter. At the time that he was finally named Count of Aversa, Richard was actually being held prisoner by Drogo, following an unsuccessful raid on Hauteville land. Chalandon, p. 117.

    2. Amatus of Monte Cassino, I, C. 2, p. 9, as cited in Wolf, p. 91.

    3. Amatus of Monte Cassino, III, C. 9, p. 122, as cited in Wolf, p. 104.

    4. William of Apulia, II, lines 302–4, p. 148, as cited in Wolf, p. 132.

    5. Loud, p. 113.

    6. Anna Comnena, Book I, p. 27.

The Pope's Wrath

A new pope had taken the seat of Saint Peter in Rome, a man who rapidly showed that he was not only interested in the situation in southern Italy, but intended to do something about it. The Normans' political isolation began to be uncomfortable. The new pope had been chosen by Emperor Henry, the third pope he had selected in his reign. He had made a seemingly safe bet: Bruno, Bishop of Toul and his own second cousin. But this active and zealous bishop, who took office as Leo IX, was cut from a different cloth than that of his docile predecessors. To start with, he insisted that he assume office only after acclamation by the Roman clergy. This small act of independence (if not yet of defiance) was a subtle challenge to his cousin the emperor's presumption in having named a pontiff single-handedly, a sign that this was a pope who intended to fight for the Church's rights. Leo of course was neither in a position to challenge the powerful emperor directly, nor did he wish to: they agreed on the priority to be given to reform of the corrupt and discredited Church.

Both Leo and Henry had been strongly influenced by the reformist teachings of the Benedictine monks of Cluny, in France, who for over fifty years had argued the need to return to celibacy in the priesthood, to eliminate the sale of Church offices, and for other reforms designed to strengthen the Church's moral standing as well as its autonomy. Leo in time made those reforms the centerpiece of his tenure, and his actions while in office paved the way for the later flowering of the reform movement. The emperor, on the other hand, sincere as he may have been in an abstract wish for reform, did have something to lose by its reality. In feudal Germany, a large measure of his power and influence came from the ability to appoint Church officials, even to sell them their offices. So for the new

Pope Leo, anxious to begin reform, a direct assault on simony in Germany was not a sensible place to start. He had to look elsewhere.

Leo's initial focus was on the situation of the Church in southern Italy, which was both near at hand and rife with abuses needing correction. In early 1050 he held a synod in Siponto,[1] near the shrine of Saint Michael in Monte Gargano, an area in which Norman abuses had disrupted both the local Church properties and the pilgrimage traffic. In Siponto and at a subsequent synod at Salerno, Leo moved cautiously — being careful to respect the authority of the Patriarch of Constantinople over the Greek rite churches in Apulia, as well as to recognize the peculiar status of the Lombard metropolitans. But he was determined to bring the Latin rite churches of the area back into Rome's orbit, and for that reason he reviewed the election of certain bishops, insisted on payment of tithes to Rome, and in general sought to reestablish the Holy See's authority in the region. He could not do so, however, without also showing himself to be the protector of local Church property, and in that connection he was obliged to hear first-hand of the Norman confiscations and pillage of the region's monasteries and churches. There were ecclesiastical complaints against the Normans, as well: they had sold both Church offices and dignities, refused to pay tithes, and generally bucked the tide of reform. Leo was not yet ready to take on the Normans, limiting his intervention for the moment to internal Church affairs. Nonetheless, he let his frustration show in his correspondence with fellow rulers, in which he accused the Normans of impiety and pagan behavior.

After consultations over the winter with his cousin the emperor, Pope Leo returned to the south in the following summer. This time he intended to deal more directly with the problems caused by Normans, and indeed he had a new and pressing reason to do so. He had just become the lord and protector of the state of Benevento, itself under attack by Norman barons (including Guiscard's father-in-law Girard of Buonalbergo), who had occupied substantial portions of its territory. The pope had been invited by the commune to be lord of Benevento after they had thrown out the feckless Lombard ruling family, which had passively overseen a disintegration of the state's power. The commune knew only too well that their state badly needed a strong protector, one who could defend them against both the distant but angry Emperor Henry, and the nearby and predatory Normans to whom he had given such a free hand. The only alternative for the Beneventans was the protection of Constantinople, clearly a poor choice as its power in the region continued to wane. Leo was entirely willing to accept the rich prize, which the papacy had long claimed, even though it would require considerable effort to protect such a weak state. In July 1051, the pope entered his new domain to obtain its homage and to install his rector. He summoned Guaimar of Salerno and his vassal Drogo, Count of Apulia, to his court to recognize his new holding and responsibilities in the region

The pope's immediate demands were that the Normans cease their depredations against Church property (now including all Benevento), respect the peace, and apply the reform measures. His broader aim, which was to maintain the existing political balance and reassert Rome's authority in southern Italy, was unstated but equally clear, and equally antithetical to the Norman desire for continued expansion. However, Leo could only use persuasion to bring the Normans into line. He was, of course, supported by the authority of his position, but by no threat of force: Emperor Henry, potentially the sword of the Church, was all too clearly occupied with his problems in Germany, and not overly concerned over the Normans' behavior in any event. Both sides recognized the conflict of their aims, but wanted to avoid a break. Leo reviewed for Guaimar and Drogo the Church's complaints, and, in the end, obtained some satisfaction: they solemnly promised that they and their followers would respect papal and Church property in the future.

For the upstart Count Drogo, semi-legitimate leader of a new, contested, and disorganized frontier county, refusing such an appeal from the Holy Father in person was all but unthinkable. Like most of the Normans, Drogo was pious if not necessarily dutiful; his respect for the pope's august office obliged that he at least attempt to honor his word. But his realism — another Norman trait — allowed him to qualify the extent of his obedience. In fact, he controlled the behavior of few of his nominal barons, who had spread their private wars throughout the province of Apulia and even, to the north, into lands belonging to the state of Benevento and the Lombard *gastaldts* of the Abruzzi region. It is scarcely surprising that few of them paid heed to what Drogo had promised the pope.

Within a very short time, petitions concerning new incidents of Norman aggression flowed in to the papal secretariat. The pope was furious, and complained to Prince Guaimar about the perfidy of his vassal and son-in-law. Guaimar, putting a good face on the circumstance, tried to explain how little control Drogo actually exercised over his barons, but was unable to appease the disappointed and angry pontiff.

Whether the situation would have escalated under Drogo's diplomatic and cautious leadership is moot, for within a month he was dead, assassinated in his private chapel. Responsibility for the deed was unclear, as the assassins died in the ensuing fight, but the fact that a number of other prominent Normans were killed at the same time, in what appears to have been a concerted attempt at a general uprising, pointed the finger at the Byzantine authorities. If conspiracy it was, the lead had been taken by the newly appointed Byzantine governor — none other than the Normans' erstwhile leader, Argyrus the son of Melo.

Argyrus, the first Italian to have been elevated to the rank of *katapan*, had developed a close relationship with Basileus Constantine during a long stay in the capital city. In the Byzantine court, he had argued against those who still hoped that the Normans could be managed, or their threat diverted, by the time-hallowed Byzantine tactics of co-optation and bribery. He had not, however, won that argument, and his initial instructions as *katapan* were to try to buy off the Normans by offering them lucrative service in the imperial armies in Asia. Argyrus' efforts to that end evidently failed, and it seems indeed that he had pursued them only halfheartedly. Neither co-optation nor a popular uprising could, in his opinion, drive the Normans out of Byzantine Italy. He had become convinced that the Norman advance could only be stopped by a military alliance with the papacy. With the support of Constantine, Argyrus now proposed an alliance with Rome and — following the pope's disappointment with broken Norman promises — found a ready ear.

The pope had good reason to be angry, since Drogo's assassination had loosed the Norman barons on a new spate of aggressions, as each knight tried to take advantage of the situation to extend his holdings, or simply to raid his neighbors. Norman knights raided into Beneventan territories even while the pope was in residence, and complaints to Rome reached a new crescendo. The pope and his advisors, among them a rising young functionary called Hildebrand, had already come to the conclusion that the Normans had to be put in their place, and now agreed that a grand alliance including the Greeks was necessary for the purpose. In spite of the ecclesiastical differences between the two churches, the pope wanted to cooperate with Constantinople in protecting Christian interests in southern Italy, and was prepared to countenance a possible Byzantine resurgence in Italy as a cost of their aid in controlling the troublesome Normans. By the beginning of the year the alliance was beginning to take shape, as papal diplomacy, with Byzantine support, gathered promises of troops from most of the rulers of the south, and some from north of the Alps as well.

The lone regional holdout to this Papal-Byzantine alliance was Guaimar. The Prince of Salerno could scarcely abandon his Norman allies, with whom he had had a successful collaboration for over fifteen years — and who, incidentally, might not take a defection on his part passively. Nor could he acquiesce in the formation of a Rome-Constantinople axis that would surely, if it successfully put down the Normans, then turn on Salerno. Guaimar rejected the pope's overtures, and his opposition proved fatal to the alliance. Neither Capua nor Benevento could provide the troops or the lines of communication necessary to attack the Normans, and by late spring Argyrus and the pope had to shelve their plans, at least for the moment. Guaimar, patron and protector of the Normans, had performed a last vital service. He had gained them a reprieve.

The Normans, under pressure of the impending expedition against them, had elected a new leader. The new count was Drogo's brother Humphrey, but the election of a Hauteville had once again been strongly contested by the sons of Ami. Humphrey's success probably owed more to the external threat, his familiarity with Drogo's policies, his connection with Salerno (he had married Guaimar's sister), and a lack of enemies, than to any particular qualities of brilliance or statesmanship. With his election, the sons of Tancred had succeeded in maintaining their leadership of the Normans in Apulia.

The title of count still gave its holder little real ability to govern effectively — real power in the Norman-held areas of the province remained too divided among the fractious and opportunistic barons. What the title of Count of Apulia did provide, however, was the potential of patronage, and the authority to raise Norman armies for the common defense. For the plain, blunt, and soldierly Humphrey, the latter power in particular would work to his great advantage over the coming years of challenges.

Almost immediately, a Norman expeditionary force was needed, although not to defend Apulia against a papal coalition. A more immediate problem had arisen. Less than a year after Drogo's assassination, Prince Guaimar was in turn murdered. The loss of their patron, the man whom they almost universally respected and called their "father," was a severe blow to the Normans. If a hostile leader emerged in Salerno, it would leave them perilously isolated both politically and militarily. They had to intervene.

Guaimar's death had come at the hands of his own family, or more specifically four brothers-in-law. They had joined with the Amalfitans in a pro–Byzantine plot to overthrow Guaimar and his house, to make Amalfi independent again, and to install the eldest brother, the Count of Teano, on the princely seat. They were all but successful, assassinating Guaimar and capturing the major part of his family. But Guaimar's brother Guy had been able to escape, and rode off to rally the Normans. He found Humphrey (who was his brother-in-law) already in the field with a small army. Humphrey moved rapidly, and within a week the leaders of the coup found themselves besieged in the citadel of Salerno. The speed of the

Normans' counterattack had been such that they even succeeded in capturing some of the rebels' family members, whom they used as bargaining chips to obtain the release of Guaimar's son, Gisulf. The Normans would have preferred to see Guy assume the rule, as he was much more inclined to maintain the old alliance than young Gisulf, who was not known to be friendly. But when Guy deferred to his nephew as legal heir to the slain Guaimar — Lombard tradition was strongly in favor of patrilineal succession — the Normans reluctantly acquiesced. They dutifully did homage to Gisulf, but at the same time weakened him by seeing that Guy was made lord of Sorrento, virtually removing that town from Salerno's control. Gisulf in turn confirmed them in such fiefdoms as they held in Salerno's territory and thereby, at least in form, renewed Salernitan-Norman solidarity. But it would never be the same. The Normans, who had respected and honored Guaimar as their patron, distrusted Gisulf and had become strong enough to dominate the relationship.

With both the political and military circumstances thus turned decisively against them, the leaders of the coup had little choice but to yield their citadel stronghold. Gisulf and Guy, showing remarkable magnanimity for the times, considering in particular the brutal way in which their relative had been butchered in the prime of his life, agreed to spare the plotters' lives. But Humphrey and the Normans, enraged by the murder of their patron and employing a Norman trait of self-serving lawyerly argumentation, claimed that they themselves had made no promises, and struck. They were vindictive in addition, killing not only the brothers but as many of their followers as there had been knife wounds in Guaimar's body — thirty-six. Brutal tactics indeed, but useful in terms of cowing any remaining opposition, and in convincing their many opponents that they were ready to fight.

Fight, it appeared, they would have to do, for during the winter of 1052-3 the pope and his Byzantine allies had cobbled together a new coalition, preparing to come south and settle affairs with the Normans once and for all. Humphrey did not wait passively, but instead took the offensive against the Byzantines in both Apulia and Calabria. He defeated Argyrus' force in an engagement near Taranto, while Robert Guiscard bested another Byzantine detachment near Crotone on the southern coast. While neither of these engagements was decisive, together they proved that the Normans were still capable of working together against their foes, and that they remained a formidable force on the field of battle. The Norman successes most probably occasioned the remarkable lack of initiative shown by the Byzantine armies in the coming campaign.

Pope Leo came south with a numerically superior but motley force.

Emperor Henry had not, in spite of promises, contributed any fighting men to the expedition. In fact, it was only through the efforts of the papal chancellor, the warlike Frederick of Lorraine, that the pope had recruited any contingents at all from north of the Alps. That, however, was a satisfactory nucleus for an army: a detachment of some seven hundred Swabian infantry, huge warriors who fought in tight masses, using their two-handed swords with deadly effect. Around this German core, the pope had gathered as he proceeded south an array of allies from the Lombard and Italian states of the central and southern peninsula. Although numerous, these contingents fought largely under their individual banners and were, in the event, poorly coordinated and led.

The papal force did have a key advantage: it could count on the neutrality of Salerno, since the newly installed Prince Gisulf cautiously had decided to stay on the sidelines for the coming showdown. His excuse was his engagement in the continuing struggle with Amalfi, but more than a dash of anti–Norman opportunism can also be discerned. Be that as it may, Salernitan neutrality, a role that Guaimar had refused to play, protected the flank of the papal progress and allowed the army to move easily into Apulia. The pope, who had led armies in the field before, planed to link up with a promised Byzantine force somewhere near Siponto.

To face this threat, the Normans had rallied virtually every knight of theirs who could ride. Guiscard brought his men from their strongholds in Calabria, fresh from their victory at Crotone. Humphrey led the vanguard of knights from Apulia, which included even his rivals— so great was the threat to the Normans collectively — Pierre and Gauthier the sons of Ami. Richard of Aversa as well, recognizing that the Norman cause in southern Italy could well be decided by the outcome of the coming battle, hastened to put his knights under Humphrey's overall command. The Norman leaders decided to move rapidly, in an effort to confront the hostile army before it could join up with the Byzantine one. In that they were successful, with the result that the Greek army was maneuvered into a position of passivity— some said treachery— and wound up playing no role in the battle.

Nonetheless, the Norman army that finally intercepted the papal army near Civitate was not in peak condition. The men were exhausted from weeks of forced marches in the summer heat. They were also hungry, because the hostile citizens of the area had hidden provisions or refused to provide them to their persecutors. The chroniclers tell us that the knights and soldiers, the evening before the battle, had to make do with eating grain fresh from the fields, dried before the fires to make it somewhat edible. They knew that, if obliged to fight, they had to win — any other conclusion would almost surely end the glorious freedom, and license to enrich themselves, from which they had profited over the past decade.

The day before the battle was occupied with parleys, initiated by the Normans. Perhaps they needed the rest; perhaps they sincerely wanted to avoid a pitched battle against a superior army led by the Vicar of Christ. Their efforts to explain their position and promise future loyalty and obedience however were derided by the hard-liners in the pope's entourage. Of course, the Normans didn't offer very much, either; they promised, for example, to do homage for the Beneventan lands they had seized — but not to return them. Nonetheless, their overtures were rejected in a manner that they considered offensive, while their warrior qualities were mocked by the cocky Swabians. The chroniclers tell us that the Normans felt that they had been given a virtual ultimatum: surrender and agree to give up their conquests, or be destroyed in battle. Never lacking in self-confidence, the Normans felt that there was still a better alternative. They drew up plans to fight early on the following morning.

Their attack came early, and was fiercely effective. It began, the pope's apologists were later to claim, before the parleys were over. In view of the fact that the pope was playing for time in the hope that the Byzantine army would make its promised appearance, however, the papal complaints are unconvincing. Given the scope of the pope's defeat, they sound even more like sour grapes. The battle of Civitate, contrary to most expectations, turned into a total victory for the Normans.

The key to the Norman victory was not their superiority as heavy cavalry — they were known to be almost unmatched in that element of warfare. Nor was it their ferocity or will to prevail, even though the chroniclers tell us of extraordinary feats by Norman heroes— such as the repeated charges by Humphrey's knights against the Swabians' unbreakable ring of steel, or Guiscard's three returns to the melee after having horses killed beneath him. Ultimately, the prize for valor should have gone to the Swabians who fought to the last man, even after their lines had finally been broken. The main reason why the Normans finally won the day was, rather, because they could fight a battle of maneuver while maintaining good battlefield discipline. Guiscard's decision to bring his horsemen from the left wing into the struggle at the center cracked the Swabian lines at a crucial moment. The Normans' ability to break out of the melee six times, rally and charge again showed remarkable battlefield cohesion. Most importantly, Richard of Aversa's routing of the Italian contingents in the early stages of the battle could easily have turned into a disorganized pursuit, but did not. The Norman knights, even if belatedly, regrouped and then rejoined the fiercely contested main battle just in time to make the fatal difference. The Normans had earned their victory on the field.

As we have seen, victory was not immediately translated into a political triumph. Indeed, months later when Leo finally did submit to Norman demands and acknowledge their territorial holdings in southern Italy, he did so in an obscure and grudging manner. The Normans were recognized, but not invested, in their conquered territories. Of course, the pope had no actual right to dispose of Byzantine or Lombard lands in any event, other than through the hoary and somewhat suspect terms of the Donation of Constantine. He could scarcely enfeoff the Normans in their new conquests nor, for that matter, did he wish to. Emperor Henry had, six years earlier, relied on his right as King of the Italians and successor to the Lombards in all Italy to grant fiefs and titles to the Normans, but the pope apparently chose not even to confirm those in public. The reason was not hard to discern: Leo would not legitimize the Norman conquests any more than he absolutely had to. He wanted revenge, and until his death was actively engaged in efforts to set the stage for another assault on the upstarts who had defeated his army. Reinforcing the alliance with Byzantium became his first priority to that end.

Pope Leo's political efforts, however, were to bear no more fruit than his military ones. Throughout his virtual captivity in Benevento, he maintained contact with the Byzantines in the hope of keeping the anti-Norman alliance alive. Constantine and his party, which included Argyrus, favored the alliance for strategic reasons. But the Basileus was ill and the alliance's opponents were powerful, headed by Patriarch Cerularius, who not only opposed the policy of reconciliation, but the Latin Church in general. The doctrinal and theological differences between the two churches had indeed grown over the years and were deep-seated, but what Cerularius opposed above all was Rome's assertion of papal supremacy. The Bishop of Rome was seen by the Patriarch as simply another bishop, perhaps the first among equals, but certainly not the head of a universal church.

Cerularius took the offensive with a long broadside in which he charged the pope with duplicity. The very Normans whom the pope was trying to drive out of Apulia were, he claimed, virtual agents of Rome in ecclesiastical terms, because they had forced the Greek parishes there to follow Latin practices such as the use of unleavened bread. In retaliation, he demanded that all Latin communities in Byzantine territory follow the Greek rite or be shut down. The pope and his counselors were all too ready to pick up this gauntlet; intemperate responses were considered and drafted. But in the end they were constrained by their need for the alliance, as well as by the arrival of conciliatory letters from Emperor Constantine and, surprisingly, Cerularius himself. A confrontation was avoided, temporarily.

Pope Leo then decided to send a high-ranking delegation to Constantinople in an effort to resolve both ecclesiastical and political issues, but he made a crucial error when he named emissaries chosen for their ability to stand up to the redoubtable Patriarch. The tragedy was that they did so all too well. The papal legates included his chancellor Frederick of Lorraine and Peter, Archbishop of Amalfi. Both had fought at Civitate, where to their previously held anti–Norman sentiments they appear to have had added resentment at what they considered to be an all but treacherous Greek performance in missing the battle. The third legate was the pope's secretary, Bishop Humbert of Mourmoutiers, anti–Greek and hard-headed, who scarcely added the necessary balance to this crucial delegation. Anxious to put their case before the Basileus and avoid being undercut by Cerularius, they immediately got off to a bad start in Constantinople — storming out of their initial meeting with the Patriarch over alleged protocol slights. They then made the fatal mistake of releasing the text of the original, but never approved, papal response to Cerularius' charges, which was both quarrelsome in the extreme and offensive to the Patriarch's personal sense of dignity. From then on, their mission was scarcely redeemable, in spite of the efforts of the emperor's party. Popular sentiment had been aroused by the legates' arrogance, the Patriarch was able to expose them to ridicule, and the legates' argumentation with the Greek bishops became increasingly intemperate and inflammatory.

Even when the legates learned of the death of Leo, which could have allowed them to bring their mission to an end inconclusively but honorably, they doggedly persisted. Finally, frustrated undoubtedly by Emperor Constantine's unwillingness to openly take their side, as well as by the Patriarch's delaying tactics, the legates lost their composure entirely. Clad in the full panoply of their offices, they interrupted the Eucharist service of Santa Sophia in July 1054 to deliver, on the High Altar, a bull of excommunication against dignitaries of the Greek Church, including, of course, Patriarch Cerularius.

The damage was done. Even though the bull, in addition to being tendentious and inaccurate, was without authority because there was no living pope in whose name it was issued, it caused a permanent break in the relations between the two Churches. Rather than obtain a rapprochement between the two capitals and two Churches, the ineptness of the papal legates, assisted indirectly by the equal obstinacy and fanaticism of Patriarch Cerularius, had created a schism of historic proportions.

For the Normans, the schism was the culmination of an amazing year. Their victory at Civitate, thirteen months earlier, had guaranteed military possession of their existing territorial gains. They consequently stood poised, with an enhanced reputation for invincibility, to successfully increase pressure on their neighbors. Pope Leo, their determined opponent, had been humiliated and then died. And now, as the result of the tragi-comic confrontation in Constantinople, they were forever relieved of the threat of a military alliance against them by the only two regional powers that had the ability to restrain them. Their opponent Argyrus had been disgraced by the failure of his policy of entente with Rome, while the incessant power struggles in Constantinople virtually ruled out any meaningful Byzantine intervention in Italy. The schism between the two Churches provided another benefit, moreover to the Normans, for it suddenly offered them the opportunity to transform themselves, in Rome's eyes, from persecutors of the Church, to its champions in those areas of Italy still under the waning domination of Constantinople.

Notes

1. Siponto, settled since Roman times, was the main seaport of northern Apulia in the early Middle Ages, but had to be abandoned in the thirteenth century because of earthquakes, tectonic subsidence which created marshes, and the consequent spread of malaria. Only ruins and a cathedral remain.

Consolidation

Propelled onto the political stage of Europe by their victory at Civitate, the sons of Tancred could well marvel at their success. In twenty years, they had progressed from hireling adventurers to lords of rich and expanding lands, owed fealty by numerous warlike barons. As their wealth had grown, so had their munificence, and through their donations and the changed political situation they had even begun to emerge as potential paladins of the Latin church in southern Italy. Humphrey, Count of Apulia and leader of the victorious army, had become a key player in the politics of the region, his friendship sought and his enmity to be avoided.

Paradoxically, the victorious Normans seemed unwilling at first to progress beyond the role in which Pope Leo had cast them, that of rapacious and ruthless opportunists. Statesmanship and political finesse might, and indeed would, come later. Humphrey, however, was not the man for it. That blunt and soldierly knight was much more interested in following up his current advantage, by consolidating the Norman position amongst a hostile Apulian population, and by obtaining retribution against his enemies—particularly those who had murdered his brother Drogo, or otherwise assisted the Byzantine and papal cause.

Help was readily available. As the news of their victory reached Normandy, the three hundred knights who had fought at Civitate were soon reinforced by newcomers from the old country. Every baron in Apulia saw his household force increase by an influx of these new, eager, and land-hungry recruits, but none more so than Count Humphrey, whose position gave him more to offer the newcomers. As the Count's personal army grew, so did his ability to conduct sizeable operations on his own account, without need to call on his barons to fulfill their military obligations. Three additions to his household must have been particularly welcome to

Humphrey, who was joined at this time by more of Tancred's sons: Geoffrey, a full brother, and two half-brothers, Mauger and a second William. Useful they could be in strengthening the family's hand in the evolving regional situation, and indeed Humphrey was to deploy them to further his strategic aims. They may also have been helpful in cushioning the often contentious relations between Humphrey and his other half-brother in Italy, Robert.

Robert Guiscard's obvious talents, but equally obvious ambition, had led both Drogo, and now Humphrey, to keep him at arm's length in Calabria as much as possible. There, he could pursue family objectives while being far enough from the seat of power not to be a threat to it. But Robert and his knights had played a key role in the battle at Civitate, and afterwards enjoyed their victory at leisure in Apulia. It was a longer period of enjoyment, it seems, than Humphry would have liked, particularly as they were living luxuriously and arrogantly off the fat of his lands. Aggravations built up, culminating at a banquet at which harsh words were exchanged between the two proud brothers. When Humphrey threatened his younger brother with imprisonment for his misdeeds, Robert — hotheaded for once, rather than wily — drew his sword to challenge his liege lord. A household knight, Jocelyn de Hareng, subdued Robert before he could do anything still more rash — unfortunately earning not gratitude, but rather Robert's permanent enmity. The incident soon enough was papered over, and a reconciliation of sorts achieved between the brothers — family solidarity was far too useful to be broken. Robert and his band, now reinforced by newcomers from the north, were sent back to Calabria to continue the process of driving out the Byzantines and expanding the family's fortunes.

Humphrey's first move against his enemies was to raid into papal Benevento. While the Norman army was not prepared for a long siege of the city and withdrew after the habitual pillage of the countryside, the expedition had made its point to Pope Leo's successor about Norman superiority on the ground. After seizing a few minor towns in the Gargano area, Humphrey's army began in earnest to intimidate the population of Apulia. Conversano, on the plain south of the Byzantine capital of Bari, was seized, while other Byzantine towns along the plain, in Calabria, and even in the Tarentine "heel" of Italy were sacked and obliged to recognize Norman might, if not necessarily their right to rule. New Norman forts sprang up throughout the province, designed to dominate their immediate surroundings and extract a price for non-cooperation.

The regular military forces that the Byzantines were able to put into the field to oppose this expansion were defeated repeatedly, specifically in engagements at Matera, Oria, Lecce, and Taranto, while the town militias were as often cowed into surrender as defeated. Otranto, Lecce, Nardo, Gallipoli, and Minervino were plundered, and even the strong cities of Trani and Bari were forced to pay tribute to the Normans to avoid pillage of their fields and orchards. At Otranto, the town was won by a ruse. Robert, commanding the Norman force, had won the confidence of a citizen whose house adjoined the city walls (but which had not been pulled down in preparation for the siege because it belonged to a relative of the governor). After talking his way into the house, Robert let in his troops, who then used its roof to scale the city's ramparts and capture the town.

This was a Hauteville campaign of conquest. Geoffrey and Mauger were regularly in the field with their brother the Count, while Robert left Calabria periodically to cooperate with his brothers in the campaigns. Family coffers were greatly enriched by the booty from the two-year campaign. Much less to the family's credit were the savage retributions demanded by Humphrey against those whom he considered his enemies: public executions and display of the corpses along the roadsides of the province became all too common. Norman domination of the province was strengthened by this display of cruelty, but it only delayed popular acceptance.

In the eyes of the resentful inhabitants, as well as of the surrounding powers, the Normans remained no more than military usurpers. The legitimacy of Humphrey's title as Count was still questioned by the rulers in the region, who questioned either the Holy Roman Emperor's or the pope's authority to have granted the title. Even among the Normans themselves, the right of the Hautevilles to the leadership remained contested by a number of the more powerful barons, who had also carved out rich personal fiefdoms in the province and were ready to fight for their autonomy.

Fortunately for Humphrey and his brothers, their external opponents were for the moment unable to stop their subjugation of Apulia and expansion into Calabria. Byzantine power in Italy, in particular, was at a low ebb, drained by years of faction and rapid regime changes in Constantinople, conscious neglect of the military by Basileus Constantine, and higher defense priorities in the Balkans and Anatolia. Even when the imperial armies finally succeeded in halting the invading Pechnegs in Bulgaria and Seljuk Turks in Anatolia, and the anti-military policy was reversed by a strong new emperor, Isaac Comnenus, the gains were fleeting. Comnenus was all too soon replaced by Constantine Ducas, who reverted to the policy of neglecting the military. While such a policy may have made sense in Constantinople as a way of limiting the military aristocracy's pretensions to rule, it was disastrous for what was left of Byzantine power in Italy during the very period when the Normans were readying to complete their conquest. Faced with shrunken budgets, reduced strength and fickle leadership in Constatninople, Byzantine garrisons were all too often left to their own devices, or reinforced too late with too little. For the population of the area, the waning of Byzantine power engendered the growth of faction. Within the towns remaining loyal to the empire, proponents of accommodation with the Normans, often of Lombard stock, undermined the Greek loyalists. Thus, and in spite of their bad record of governance, the Normans had a growing fifth column amongst the citizens of the cities and towns that they sought to conquer.

The papacy remained hostile to Norman ambitions, yet virtually powerless to do anything to counter them. The new pope, Victor II, a German like Leo, was elected after a year's political maneuvering, with the support of both the reformers in the Church and Emperor Henry. His election assured a continuation of Leo's reform policies, and blocked the aspirations of the Roman families, who had wanted the return of an Italian papacy. Victor's major objective was Church reform, and events in north Europe seized his attention more than the problems of the Latin communities in the south. Moreover, he had few means at his disposal to influence events in Apulia. The religious schism had ruled out any alliance with Constantinople. Even the papal base at Benevento had less value in Victor's eye's since the city's commune, resentful at the papacy's lack of support when Humphrey had besieged the town in 1054, kicked out the pope's regent and invited back the old rulers, Pandulf and Landulf. Powerless to reverse the defeat at Civitate and preoccupied elsewhere, Victor could only swallow his resentment at Norman arrogance and practices. Moreover, with the death of Emperor Henry in 1056, the pope lost his only possible ally in extending the reform program into the south. The nine years of a weak and ineffectual regency which followed (Henry's son having acceded to the German throne as Henry IV at the tender age of six) meant the virtual suspension of imperial pretensions in southern Italy.

Pope Victor died in 1057. The reformist bishops engineered the election of his successor, without seeking the blessing of the child emperor-designate. Indeed, it was unlikely that the successor, Frederick of Lorraine, could have obtained imperial support even had he tried, as the house of Lorraine was in fierce competition with the German royal family. Frederick's election was not good news for the Normans; he had always taken a strong anti–Norman position as counselor to Pope Leo, and had also been one of the ill-fated legates to Constantinople. When he took office as Stephen IX, he immediately sought to bring the Normans into line with

Rome's reforms, even confiscating the treasure of his old abbey of Monte Cassino to finance a military effort. He could expect no help, however, from young Emperor Henry, given the hostility of their two families and the circumstances of his election. Stephen instead sought to renew the alliance with Constantinople, where Patriarch Cerularius had lost his position as a result of the accession of Isaac Comnenus, and Argyrus was also beginning to regain his influence. Stephen was determined to avenge the Church's defeat at Civitate.

Pope Stephen found a potential ally in a seemingly unlikely place, in Salerno. Long gone were the days when alliance with the Normans was the bedrock of Salerno's power, or when Prince Guaimar had refused to join Pope's Leo's expedition against the Normans. Instead, since the death of Guaimar, Norman-Salernitan relations had veered from grudging cooperation toward a more normal relationship between contemporary states: that is, competitive near-hostility.

Guaimar's two-decade alliance with the Normans had been highly beneficial to both sides. The Normans had first enjoyed the protection of Gauimar, and later gained some acceptance and legitimacy through the marriage ties between the ruling house of Salerno and the Hautevilles. But, following the death of Guaimar and the victory at Civitate, the Normans had outgrown their need for Salernitan sponsorship and, instead, began to look at Salerno as potential prey. Salerno, for its part, had used the military strength of its Norman allies to rise to predominance in the region; its golden age was a result of Guaimar's Norman connection. But the policy had been costly. The taxes that Guaimar had levied to pay for his expensive and sometimes troublesome auxiliaries, coupled with some extravagances of his own in his latter years, had harmed prosperity and were resented by the population. In addition, Guaimar had perhaps been too generous, both to his Norman allies on whom he had kept few controls, and to his internal allies, to whom he had granted much of the revenue, and even the power, of the state.

The new ruler, Gisulf, saw these problems and was anxious to rectify them, but had neither the political leverage, nor perhaps the skills, to move decisively. To begin with, he could resolve the state's financial problems only by losing domestic support, since he would have to withdraw many of the privileges that his father had given the church and local gentry. Rejecting the Normans could be even more costly, no matter how much he may have wished to do so, for had they not shown their power by putting him on his throne? Gisulf, it can be imagined, was not entirely grateful to the Normans for their role in putting him in power, for they had — in typical fashion — made a good profit from their support, grudging as it was after their initial support for his uncle Guy. Guy, indeed, had become head of a faction of Salernitans who militated for a renewal of the Norman tie. Gisulf's reign had begun on a bad note as far as his relations with the Normans were concerned, when he had chosen to sit on the fence during the Normans' struggle with Pope Leo. His excuse had been his troubles with Amalfi, but the Normans would not forget his equivocation.

The Normans themselves brought the conflict into the open. The first to move was Richard of Aversa, who shortly after returning from his key role in the battle of Civitate began to levy demands on the new ruler of Salerno. His tactics were typically Norman: presentation of a claim based, however loosely, on law or custom, and then application of force to extort a payoff. Richard argued on this occasion that the annual gifts that Prince Guaimar had given him should also be paid by Gisulf — presumably in perpetuity. On Gisuf's not unreasonable and perhaps expected refusal, Richard began to harass Salerno's territories, and skirmishes ensued — in which Gisulf was almost captured by his nominal vassal. Before the affair could become serious however, Gisulf was able to forge a defensive alliance with the Amalfitans that had the effect of diverting Richard away to an easier target. That was Capua, long an opponent of the Normans in Aversa but no longer powerful. Richard had tried once before, in 1052, to lay claim to Capua, but had put his ambitions on hold when bought off with an extortion payment of six thousand gold bezants. However when Prince Pandulf V died in 1057 and was succeeded by a minor, Landulf V, Richard lost no time in seizing the opportunity. Within months, he had starved the capital city into recognizing him as its Prince — even though the town retained its own garrison, citadel, and control over commerce in the settlement.

By seizing Capua, Richard became the first Norman to rule a preexisting Italian state. Married to Humphrey's sister Fressenda, this gifted and personable ruler was both kin and competitor to the Hauteville brothers in Apulia. After reinforcing his victory over Capua by obliging the statelet of Gaeta to enter into an unfavorable alliance, Richard emerged as the predominant ruler in the rich Campania region, and the most accomplished of the Normans of southern Italy.

Ever opportunistic, the Normans of Apulia were not slow to follow Richard's example in making demands on Salerno. Humphrey's pretext, in addition to the payment tactic followed by Richard, was to claim that Gisulf had promised him certain castles in compensation for his help at the time of Guaimar's assassination. Gisulf, as Humphrey probably expected, refused to yield the castles. Humphrey's response was both tactical and strategic. He invaded, and rapidly seized lands around Policastro in the south, and Eboli in the very heart of Salerno's lands. Then, to show that he intended to stay and to seize still more, Humphrey enfeoffed his recently arrived brother William as Count of a newly invented county, the Principata, a Norman thorn in the very flesh of the historical princedom. William would, over the coming years, succeed in enlarging his county through incremental acquisitions of Salerno's weakly defended and administered lands in the Cilento hills, between Eboli and Policastro. Nor was that all the damage done by the Hautevilles, for by 1057 Robert Guiscard had forced the submission of Cosenza and other towns on the borders of Calabria that had long been claimed by Salerno.

Bit by bit, the Hauteville brothers were expropriating most of Salerno's southern lands, leaving Gisulf to sulk impotently in his capital. Small wonder, then, that Gisulf welcomed Pope Stephen's efforts to turn the tables on the Normans. He became an enthusiastic supporter of the hoped-for alliance with Byzantium.

The Normans, foremost among them the sons of Tancred of Hauteville, were also expanding elsewhere. To the north of Apulia, in the loosely held Lombard territories of the southern Abruzzi, Norman knights had been carving out independent holdings since the early days after Melfi. But Humphrey now made expansion in this area a new Hauteville family goal, by enfeoffing his brother Mauger in another newly created county called the Capitanata. When Mauger died, not long after his arrival in Italy, the title passed to the elder brother Geoffrey. It was Geoffrey's son, however, Robert of Loritello, who would in the coming years most actively expand the Hauteville holdings in the north.

For the moment, it was Robert Guiscard in Calabria who was most successful. From his fortress at San Marco he had succeeded in dominating if not yet conquering the cities of Calabria's one major agricultural area, the Val de Crati. Cosenza, Bisignano, Martirano all paid him tribute, as well as providing him with military service and hostages to guarantee good behavior. His band of knights grew with his successes, supported by his reputation for generous distribution of the spoils as well as his air of affability and courtesy. With each increase in strength, Guiscard was able to erect and garrison more fortresses to dominate the region, and to exact more plunder from those areas that remained loyal to Byzantium.

The Normans, led by the Hauteville brothers and Richard of Aversa, had, in a few short years, followed up the victory at Civitate by solid gains on the ground. The power and seeming invincibility of the Normans was recognized throughout Byzantine Italy and the Lombard states. Where the Normans had not yet conquered, they often dominated and exacted tribute. The Hauteville brothers had been particularly successful in expanding the family fortunes to the north, south, and west of the province.

But while the military promise of the victory at Civitate was being consolidated, the political payoffs had been few. Apulia was pacified but far from stable; the fractiousness of the Norman barons was as much an element of insecurity as the hostile population. The cruelty of Humphrey's repression in Apulia had done much to keep anti–Norman sentiment alive, and Norman arrogance and exactions against their neighbors threatened to rekindle a hostile grand alliance between the papacy and the eastern empire. Pope Stephen was a determined enemy, and the Normans had reason to fear that their gains were not yet assured.

Against this uncertain backdrop, Humphrey in 1057 fell mortally ill, the probable causes being malaria and the hardships of a military life punctuated by excesses. Recognizing that his end was coming, and that consolidation of the Hauteville fortunes would require strong leadership, the Count swallowed his personal feelings and summoned his younger half-brother Robert to his deathbed. There, he put his sons Abelard and Herman under Robert's protection and supposed regency. Robert, who knew well how to make himself agreeable, wept and made indeterminate promises. In this dramatic scene of family tension, the two brothers, never close, did at least have one common interest and objective in the time remaining: that the leadership in Apulia remain in Hauteville family hands. In that they were successful, and Humphrey died knowing that his family would inherit the title and the lands that he and his brothers had carved out in this new land.

Humphrey's death marked a transition. The sons of Tancred had originally emerged from the ranks of their peers as effective military leaders. But their very successes had now put them in an immensely more complicated position, one in which the stakes were higher, involving much greater diplomatic finesse, and requiring need for statesmanship and vision. Humphrey, gruff and uncomplicated, had recognized the new requirements in putting forth Robert the Guiscard, already renowned for his skill in political maneuver as much as for his skill in warfare, as his successor. History vindicated his choice.

In the short run, it was Humphrey's sons who paid for his choice, since Robert's skills were now used to deprive them of their inheritance. Moving rapidly after Humphrey passed away, Robert maneuvered to have his election as Count made, not as regent for his nephews, but in his own right. Once again the sons of Ami, Pierre and Gauthier, contested this succession from one Hauteville to another, but once again they were outmaneuvered. Robert Guiscard was elected as the new Count. Perhaps his selection could be seen as a tribute to Robert's skills as a negotiator and politician. But it also could be attributed to the Norman barons' reluctant recognition that the recent election of the strongly anti–Norman Pope Stephen posed a threat that required them in turn to have firm leadership. Either way, Robert's election did not sit all that well with many of the barons who either supported the sons of Humphrey or, more fundamentally, resented Hauteville pretensions to rule them. That resentment would cause problems, time and again, during Robert's long rule.

Guiscard

Robert Guiscard had become Count of Apulia, but he could not yet
enjoy the title in security. Pierre of Trani, powerful and resentful, refused
to accept the results of the election. Waiting until Robert's back was turned
in Calabria, he raised a revolt, seized the communal capital of Melfi, and
was only driven out when Robert returned in person to take up arms. And
even though Robert then called a conclave of all the barons of Apulia and
got them to reaffirm his leadership, he would be faced with resistance and
periodic revolt from a number of them for more than two decades. The
spirit of independence that had led the original Norman adventurers to
Italy and the enterprise that they had shown in carving out their individual fortunes in Apulia, coupled with resentment at the successes and pre-
sumptions of the Hautevilles, would long keep the spirit of rebellion alive
among the unruly barons of the south.

The new Count Robert wasted no time in assuring his personal fortune. He quickly accomplished the transfer of Humphrey's estates, including most of those intended for the young nephews. With these additions
to his already existing holdings in Calabria, he became the premier Norman landholder in Italy, to be exceeded only by his rival Richard of Aversa
when the latter took over Capua the following year. But Robert's holdings
were widely spread, often in poor regions, and could not form the basis
of a coherent polity. For that, he would need to control more land — his
ambition knew few limits on that score — as well as more contiguous holdings. Never one to lose time, he returned to Calabria to continue his work.
This time, he went beyond his previous field of action in the Val di Crati
to harry the Byzantines in the very toe of Italy, obtaining subjection and
payments of tribute from the towns of Maida and Squillace.

During that summer's campaign, Robert was joined by the last of the sons of Tancred to come to Italy, in fact the youngest of them all, Roger. About twenty-five years old at the time, Roger rivaled his elder brother in good looks, ability and ambition, but the two had quite different personalities. Where Robert was calculating, often distant and arrogant, Roger was of a much sunnier disposition, inclined to merriment and at ease with his companions. The description by Roger's most loyal chronicler Geoffrey Malaterra, as laudatory as most chronicles are, nonetheless finds corroborating echoes among other, less partisan, contemporary observers:

> ... a handsome youth, tall and well built. He was very ready of speech, but his gay and open manner was controlled by a calculating prudence. Brave and valiant himself, he was fired by the ambitions proper to his years, and he sought by means of lavish gifts and favors to collect a party of adherents who would be devoted to furthering his fortunes.[1]

Two brothers with such similar ambitions seemed bound to clash, and indeed they would. But they began in exemplary cooperation. Roger first helped his elder brother mount an unsuccessful, and half-hearted, attack on the rich city of Reggio at the end of the peninsula, controlling the Straits of Messina to Sicily. Afterwards, when Robert had to return to Apulia to put down Pierre of Trani's revolt, Roger continued the campaign in Calabria and then, when Guiscard needed more help, went to Melfi to make a key contribution in defending the family's interests. His brother's succession as Count finally assured, Roger returned to Calabria with fewer than a hundred men. There, he set up in a new castle near Mileto, a site from which he could control the old Roman road to Reggio, and which would be his preferred home for many years. Robert joined him during the winter with more men, to make another effort at subduing Reggio, but once again they found the fortifications too well defended to take easily. Some compensation for that disappointment was gained in capturing Nicastro and forcing the town of Gerace to pay a generous tribute. Following this short campaign, Robert returned to Apulia, leaving Roger in charge of pursuing the family's interests in Calabria.

In the spring of 1058, the external threat to the Normans in Apulia suddenly receded, for Pope Stephen was taken ill in Rome and died. So sudden was his illness, in fact, that there were suggestions that the Normans might have had a hand in removing their enemy. Unlikely as it was that the Normans at the time could have managed a sophisticated poisoning plot, they most surely welcomed the development. As the throne in Constantinople was changing hands at the same time, it meant that the threat of a Byzantine-papal alliance was removed. Election of a successor to Pope Stephen would create an imbroglio into which the Normans would eventually be drawn, but for the moment they were free to pursue their own interests, namely the consolidation of Apulia, and the effort to bring still another province into Hauteville hands.

Their own interests soon became complicated enough. Robert and Roger, even though they had subdued most of Calabria and softened it up for eventual conquest, began to lose the warmth of their first phase of cooperation. The check at Reggio, and the beginnings of a dispute about sharing the booty, were eroding the brotherly relationship first established. Robert had granted Roger no land of his own or private source of income, while Roger for his part was anxious to build up his wealth rapidly so he could afford to marry. Then Robert began to slow down payments to Roger for his garrisons, motivated perhaps by thoughts of how he had had to live from hand to mouth in his own first years in Italy, and trying to oblige his younger brother to take the same harsh medicine. Equally likely, Robert may simply have been careful to see that his ambitious younger brother not have the wherewithal to build a large and loyal following at his, Robert's, expense. Proud Roger, quick to take offense at what he considered his brother's lack of respect, first complained, and then decided to make Robert pay for his supposed mistreatment, by going into revolt.

Roger found support from another brother, William, Count of the Principata. We do not know the reasons for William's dissatisfaction with Robert, but grievances he must have had. It seems that Robert, whatever his skills with outsiders or his affection for his brothers may have been, was not an easy man, and his brothers repeatedly were driven to the necessity of violence to make him hear their complaints. In any event, at this point William offered to the rebellious Roger a secure base of operations in Scalea, a castle town at the south end of the Bay of Policastro, from which Roger began to attack Guiscard's properties. The elder brother quickly retaliated, bringing forces into Calabria to lay siege to Scalea. He in turn was attacked outside the town by Wiliams's troops, and thus an unseemly war between the brothers continued across the province throughout the early part of 1058. The Normans, thoughtlessly it would seem, employed against each other their familiar tactics of destroying crops, pillaging the countryside, and abducting merchants for ransom.

The principal victims, as usual in wars of this period, were the local peasantry whose crops were destroyed, and the towns whose commerce was disrupted. This wanton damage, coupled with a severe drought, created a famine of Biblical proportions and, in turn, a true popular uprising in Calabria against the Normans. The uprising eventually threatened the fragile stability of Apulia, also suffering from drought as well as the exactions of the count and his oppressive barons. After a garrison of some sixty Normans at Nicastro was overwhelmed and slaughtered by its irate citizens, the Hautevilles finally realized that their internecine fighting could no longer serve any logical family purpose, and a reconciliation of sorts was arranged.

It was an ambiguous settlement. Robert agreed to give Roger the lead in subduing Calabria, and agreed to split any new conquests, beyond a line at Squillace, on a 50/50 basis. But Robert's terms were grudging, and not very generous: Roger would get half the revenues, but neither ownership nor control, of new lands and towns. "While generous with money, [he] was stingy in giving out the smallest portion of land, and found all sorts of roundabout ways to drag matters out,"[2] commented a chronicler about Guiscard. Robert's caution and cunning were directed even at his younger brother, in this case by depriving him of a territorial base, and also denying him the sufficiency of fighting men that might prompt greater ambitions. Nonetheless, with their quarrel patched up for the moment at least, the brothers were free to look to how they might gain family advantage from the major political developments that had been taking place in Rome.

In the Holy City, events had tumbled out of control since the death of Pope Stephen. The old Roman families, frozen out of the last three papal selections and eager to reclaim their earlier dominance of the process as well as the person of the pontiff, had moved swiftly. Taking advantage of the temporary absence from Rome of the principal reformers, and the weakness of the distant emperor's position, they arranged the election of a fellow Italian as Pope Benedict X. While Benedict himself was an acceptable choice, the reformers found both the method of his election, and the resurgence of the reactionary Roman clique, to be unacceptable for their reform aspirations. The reform-minded bishops left Rome to confer as to next steps with the acknowledged leader of the reform movement, Cardinal Hildebrand.

Hildebrand had been the leader of the reform movement within the Vatican since the days of Pope Leo. A Benedictine monk from Siena, he was gifted with such extraordinary intelligence and strength of character that he had risen fast in the Church's service and become principal counselor to the recent popes. In fact, he probably could have had the job himself had he not preferred to work from behind the scenes. An ardent champion of the reforms, which later in his career he would push to their logical extremes, he counseled a strong reaction to the coup by the Roman families. The bishops decided to put forth their own papal candidate, and after consultations with their allies, the Regent Empress Agnes and the powerful Duke of Lorraine, they proclaimed a Burgundian, Gerard, Bishop of Florence, as the new pope. He took the name of Nicholas II, and in short order advanced on Rome with the support of the Duke of Lorraine's troops.

Rome now had two rival popes. Even though Benedict was soon forced to evacuate the Lateran and flee, under the protection of the Roman families, to suburban Galeria, both the population and the clergy had split their loyalties between the two claimants, and Church business came to a full stop. The reformers had their man in the Lateran, but he could not exercise full power, and they foresaw that they could not succeed unless they drove Benedict from his rival office. But Hildebrand, who increasingly believed that the reforms could only succeed if the Church was more independent, was hesitant to call on the emperor or the Duke of Lorraine to expel the Roman pope. To do so would compromise the degree of autonomy that the Church had managed to wrest since Henry III's death, and make it once again dependent on balancing between the Roman families and the empire. The Church needed, in short, a champion powerful enough to cause the Roman families to back down, yet one who would not seek to interfere in the Church's business. For this unexpected role he was prepared to consider, on the advice of his close advisor Bishop Desiderius, none other than the Normans.

Desiderius' role in promoting the advantages of a Norman connection was a key one, and seemingly unlikely given his background. A Lombard, and a member of the Beneventan princely family at that, whose own father had been killed in a skirmish with Normans, he could scarcely have been expected to be pro–Norman. But Desiderius was a thoughtful man, given to the contemplative life; his skills had made him in demand as a Church administrator, and he had begun some years earlier to recognize that the future of the region lay more in the hands of the new Norman settlers than in the decaying and fragile Lombard aristocracies. A chance earlier visit with Robert Guiscard had also brought him to consider that the Normans, in spite of their crimes and mistreatment of Church property, might yet become bulwarks of that very establishment because of their basic piety and respect for papal authority.[3] Desiderius finally became convinced of the potential usefulness to the Church of a Norman connection once he had succeeded Frederick of Lorraine as abbot of the monastery of Monte Cassino. That important Benedictine center, with rich properties situated in the middle of Capuan territory, had long been preyed upon by the rulers of that state, most particularly the notorious Pandulf IV. Even the Normans of Aversa, hired by the monastery to defend it against the Capuan demands, had taken advantage of their situation until forcibly driven off monastery lands by a previous abbot, Richer. As the emperor was both too far away and too feeble at the moment to be an effective protector of the abbey, Desiderius needed a closer protector or, at a minimum, pledges of non-interference from his neighbors.

When Richard of Aversa had become ruler of Capua, the recently appointed Abbot Desiderius realized that a new relationship with this imposing ruler could give the monastery the powerful protector it needed. He invited Richard to pay a visit to the abbey during one of his campaigns in the area, and was careful on the occasion to receive him with all honors, even washing the Count's feet with his own hands. The strategy worked. Richard, who realized that the abbot's blessing could strengthen his legitimacy (which was shaky after his having deposed the traditional Lombard dynasty of Capua), apparently decided that he could play a greater role as the monastery's protector than as its despoiler. Within weeks, he issued a formal charter that confirmed the great abbey in all its lands and possessions. The abbey's future was secure, and under Desiderius it would go on to its golden age. But, more important for our story, the Normans had found an influential ally in the heart of the Church, one who would speak in favor of alliance with, rather than hostility to, these troublesome knights.

Hildebrand would need some convincing. While he had softened somewhat the virulent attitude toward the Normans that he had displayed during Pope Leo's time, he was scarcely inclined either to like or to trust them. But, under Desiderius' urging and with the reform papacy in peril, the pill of necessity was swallowed. Even though the Church had long reviled the Normans as scarcely better than pagans, renegades who had abused the Church and violated its property, who had taken up arms against the pope and held him captive for nine miserable months, Hildebrand agreed, on behalf of that Church and in its hour of need, that he would go and ask those Normans for their assistance. It was a fateful decision, but Hildebrand was if nothing else a man of action and determination. He set off for Capua, thinking heaven knows what thoughts, but determined to get the necessary Norman assistance. Richard, on the other hand, did not need convincing that this was an opportunity he could not pass up. Only a year earlier the object of Pope Stephen's schemes, he was now being petitioned to become the new pope's sponsor, a position that would enhance his status and legitimacy immeasurably. Hildebrand quickly got the agreement he wanted, and the two men together, accompanied by three hundred of Richard's troops, marched to Rome. The presence of the Norman troops intimidated the Romans sufficiently to assure a successful consecration of the new Pope Nicholas, even though the rival Pope Benedict remained holed up in his stronghold at Galeria.

The new pope acted decisively. Less than a month after his consecration, and urged on by the energetic and forceful Hildebrand, Nicholas called a synod at the Lateran. There, a far-reaching and dramatic reform was enacted. In a direct challenge to both the Roman families who were still protecting the antipope, and to the Holy Roman emperors who had traditionally interfered in papal selections, the Lateran Synod of 1059 declared that papal selection in the future would be the prerogative of the Church elders alone. The cardinals of the Church, supervised by their own officers, were to make the selection, which would, subsequently, be submitted to the emperor and the public for passive assent only. This system, which with a few changes has lasted until the present, was a daring move at the time. In denying the emperor's right to a voice in selection of a new pope, the synod undermined the relations of interdependence that had so long existed between pope and emperor. Future emperors might now find themselves less inclined to support the papacy; they might even oppose it. Pope Nicholas may not have been as concerned, however, about the future as his own tenuous present. He was ready to take his chance on the future because he could take advantage of the actual weakness of the empire, as well as the passivity imposed on the Roman clans by the threat of his Norman allies. His action, even so, was a risky one and he was exposed, needing support from a powerful regional ruler to maintain the ground that he had staked out. He needed the Normans even more than before.

With strengthening the Church's position in the south as one of his absolute priorities, Nicholas began a trip to the region less than a month after the Lateran Synod. Traveling with the full dignity and display of the papal office, Nicholas' retinue made its first stop in Monte Cassino, to honor the great abbey as well as Abbot Desiderius, whose policy recommendations had so far borne such good fruit. After a stop in Benevento to hold a synod and, not coincidentally, renew papal claims to that city, Nicholas proceeded toward Melfi where he proposed to hold another synod on the deplorable state of the Church's affairs in the region. That he chose Melfi, the capital of Norman Apulia, was no accident. It emphasized to the Normans, in their own territory, the importance which the papacy placed on reform in the local dioceses. At the same time, it gave him and his entourage a chance to have some side conversations, and perhaps reach agreements, with these new or potential allies. Count Robert may even have invited the pope to Melfi, for there are hints in documents of the time that he had followed Richard of Capua's new relations with the Church with great interest, and perhaps even sent tentative feelers to Rome on his own. The Hauteville brothers hurried to Melfi to honor the pope: Robert from the Capitanata where he had been helping his brother Geoffrey gain control over his new county, and Roger from Calabria, where he had just put down a Byzantine-inspired revolt in Gerace.

Before opening the synod at Melfi, Pope Nicholas performed a highly symbolic act: he consecrated the new church of Santissima Trinita at Venosa. The rebuilding of that church had been begun by Drogo, and both he and his two brothers William and Humphrey had been buried there in what had become for the Normans, and certainly the Hautevilles, an important place of veneration. The ceremony buried, at a symbolical level, Pope Leo's old policy of total opposition to the Normans.

The Synod of Melfi dealt with pressing ecclesiastical matters, in view of the fact that the reforms on matters of simony and celibacy among the clergy had so far been widely ignored in the south. Nonetheless, and in spite of the public defrocking of several bishops, the synod achieved little of lasting value in reforming the Church. What happened in the side conversations, on the other hand, was historical in its significance. The dealings between Hildebrand, the determined moralist, and Guiscard, the pious but amoral opportunist, must have been fascinating, and owed their eventual success to the traits of statesmanship which the two participants shared. For at Melfi the Church and the Normans reconciled, and indeed went beyond. They laid the foundation for a new alliance that would provide important benefits to both sides for years to come.

Both Robert Guiscard and Richard of Capua swore formal oaths of support and loyalty to the pope, in return for which he invested them in their existing territories and, for Guiscard, territories still to be conquered in Italy and even in Sicily. The implications of this bargain were far-reaching. For the pope, it meant that he was promised the support of the most dynamic and capable rulers in the south of Italy, and with their strength behind him he could pursue his reforms with much more assurance. Norman promises to support him in matters ecclesiastical was also important, as it could help produce the reforms he wanted in the southern dioceses, as well as an expansion of the Latin church in the lands that the Normans would come to rule. He also had reason to hope, as events in Apulia were beginning to indicate, that Norman rule was maturing and that, by bringing them into the circle of power and responsibility, their excesses could be abated. Finally, the pope had retained a slight lever over the Normans, whose potential for disruption he could not ignore. By obtaining parallel pledges from the rival Norman rulers, Robert and Richard, the pope had retained a possibility of playing them against each other in the event that one failed to perform the obligations of his oath.

For the Normans, the pact at Melfi opened the door to a different sort of world. No longer quasi-outlaws, they had suddenly been invested in their existing lands by the very authority which had, not too long ago, been trying to drive them out of the region. Moreover, Robert had been invested with a new title: Duke of Apulia, Calabria, and Sicily, which amounted to an open invitation from the papacy to conquer those lands in his name and, that of the Church. Not only did the new title give Robert greater precedence over his fellow counts in Apulia, it also legitimized the eventual conquest of Calabria and Sicily as Hauteville land. It probably bothered Robert little that the pope had very slight actual authority to make such a sweeping investiture. Even if the ancient and spurious Donation of Constantine might be interpreted to cover Calabria, it covered Sicily scarcely at all, and the pope's investiture ignored equally the rights of both western and eastern emperors in southern Italy, not to speak of the Muslims in Sicily. But Guiscard was, like most Normans, ready to invoke a law against others when it could be interpreted to suit his own purposes. He was not going to question the propriety of such a sweeping papal grant, given that it eminently suited his own present as well as future ambitions.

The text of the oath taken by Robert (Richard's was probably very similar) has survived in the Vatican archives, and is interesting:

> I, Robert, by the Grace of God and of Saint Peter, Duke of Apulia and of Calabria, and, with the aid of both, future Duke of Sicily, shall be from this time forth faithful to the Roman Church and the Apostolic See and to you, my lord Pope Nicholas. I shall do nothing by word or deed whereby you lose life or limb, or be taken captive unlawfully. Nor shall I knowingly betray, to your injury, information which you have entrusted to me instructing me not to share it. I shall everywhere and to the best of my ability help the Holy Roman Church hold and secure the rights of Saint Peter and his property, against all men. I shall help you hold the Roman papacy securely and honorably. I shall seek neither to invade nor acquire the land of Saint Peter and the Principality [Benevento], nor shall I presume to plunder them without the clear permission of you or your successors who may enter into the honor of Saint Peter, with the exception of what you grant to me, or your successors shall grant. I shall endeavor in good faith to see that the Holy Roman Church receives annually the agreed tribute from the land of Saint Peter which I hold or shall hold. All churches which lie under my lordship, with their possessions, I transfer into your power, and I shall defend them in fealty to the Holy Roman Church. And I shall swear fealty to no one except with the reservation of my fealty to the Holy Roman Church. If you or your successors shall leave this life before me, I shall, in accordance with the instructions I am given by the foremost cardinals, Roman clergy and laymen, assist in the election and ordination of a pope to the honor of Saint Peter. I shall observe all the above in good faith to you

and the Holy Roman Church, and I shall observe this fealty to your successors who are appointed to the honor of Saint Peter, and who shall have confirmed to me the investiture which you have granted to me. So help me God and his Holy Gospels.[4]

With this oath, a new page was opened in Norman relations with the Vatican, and huge new possibilities for the future were opened up to the sons of Tancred. For Richard of Capua and Duke Robert Guiscard, investiture by the pope imparted a new kind of respectability, and opened up for them, and the states which they were building, a new kind of role in the region's politics. How well they would play those roles remained to be seen, but alliance with the papacy would give the Normans, for the first time, a secure moral and legal basis for the power that they already exercised.

But, for the moment, there were some immediate problems to be faced, the first of which was the persistent problem of the rival pope. In keeping with their new status as sworn allies of the papacy, Robert and Richard soon lived up to the first of their responsibilities by obliging the Romans to accept Nicholas as pope. Norman detachments descended on Rome, besieged the Galeria stronghold of Benedict, and looted the surrounding countryside. Those strong-arm tactics resulted in the capture and imprisonment of the unfortunate bishop, whose only crime had been to be the instrument of the losing side. Pope Nicholas, finally secure on his seat in the Lateran, could resume the Church's business unchallenged, and with some gratitude to the Normans for putting him there.

For Guiscard, ever the realistic politician, the pope's blessing presented opportunities to be seized and an impetus not to be lost.

Notes

1. Geoffrey Malaterra, I, C. 19, as cited in Douglas, p. 42.
2. Geoffrey Malaterra, II, C. 21, p. 35, as cited in Loud, p. 132.
3. Desiderius' sojourn with Guiscard had taken place when the churchman, as a leading member of the delegation that Pope Stephen was sending to Constantinople to propose an anti–Norman alliance, was obliged to cancel the trip because of Stephen's death. From Bari, he needed to return rapidly to Rome, and accordingly applied to Robert for a safe-conduct to cross Norman-held Apulia. Desiderius was not only granted safe conduct in spite of his hostile mission, but entertained and courted by the politically astute new Count.
4. *Le Liber Censuum de l'Eglise Romaine*, i.422, as cited in Loud, pp. 188–89.

Calabria

The new Duke of Apulia, Calabria, and Sicily did not yet, in fact, have much of a duchy. Robert Guiscard had undoubtedly become the greatest individual landowner in Apulia and Calabria, even as his brothers Geoffrey, Mauger, William, and Roger were busy adding to the family's holdings in various parts of southern Italy. But, as yet, those holding were scattered, sometimes contested, and still far from consolidated into a single polity. Moreover, the major part of Norman Apulia and the southern Abruzzi remained in the hands of other Norman barons, most of whom had earned their fiefs through their own efforts, and whose acceptance of Guiscard's lordship — either as count or duke — was grudging at best. For most, he was still their military leader, to whom they owed the expected oaths of fealty and assistance in time of common threat. But, as far as they were concerned, their status as nominal vassals did not necessarily encompass absolute loyalty, or even obligations of military service if not in an agreed cause.

The reality was that the Byzantines still controlled substantial areas of the prospective duchy, including their provincial capital of Bari. Moreover, Muslim control of Sicily had been uncontested since the failure of the Byzantine expedition led by Maniakes some 17 years earlier, and whatever ambitions Guiscard and Pope Nicholas may have nurtured to return the island to Christian rule seemed, at the moment, farfetched.

To establish his dukedom in reality, Guiscard faced a formidable set of challenges. He would have to consolidate existing Norman holdings into a coherent entity, drive out the remaining Byzantine forces, invade and conquer Sicily, and obtain acceptance from his subjects as well as his fellow rulers. The man's ambition, however, was every bit as large as the challenges that faced him.

The papal alliance and the new ducal title did provide, to begin with, new diplomatic opportunities for both of the major Norman leaders, Duke Robert and Prince Richard. Their status had never been higher, their power had now become legitimized, and they were the most dynamic and powerful rulers in the area. The situation nonetheless was delicate; the two proud men could, by cooperation, dominate the region or, in competition, keep it in turmoil. Their opponents may occasionally have been tempted to stir up the known rivalry between the two Norman leaders in the hopes of weakening both, but most abjured such a tactic as too risky and fraught with potentially lethal consequences. And while both the western and eastern emperors were unhappy that the Normans had been given new legitimacy by Pope Nicholas, each was preoccupied by matters closer to home and the two were unlikely to make common cause to reverse the situation in Italy. The Byzantine authorities in Italy consequently were limited to largely defensive operations, even though they retained considerable military and political capability. As a result of these considerations, the native states could find no viable allies, and realized that accommodation to the Normans — or at least obtaining their neutrality — was the best strategy available.

The most important of the neighbors to seek an alliance was Gisulf of Salerno, who had been estranged ever since his conspicuous absence at the battle of Civitate some six years earlier. Now, prompted by the new situation, Gisulf found it necessary to overlook (if not abandon) his aversion to the Normans. His preferred strategy of an anti–Norman alliance with Rome had died the year before, along with Pope Stephen. Gisulf had also sought to capitalize on the spat between Robert and his brothers Roger and William, and had made overtures to Robert in an effort to widen the split between his adversaries. Reconciliation among the brothers, however, had put an end to that gambit. Subsequently, Gisulf had been seeking insurance elsewhere, trying to enlist Richard of Capua as his ally. But those tactics, too, had failed, and Gisulf in the end was faced with the unpalatable necessity of making up with the Hautevilles. Only by doing so could he stop the continual territorial encroachments of William, Count of the Principata, and obtain the neutrality, or perhaps even the friendship, of his even more dangerous neighbor, Robert.

Robert, as chance would have it, had also been thinking of renewing the traditional alliance with Salerno for his own purposes. He also had in mind an advantageous mechanism. He would, as had his elder brothers and predecessors as Counts of Apulia, seek a marriage alliance with the Lombard ruling house. There was, of course, the small embarrassment that he was already married, but a solution was found. His rapprochement with the papacy had obliged the pious but basically amoral Guiscard to show a greater respect for the Church's teachings. Among those strictures, he suddenly discovered, was a recent ban on marriages within seven degrees of consanguinity, a category within which, it fortuitously turned out, his wife Alberada fell. Robert declared that his conscience and his faith required that he disown his wife who, in spite of a dozen years' marriage, had only given him one living child, a son Bohemund. Robert's suddenly discovered conscience fortunately corresponded with his interest, for a remarriage at this time would give him the opportunity to make an alliance more in keeping with his new prospects. Moreover, there is a hint that Alberada herself, who still was both young and attractive, and perhaps a bit of a flirt in addition, did not oppose the idea. Be that as it may, she and her father went along, she was given a rich settlement, and the marriage was annulled in full amity. Alberada rapidly remarried a son of Drogo, Richard, for whom, the rumors had it, she had already set her cap; she continued her life on good terms with Robert, later married yet again, for a third time, and lived well into the next century. The only one to suffer from this politic separation was the young son, Bohemund, who found himself legally a bastard by this act of his father, and was obliged to struggle for his right to a place in the sun.

Robert's status as eligible bachelor did not last long, as he and Gisulf soon agreed on a wedding alliance. The bride to be was Gisulf's own elder sister, Sichelgaita, and such a marriage would once again link the Hauteville family with that of the princely house of Guaimar, the Norman newcomers with the traditional Lombard rulers. Gisulf, it seems, at first disliked the idea of marrying his sister to any Norman, as he considered all of them "a fierce and barbarous race, without pity, and lacking in human spirit."[1] Putting his dislike and distrust of the Normans aside, Gisulf saw potential political advantage in the wedding; it would create a tie of blood and obligation that might protect his principality from Hauteville covetousness. Gisulf made the point very clear: one of his conditions for the marriage was that Robert should actively oppose his own brother William, and force him to give up recent conquests in the Principata. The marriage, of course, was no less a political act on Guiscard's side, since blood ties with the ancient ruling house would provide him with a greater legitimacy among his Lombard subjects than he could hope to achieve by force alone.

Arranging the wedding was not without its complications and crises. As agreed, Robert actually had to send troops to fight his brother William, forcing him to yield back to the princely family some of his more recent conquests in Salernitan territory. In angry response William, always slightly at odds with Robert, strengthened his own alliance with an opposing branch of Salerno's princely family. He married Gisulf's cousin, a daughter of that uncle Guy who led the anti–Gisulf faction.

With such complicated infighting under way, the marriage was scarcely assured to create peace and harmony between the two families. Sensitivities were high, the arrangements intricate. The agreement on return of the seized castles, for example, was a carefully crafted compromise that probably pleased no one: William returned half of his recent acquisitions, but swore his fealty for the remainder, not as Gisulf's vassal, but rather as his adopted brother. According to Lombard custom, that gave him status almost equal to that of the prince.[2] There was even trouble over Sichelgaita's dowry. When Gisulf, short as always of cash, had difficulty in raising the dowry that would be expected under Norman custom, Robert upstaged him, and gave his new bride lavish gifts under the Lombard custom of *morgengab*. Even though Robert's gesture could be seen as culturally sensitive, and indeed may have facilitated the spread of the *morgengab* custom among the Normans of southern Italy, it was, in the circumstances, an insult to his new brother-in-law. The diplomacy and arrangements for the wedding in fact got so tense that Gisulf at one point demanded a postponement.

Nonetheless, the wedding did take place, and the outcome was much to the benefit of Guiscard. In Sichelgaita he gained a remarkable wife and helpmeet, a woman of redoubtable presence and courage who would accompany him on his travels throughout his life, who fought in his battles, bore him ten adult children, and assured his succession. Contemporary descriptions tell us of a woman of striking appearance and strong behavior, a true Valkyrie type who apparently had inherited more of the ancient warrior traits of her Lombard ancestors than the rest of her family.

If Gisulf had hoped to have his sister act as his agent within the Hauteville family councils, he was mistaken, for Sichelgaita came to identify completely with her new husband's interests. Robert, it appears, was a good family man, no matter how forbidding he may have been to outsiders, and the warmth of his relationship with his brothers seems to have been genuine in spite of the numerous fallings out they had over money or sharing power. While his brothers Roger and William sometimes contested him and even fought against him, they consistently pulled together against outside threats, and none of Robert's brothers ever betrayed him — as was so often the case in other knightly families. Sichelgaita became a trusted member of this family group, and began to provide Robert with the appurtenances of a proper ducal household that would serve him well as he became a regional power.

Even during this period of diplomacy and alliance building, Robert, with his usual energy, was actively expanding his lands by military means. Cariati and Rossano, on the southern Calabrian coast, fell to his troops, while Gerace was once again forced to pay tribute and accept Robert as its lord, even though its commune continued to retain control of the city fortifications. Only another short-lived revolt by Pierre of Trani, and then the wedding, interrupted Robert's military campaigns. Shortly after the wedding, in the spring of 1060, he and his brothers were once again on campaign. While Roger stayed in Calabria to prepare supplies and siege weapons for the coming campaign there, Robert led troops to the Capitanata to aid his brother Geoffrey subdue a few of the more difficult Lombard *gastaldts*, who were holding out against the piecemeal Norman conquest of the southern Abruzzi. That achieved, he and Mauger turned to the south, moving with the speed which characterized most of Robert's campaigns. They soon had obtained the submission of Taranto and Brindisi, and capped their successful campaign in southern Apulia when Mauger defeated a Byzantine army in a battle near Oria.

Robert did not wait to consolidate his gains; conquest was always higher on his list of priorities than governing. Instead, he led his successful and confident army into Calabria, where he joined up with the forces and equipment that Roger had been marshaling there. Together, the two brothers then descended once again on Reggio, to invest it with their combined armies and a number of carefully prepared siege engines. Those machines, which were used extensively by the Normans for the first time at Reggio, finally brought about the surrender of this last Byzantine stronghold in Calabria. The Byzantine garrison and officials escaped and were briefly besieged in a neighboring castle, but managed to slip away by boat to return to Constantinople.

With the flight of the Reggio garrison, the only remaining Byzantine forces in all of southern Italy were those in Bari, still the nominal capital of the much-shrunken imperial province. Elsewhere, from Troia in the north, to Otranto in the south, to Reggio in the west, the Normans—and in the cases of Calabria and southern Apulia, the Hautevilles—were victorious. A summer's campaign had conquered Calabria, where Byzantine forces would never again hold sway. But Apulia was, as always, the tougher nut to crack. While the Hauteville victories had established Robert as the preeminent lord of the region, it would require another twenty years before the sons of Tancred were able to establish effective control in the province over their Byzantine adversaries and Norman competitors.

With his summer's conquests, Robert's duchy was beginning to take shape. In the Tarentine peninsula of south Apulia, in Calabria, and in the Capitanata, he and his brothers had conquered vast territories to add to Humphrey's original holdings. In the rest of Apulia, Robert as duke was owed fealty by the other Norman barons, however grudgingly some might admit it. The wealth that flowed from these lands and relationships was immense and most useful; Robert had always known how to win and impress followers with lavish displays and a generous hand in the division of spoils. His gifts were legendary, nor was his generosity limited to his Norman colleagues. Peter of Tyre, for example, the ex-governor of Bisignano whom he had kidnapped and ransomed in his brigand days, was compensated many times over at this time by a rich gift. The Guiscard household, still peripatetic, expanded with the duke's new wealth and status. Byzantine luxury, and the display expected from rulers in the east, began to take root in the new conditions of wealth; Norman knights decked themselves in the robes that their predecessors had found effeminate, and the duke's *mesnil* began to take on the trappings of a court.

Robert now enjoyed an immense capacity for patronage, having the right to grant fiefs in his newly conquered lands to deserving colleagues. Yet he was slow to provide his followers with major grants, preferring to give generously of his money but sparingly of that which gave him power, his land. By giving small, direct fiefdoms, he created links of personal loyalty to himself, rather than creating powerful barons with landholdings and vassals of their own sufficient to give them a sense of independence. Even Roger was subjected to this discipline, though he did not accept it easily or long. Robert was generous in land grants only with respect to the Church, where he established and endowed numerous Latin churches and monasteries in a conscious effort to build up an institution that would be loyal. (Too loyal, Rome occasionally said, objecting to Robert's tendency to appoint Latin bishops with only minimal consultation with the Church elders.[3]) Generosity to the Church also served the duke's purposes by spreading, through the monastic affiliations that were one of the principal information networks of the period, favorable news of Norman exploits in the south that would raise the prestige of the Hauteville state and bring in new and enterprising recruits.

Other than the expanding Latin Church and the growing but still modest ducal *mesnil*, however, the duchy had little in the way of central institutions. In the countryside, Norman fiefholders maintained justice and collected taxes quite independently of the duke. In the towns, Lombard or Greek administrative mechanisms and law had been largely left in place under treaty or other arrangements that spelled out the towns' obligations by the way of taxation, military service or, in the case of the seaports, provision of naval auxiliaries. Leaving the existing administrative apparatus in place had a benefit for the Normans, always short of manpower as they were, but it also had a danger: the communes felt free enough to rise in rebellion whenever they saw a Norman weakness, and they did so frequently. The Normans attempted to control the towns, as they did the countryside, through permanently garrisoned strong points at the edges of the towns or in commanding positions along the lines of communication, and they were able to put down most rebellions with ease and minimum force. Robert himself had a reputation for a lack of animosity toward his enemies. Nonetheless, on occasion his soldiers were brutal in suppressing a revolt, as when they burned the town of Policastro and deported its inhabitants to Nicastro. At this stage, the Normans were still very much military occupiers of the country, living largely apart from the local populations except at the more polyglot court of the duke, and often marrying women from the north rather than intermixing with the Lombard or Greek populations.

The governance of his new lands, however, was not the primary subject on Guiscard's mind after his victorious march through Calabria. Much, much more heady prospects had now opened up. Ever since their unhappy participation in the Maniakes expedition to Sicily in 1042, the Normans of Apulia had retained the thought of returning to that rich island, defended by Muslims who, the Normans were convinced, could be beaten in battle. With Reggio and the maritime resources of Calabria now at their disposal, the Hauteville brothers could actively consider their prospects across the narrow Straits of Messina.

Not only did the incomparable riches of Sicily beckon, but Robert's confidence that he could succeed had grown in light of his recent victories. His enthusiasm for such an adventure was fuelled by the attitude of the Church, in which a spirit of zealotry, particularly since the schism with Constantinople, had been growing: had he not received, from the pope himself, a license to reconquer the island for the Latin Church? That the pope's mandate conveniently reinforced his own predilections toward pious enthusiasm and greed made it all the more compelling.

What made the project of invading Sicily imperative, however, was the possibility that the Hauteville brothers might have both a sponsor, and a pretext, for an immediate invasion.

Notes

1. William of Apulia, II, line 416, p. 154, as cited in Delogu, p. 89. William's account constantly denigrates Gisulf, and can be interpreted as Norman propaganda designed to justify Guiscard's seizure of the principality.

2. Taviani-Carozzi, *La Principaute*, p. 926. Lombard law and political legitimacy placed a much higher priority on kinship issues than did Norman.

3. Taviani-Carozzi, *La Terreur*, p. 338.

Sicily

S icily in 1060 was in total disarray. The political structure had been rent by years of civil war following the deposition of the last emir of the Kalbite dynasty in 1053. Moreover, the once powerful Zirid rulers of Tunisia, patrons and protectors of the Sicilian Muslims, were severely weakened by war with Cairo, invasion of new Arab tribes from Yemen, and their own civil war. Central rule in Sicily had broken down; the ruling class had come to be divided between adherents of Tunisia and the families of the original settlers—Berbers versus Arabs—and the island was effectively partitioned between four feuding *qaids*, or leaders. In the prevailing state of confusion, rebellion, and near-anarchy which resulted, the island's native Christian communities, principally in the Val Demone region around Mount Etna in the northeast, looked for ways to gain greater autonomy and an external Christian protector. Not surprisingly, they had followed the advance of the Normans into Calabria with some interest, hoping that this dynamic new Christian power could do more for them than the Byzantines had been able to do since the debacle of the Maniakes expedition. According to some accounts, they sent emissaries to Roger at Mileto during the summer of 1060 to seek help. But it was not their initiative, in the end, that decided the Normans on immediate intervention. For that, they had a much more convincing and powerful interlocutor, one of the four *qaids* himself.

The man who offered to lead the Normans into Sicily was Ibn Timnah, the Qaid of Syracuse. IbnTimnah, a scoundrel even by the standards of the time, had reached his position by defeating and killing his predecessor, Ibn al Maklati; he then commandeered the latter's wife, Maimouna, as well as acquiring dominion over most of the island's southeastern areas. His expansionist aims quickly put him in conflict with the neighboring

qaid, Ali Ibn al Hawwas, who controlled Agrigento and much of the center of the island, and who also was Maimouna's brother. The two qaids' feud reached a crisis point when Ibn Timnah, in a drunken rage, attempted to kill Maimouna. That twice aggrieved woman then fled for sanctuary and vengeance to Ibn Hawwas, who took Ibn Timnah's assault as an insult to his family, and escalated their feud to a war to the end. Ibn Timnah's drunken mistake had proven costly; he soon found himself on the losing side of several battles, his army in disarray, and his brother-in-law hunting him down. In desperation, and tempted by the proximity across the straits of the renowned Norman warriors, Ibn Timnah traveled to Mileto where he offered Roger a deal the Hautevilles could not refuse. What he offered was no less than treason to his fellow Muslims, an alliance to capture power in eastern Sicily, and the cooperation of what was left of his army. Roger, probably more impetuous than his older brother would have been, accepted the deal.

In fact, Roger had already tried his hand in Sicily, shortly after the fall of Reggio. Audaciously, he had led a troop of some fifty or so knights across the straits, made a short demonstration before the walls of heavily defended Messina, and then been obliged to retire when the Muslim garrison mustered. While the escapade may have been futile, it by no means diminished the Hauteville brothers' aspirations. The expedition had at least shown that the Normans now had, thanks to their control of the Calabrian fishing towns, a new marine capability that would allow them to cross the straits with both men and horses. It had also taught them that Messina was too strongly fortified and garrisoned to be taken without a serious expeditionary force.

Having accepted Ibn Timnah's proposition, Roger was anxious to strike. To his regret, though, the expedition would have to wait. Robert had a major crisis on his hands in Apulia, which required Roger's help. The Byzantines had counterattacked in force.

The Byzantines had reacted surprisingly rapidly to the Norman successes of the previous year, considering the low priority accorded to the military under the government in Constantinople. But command over imperial defense of Italy had been passed to men of determination and energy: Perenos, the Duke of Durazzo across the Adriatic, and his field commander, the mercenary Abul Kare.[1] Abul Kare had landed in the Tarentine peninsula in late autumn and, taking advantage of Robert's absence in Reggio, had rapidly reversed the situation on the ground. Taranto, Brindisi, Oria, and Otranto rapidly fell to the Byzantine forces, and an army quickly raised by Robert and Mauger was defeated. By early winter, the Byzantine army had advanced the length of Apulia and settled down to besiege Melfi. This attack on their joint capital had the effect of rousing the Norman barons throughout Apulia, many of whom earlier might have looked upon the raid as a problem only for the Hautevilles. The barons sent troops to defend against the now common threat, Roger led a detachment from Reggio, and by midwinter the Normans were able to break the siege of Melfi and chase the Byzantine army southwards, winning a battle at Manduria. Most of Apulia was freed of the Byzantine army, but it would be several years before Robert could regain Brindisi, Oria, and Taranto.

Checked on the battlefield but still anxious to keep Robert from consolidating his gains of the past few years, the Byzantines accelerated their efforts at destabilization. Byzantine tactics of bribery, co-optation, and division easily struck sparks of revolt in Apulia, playing on the barons' resentment against the Hautevilles, the fractured state of governance in the province, and the dislike of the population for the Normans and the rapidly spreading Latin Church. For twenty-five more years, Perenos and his successors would provide both motivation and support for periodic revolts of the barons, and continued resistance to Hauteville rule.

For the moment, however, with Melfi relieved and the Byzantine threat removed from northern Apulia, Roger could return to Mileto and continue preparations for an invasion of Sicily. Yet the Normans, in spite of their capacity for swift and disciplined movement on land, lacked the men and the experience in amphibious operations that would allow them to mount a full-scale attack across the water. The Muslim fleets still controlled the seas, even though a major relief fleet sent from Tunisia had been destroyed in a storm.[2] In the circumstances, a full-scale invasion would have to wait, and it was decided to make, instead, a raid that would combine reconnaissance in force with plundering, long a favorite Norman activity. It was all the same a significant undertaking. Robert, who was still busy in Apulia, entrusted the command to his younger brother, but sent along a trusted colleague, Geoffrey de Ridelle, to serve as his personal representative and more or less act as a tempering influence on Roger's occasional excesses of enthusiasm. A recently arrived nephew also joined the expedition, a young man who was to have a glorious career in Sicily: Serlo, son of the Hauteville brother of the same name who had decided to stay in Normandy.

By early winter of 1061, enough boats had been rounded up from Reggio and other Calabrian towns to transport a small force of 150 knights and their mounts, plus 450 auxiliaries. The Normans reached Sicily unopposed, having chosen to land this time in undefended territory to the northwest of Messina, near Milazzo. At first, the expedition was a rousing success, the rich countryside providing much booty. The governor of Messina was tricked into an ambush and slain by Roger in combat, and when the Messina garrison sent out a force to drive off the invaders, they were mauled in a battle in which Serlo distinguished himself by leading a well-timed cavalry charge into the enemy's flank.

Then things went wrong. When the Norman troops followed up their victory on the fields outside Messina by attempting to rush the walls, they were driven off with losses. It had become time to put an end to the raid, but suddenly the straits were closed. Some of the Norman fleet had been scattered after losing a naval skirmish with the Muslims, who had rallied after their initial surprise. But suddenly, a new impediment arose: the weather. A fierce winter storm had come up which made embarkation of the Normans and their horses, not to mention the livestock they had stolen, out of the question. For three days and nights the Normans huddled on the beach, under attack by both the Messinan army and the weather, their prospects as gloomy as the skies. On the fourth day, however, the sea calmed, the Norman ships appeared and the Muslim ones did not, and Roger's force was able to make its way back to Reggio with only minimal losses, and all its plunder. In thanks for their deliverance, Roger dedicated much of the proceeds of the raid to rebuilding the earthquake-damaged chapel of Saint Anthony in Reggio, as he had promised during some desperate prayers on the beach.

It had been a close thing, and Roger had scarcely shown himself to be a provident and careful leader. But then the Normans were accustomed to risk, and their near-setback did not deter them from planning a bigger expedition, one that would be large enough to attack Messina, or at a minimum, establish a permanent foothold on the island. Robert left the preparations to Roger, on whom he had learned increasingly to rely in spite of nagging concerns about his enthusiasms, jealousy over his popularity, and fears of his ambition. By May, with the Byzantine army once again in check in southern Apulia and Roger's preparations completed, the two brothers were ready to try a more ambitious sortie into the island that they hoped to make their future property.

The invasion force this time was considerably larger, as many as 2000 men, including perhaps 450 mounted knights. The fleet, as well, was augmented; it included both transports and swifter warships to protect them, because the Muslim defenders had brought naval forces, too, to defend against a crossing of the straits. To attempt to force the crossing against such strong opposition, in fact, seemed too risky, so the two brothers developed a ruse. Robert and the main body of Normans made conspicuous preparations for embarkation near the Rock of Scylla at the northern end of the straits. The Messina garrison had, in response, deployed to the north to oppose an expected landing. But while they were keeping an eye on Robert's force, they were not mindful of their rear. Roger was able to slip across the straits some five miles south of the city in the dark of night, with some 270 men. So unalert were the defenders in that area that Roger was even able to send his boats back for a second detachment, of 170 men. At daybreak, his men fortuitously seized a supply train coming from the south, with the payroll of the Muslim garrison. With this unexpected bit of good luck to give them confidence, Roger and his men advanced on the city to carry out the diversionary raid that was their plan. There, in another stroke of luck, they found that the southern defenses were virtually unmanned. Roger showed his usual audaciousness, and attacked immediately. To their amazement, the Normans found that not only the walls but the entire city had been stripped of its defenders to oppose Robert's main body, now heading across the northern end of the straits. The city fell, virtually without a struggle, even before Robert and his men had landed.

Once again, the Normans had combined enterprise with extraordinary luck. Messina, provided it could be held, offered a secure foothold and logistical base in Sicily. While many more years would pass before the island was firmly in Norman hands, Messina was a position from which they would never be expelled, no matter the ebb and flow of their conquest. For the moment, however, the Normans scarcely had time to savor their victory. The Muslim army, once they had seen Norman banners on the walls of their city and realized that they were caught between the Normans in the town and those landing on the beach, headed inland. They could be expected to join up with Ibn Hawwas' main army and, before long, to make an effort to recapture the city. To forestall such a situation, quick action was necessary. The Normans, after attending a service of thanksgiving offered them by the city's Greek rite Christians, spent a busy week improving the defenses of the city against possible counterattack. Then, leaving a small garrison, they set out to carry the campaign into Ibn Hawwas' territory.

Ibn Timnah had joined them. Emerging from his stronghold at Catania after the Norman victory, the would-be traitor had renewed his offer to the Hauteville brothers: he would help the Normans gain control over the island, after which they would share the rule. Whatever Robert may have thought of the long-term viability of such an offer, it had immediate value in making available the logistics, interpreting, and intelligence support that his own small and inexperienced army so lacked in this new country. Proceeding to the north of Mount Etna in order to secure the western approaches to Messina, the army moved through lands more or less loyal to Ibn Timnah, the Val Demone and its largely Christian populations, and toward the central plateau and Ibn Hawwas's great fortress at Castrogiovanni.

The fortress at Castrogiovanni (or Enna, its ancient and once again its modern name) sits high above the plain, occupying an almost impregnable position which the Norman army could scarcely expect to capture by storm. They, nonetheless, began to build a necklace of fortified places around the city, to cut off its communications and perhaps intimidate it into submission. The defenders decided instead to take the initiative, and to attack the presumptuous invaders. But they had miscalculated their new enemies, and in the resulting battle the light Arab cavalry and infantry proved no match for the Norman horse formations. The battle was quick,

furious, and disastrous for the Muslims, who even though they outnumbered the Normans many times over, were killed and captured in the thousands.

The victory, the sizeable booty it gained, and the terror it instilled,
all allowed the Normans to settle down for the kind of war they knew well;
they began to wear their opponents down through massive raids and dis-
rupting the lines of communication. While the remainder of the Muslim
garrison remained penned up in Castrogiovanni, Normans under Roger
raided as far away as Agrigento with virtual impunity. The Normans soon
succeeded, through wringing payments of tribute from threatened towns
and pillage from the countryside, in enriching themselves greatly. At the
same time their strategy had its political payoffs, as Sicilians began to argue
amongst themselves as to whether to treat with or fight the invaders. Even
Ibn Hawwas, secure in distant Palermo which he had recently taken from
a rival *qaid*, sent envoys to Robert

> with a variety of gifts: ornate fabrics worked in the Spanish style,
> linen cloths, vessels of gold and silver, mules with regal trappings,
> saddles decorated with gold and, following Saracen custom, eleven
> sacks with eighty thousand gold tari.... To thank the emir for his gifts
> he had received, the duke sent one Peter the Deacon, who understood
> the Saracens and spoke well in their manner. The duke told him not
> to speak, but to listen and be alert, so as to see what the mood was in
> the city.[3]

When Peter came back from his spying mission, he was able to report that
Palermo's defenses were weak, and morale there poor.

Palermo, however, was beyond the Normans' reach, as indeed was
Castrogiovanni. The Norman army was in no position to maintain a long
siege against so formidable a fortress, particularly as winter on the plateau
was approaching. In late summer and with the harvests in, they began to
break camp. The campaign, although it had made no permanent conquests
beyond Messina, had been a great success. The Normans had greatly
increased their knowledge of the country they planned to subdue, learned
the weaknesses of the Muslim rulers, and gained a reputation for invincibility that would certainly benefit them in coming campaigns. They had
enlisted valuable local allies, and, finally, had fattened their coffers and
their ability to return with a larger force. It was time to take the largely
Apulian army back to their homes to enjoy their gains.

Robert had one last objective before departing. He determined to
build a second strongpoint beyond Messina, specifically in the Val Demone,
that would serve as a gage of his seriousness toward the Christian communities that had given the Normans such support. For this purpose, the

first Norman permanent settlement in Sicily was established, at a strategic mountain location near the north coast, and it was named San Marco d'Alunzio. That accomplished, Robert and the bulk of his army departed for Italy and a peaceful Christmas with their families.

Roger, however, was restless. After several months at Mileto, he returned to Sicily with several hundred men to launch another pillaging raid on Agrigento. He also obtained the allegiance of Troina, a largely Christian mountain town strategically located in the Val Demone, which he intended to use as a future base of operations. Then, shortly after Christmas, he returned to Mileto for an anxiously awaited reunion with his bride-to-be.

Roger's romance and marriage to Judith was a true love story in a time of political marriages. He had been looking forward, or rather hoping, for this occasion for a number of years. He had met the comely Judith d'Evreux in Normandy even before his departure for Italy; they had fallen in love on the spot and vowed to stay loyal to each other. Judith was not only attractive, she was as well placed as a young adventurer such as Roger could have dreamed of — a descendent of the dukes of Normandy and orphaned half-sister of a great lord, Robert of Grantmesnil, who was also her guardian. So great was their romance that Judith became a novitiate in the convent of Saint Evroul in order to avoid other suitors, many of whom at that time had better actual prospects or lineages than the young son of Tancred of Hauteville. But fate has its ways, and Judith was spared the necessity of taking religious orders by the fact that Grantmesnil quarreled with his ruler, the formidable Duke William; the break between the two was so severe that Grantmesnil was obliged to go into exile. Robert Guiscard, good politician that he was, saw an opportunity to help the discomfited Grantmesnil and offered him the post of abbot of a newly established monastery of Sant Euphemia. Perhaps Robert also had Roger's interests in mind in bringing Grantmesnil and his ward to Italy, perhaps not. But it certainly worked to Roger's benefit. Judith let him know of her arrival in Italy, and the marriage was agreed upon in an instant. The happy couple, separated for five years, were married at Mileto at the beginning of 1062.

If Robert had helped Roger achieve this happy conclusion, he may have soon regretted it. Roger's marriage, unfortunately, only served to open up the old dispute between the two brothers about sharing the spoils of their victories. The fifty-fifty split of properties in Calabria had not worked out well in practice, and Robert had treated his younger brother as any other knight, by refusing to grant him a significant fief. Surely, he had been generous in sharing cash, but Roger may have felt that it was no more than the minimum he was due. The embarrassing fact was that he was about to marry into one of the great families of Normandy, and yet had no land that he could gift to his bride in accordance with the Lombard tradition of *morgengab*, which had become the custom for the Normans in Italy. Roger's resentment overflowed. He sent his brother a formal request for the lands which he felt were due him, and, as the custom required in disputes between a vassal and his lord, gave Robert forty days to answer before taking up arms.

To fill the waiting time with activity, the restless young husband returned once again to Sicily for a short campaign in which he and Ibn Timnah's troops captured the town of Petralia, but achieved little else. Worse yet, shortly afterward Ibn Timnah himself was lured into an ambush and assassinated, the Norman garrisons of Troina and just-captured Petralia were forced to withdraw to Messina, and the entire Norman position in Sicily was severely compromised.

Roger returned to Mileto from his frustrating expedition in Sicily to find another disappointment. Robert, not at all accepting his demands, had instead decided to treat his brother's act as insubordination, and was preparing a punitive expedition. Once again the differences between the two proud siblings were to escalate into warfare, endangering not only their subjects who, as usual, were likely to bear the brunt of the fighting, but indeed the entire Hauteville enterprise.

Robert brought his army into Calabria and besieged Roger in his fortress of Mileto. Neither brother, however, pushed the campaign overly hard and it soon evolved into a series of inconclusive skirmishes and individual combats. In an effort to change the terms of the struggle, Roger slipped out of Mileto and set up at Gerace, a fortress hill town in which he had followers and which he could make a base of operations against his brother. Soon he was pursued there by the furious Robert, who demanded entry into the town as its duke. The commune, however, had placed its bets on the younger brother (or perhaps had little choice in the circumstance), and denied the duke his rights. Robert was not one to take the insult lightly, but decided to use wile rather than force to undermine his brother's position. The duke himself slipped into the town in disguise, where he and his partisans held a clandestine meeting in the home of one of his supporters. But at that point his luck ran out. While he and his supporters were thus plotting how to undercut Roger's position, the meeting was discovered, the duke seized, and his hosts killed on the spot.

The crowd that had broken up the clandestine meeting might well have carried out the same rough justice on the duke, had it not been for his famous self-assurance and powers of persuasion. Robert spoke out; he pleaded, he threatened, he asked their understanding, and in the end this man, who had conquered and despoiled them, succeeded in convincing the citizens of Gerace that they had better not do anything rash. Instead, they imprisoned him and submitted his fate to Roger, the younger brother sitting in judgment on the elder.

Roger, summoned from his camp outside the town, struck the perfect note in resolving the crisis. Even though he had his brother's fate in his hands, family ties were stronger than sibling rivalries. Moreover, there was no question of breaking up a partnership which, however unfair he may have thought it to be, had been highly successful. Great as Roger's ambition was, he knew that the situation in Apulia was unmanageable without his brother's political skills, and that his own ambitions in Sicily could best be met by a joint effort. But, to the citizens of Gerace, he chose to appear as an avenger, angrily demanding the immediate surrender of his brother to his justice. Neatly off the hook, the citizens gladly complied with the demand.

Roger's justice was swift but politic. Rather than throwing Robert into prison or worse, Roger dropped his anger, feigned or real as it may have been, and embraced his brother in front of the surprised, and perhaps relieved, citizens.[4] The crisis was over, and with it the ridiculous fratricidal war before it could cause lasting damage.

The incident had obliged the brothers to recognize their common interests, and their public embrace marked a virtual end to the hostilities. At a subsequent meeting on a Roman bridge over the River Crati, still called Ponte Guiscardo, Robert promised to live up to his earlier promise to share the lands and revenues of lower Calabria equally with his brother. The arrangement was more a condominium over the properties rather than an actual division, and an example will show how confusing the arrangements must have been to most concerned. When, some months later, the citizens of Gerace complained to Roger that the fortification he was having built inside their town violated the old treaty, according to which they had been left in control of the town's fortifications, he split hairs with them. Robert, he replied, signed that treaty and may well have made such a promise, which then applied to the part of the town that was his. But I, Roger, made no such promise for my share of the town. And he continued to build.

Never again would the brothers fight. The division of properties led, in turn, to a de facto division of responsibilities, with Roger given a more or less free hand to pursue the absorption of Calabria and prepare for new campaigns in Sicily. Robert had finally learned that he could trust his younger brother, as long as he gave him a fair share of the winnings and a certain amount of autonomy. From this time on, the brothers would bring troops to each other's assistance as needed, but for the most part they worked in parallel in their respective areas of the growing Hauteville state.

Notes

1. Although Argyrus was still leader of the Greeks in Bari, he had of necessity to play a more passive role, as the treaty relations of that city with the Normans required a kind of peaceful coexistence. He died in 1068.

2. Manfroni, p. 113.

3. Geoffrey Malaterra, II, C. 17, p. 34, as cited in Delogu, p. 71.

4. The square in Gerace on which this drama was acted out is, to this day, called the Piazza del Tocco, or the Square of the Touch.

Cerami

Their fight over and brotherly amity restored, Robert and Roger resumed their common effort to advance the Hauteville cause. Roger remained in Calabria to establish order in that recently conquered province, and to resume preparations for extending their gains in Sicily. A more ambitious intervention on the island would have to wait once again, however, as Robert and the major part of the army had returned to Apulia to stabilize the situation there. Although he soon succeeded in driving the Byzantine expeditionary force from Brindisi and Oria, his major troubles were political. His efforts, since Melfi, to establish ducal authority over his vassals had not been successful, and many of the barons were on the edge of revolt. The province was alive with unrest, Lombard and Greek as well as Norman, nourished by money and conspiracies emanating from the Byzantine enclave cites along the coast, and aided by Salerno and the Holy Roman Empire.

The proximate cause for the political turmoil in southern Italy was the struggle for papal succession that had broken out upon the death of Pope Nicholas in 1061. The reformer bishops, sitting in Rome and led by Hildebrand, had immediately elected a successor as Alexander II. But the empire, presented finally with a chance to challenge the Lateran Synod's decree on the election of popes, refused to accept this unilateral action of the bishops. Joining forces for once with the Roman families, the imperial regent Agnes had a rival pope, Honorius, elected. Moreover, the empire provided him with sufficient backing for his candidacy to present a real challenge to the reformers' candidate.

Once again Hildebrand and a pope he had created were required to call upon the Normans, led by Richard of Capua, to send a military expedition to Rome to put their man on the seat of Saint Peter. Once again,

Richard's troops succeeded in the immediate objective. But this time they could not assure Alexander a secure term of office, as they had done for Nicholas. The antipope Honorius would remain a threat to the reform papacy for several more years, while the relationship between pope and emperor moved inexorably from its earlier cooperation, to competition, and then to hostility. Southern Italy was thrown into turmoil by the growing conflict.

Guiscard's position was a tricky one. The backers of Honorius had determined to weaken Alexander by undermining his Norman supporters, both in Capua and Apulia. In practice, that meant a tacit alliance between the two emperors, eastern and western, against Guiscard. It would last, in one form or another, until his death.

Seeking to join that alliance, or at a minimum gain advantage from it, was Guiscard's brother-in-law, Gisulf of Salerno. Gisulf had watched apprehensively as his Norman neighbor, Richard of Aversa, expanded his power and wealth through full absorption of Capua and then Gaeta. Knowing Salerno's weakness, he had tried unsuccessfully to enlist Richard in friendship, as insurance and as a balance against possible pressure from Robert. Failure to enlist Richard only caused Gisulf to look elsewhere for an ally against Guiscard. The Prince of Salerno had never been naive about what he might expect from his marriage ties with Robert; he knew the man's ambitions and his appetite for power. The best way to keep his powerful brother in law from doing harm, he must have figured, was to keep him occupied elsewhere. Gisulf decided that he could see advantage from cooperating with Byzantium's efforts to subvert Guiscard. Undertaking an ostensible pilgrimage to Constantinople and Jerusalem, he explored the possibilities for joint anti–Norman action with the Byzantine authorities. No formal alliance seems to have been reached, and the scheme never came to fruition because one of the bishops who had accompanied Gisulf disclosed the plot to Guiscard. In addition, Gisulf himself was diverted from immediate action when his uncle Guy revolted at home. But the scheme illustrated Guiscard's problem: his expansion, and his alliance with the papacy, made him vulnerable to efforts by his external opponents to support his domestic dissidents and stir up revolt in his province.

With his brother thus occupied in Italian politics, Roger returned to Sicily in the late summer, to see what could be rescued from the collapse following Ibn Timnah's death. He found that Ibn Hawwas, preoccupied with other affairs, had not seized full advantage of the situation; the Muslims had neither challenged the garrison at Messina nor occupied the Val Demone. He was able, with only some three hundred troops, to reoccupy Troina without incident and reinforce its defenses. He then set off to carry the campaign into hostile territory, leaving his young bride in charge of the garrison. What he had not reckoned on was the feelings of the citizens of Troina, and he would pay dearly for his assumption that he could still rely on the loyalty of the inhabitants. Although they had welcomed their fellow Christians the previous year, they were no longer friendly.

Unfortunately, as had been the case in Apulia years before, the Norman armies had been short-sighted in their tactics, and disinterested in what today would be called community relations. Their enthusiasm for pillage and intimidation had once again proven more useful in conquering territory than in governing it successfully. It had been particularly inappropriate, moreover, in a region populated by fellow Christians who were potential allies. The sensitivities of the citizens of Troina, acculturated in Muslim Sicily to oriental concepts of female modesty, had been particularly offended by Norman treatment of their women. Their grievances were numerous, and their anger at renewed occupation by the Normans was real. Waiting until Roger's force was well away, they rose in revolt. They were partly successful, and after a day's hard urban fighting the brave but badly outnumbered Judith and her garrison were placed under siege. Most of the city belonged to the citizens, who had suddenly obtained reinforcements from Muslim neighbors wanting to help expel the detested Franks. Even the rapid return of Roger and his men could not reverse the situation; the Normans found themselves obliged to fall back on the citadel. There they could, and did, make a prolonged and brave defense, but it was a hard and painful one. Supplies of everything were short, communications with the outside almost nonexistent, and the rigors of the advancing winter, a particularly severe one at that, made their condition miserable.

For four months, the Normans shivered in the citadel while the citizens of Troina kept them bottled up. Hunger reduced the Normans to eating their valuable horses; cold sapped their strength. Roger and Judith, the chroniclers tell us, shared a single cloak to keep them warm, day and night. But they kept up morale and waited for an opportunity. It was provided, ironically, by the very contrast in circumstances between the besieged and their attackers. The Greek and Muslim besiegers, it turned out, were keeping warm during the bitterly cold nights by liberal consumption of the rough wines of the neighborhood, as a result of which, the Norman sentinels noticed, their tormentors developed a certain lack of acuity as the nights progressed. From that observation came the plan. One cold night in January, after the wine consumed by the besiegers had had its expected effect, the Normans sortied from the citadel. By morning, the town was once more in their hands.

Norman perseverance, discipline, and courage had again been combined with excellent intelligence and the use of surprise to gain a military victory. Their political response was also typical, and traditional: death for the rebellion's ringleaders and severe punishments for the active members. Perhaps it was not surprising, given the great hardships the Normans had suffered over the months of their ordeal and the need for the greatly outnumbered Normans to show dominance. It would take several more years, as their expansion into the island progressed, for them to accept that a politic leniency could be as effective as terror in pacifying a defeated population.

For the moment, however, Roger's punishments had had their desired effect; Troina was secure. He would use it effectively as a base of operations during the coming campaign, but first he had to make a lightning return to Calabria to bring back war horses for his knights. With a touch of bravado, or a symbolic gesture to the citizens, he once again left Judith in charge. He was soon back with horses but, as would be his problem for many more years, not enough men. This was a lack that could prove costly to the Norman force, since their Muslim opponents had finally moved onto the offensive.

The death of Ibn Timnah, and the subjugation of Palermo by Ibn Hawwas, had made the latter the virtually unchallenged ruler of the island, and he had recently received substantial reinforcements. Tamim, the new Zirid ruler in Tunisia, had freed himself for the moment from both civil war and foreign invasion, and was finally in position to make a major effort to keep the ancient Zirid dependency and its vital wheat harvests from slipping away, either into unfriendly Muslim or Christian hands. He had sent to Sicily not one but two armies, under the commands of his sons Ayub and Ali, with the objectives of bringing the followers of Ibn Timnah to justice and expelling their Norman allies. The two armies, after joining with Ibn Hawwas, began their advance into the eastern regions of the island that had so long been controlled by the rebel Qaid of Syracuse and were now partly occupied by the Normans.

The Normans in the past had scarcely been deterred by superior numbers, nor were they now. Roger and the dashing Serlo had conducted raids throughout the spring that had refilled their coffers, storerooms and confidence as well. Trusting in their heavier horses and armor, courage, and above all in the discipline in battle which had gained them victory over Byzantine and papal armies, they felt capable of taking on the much more numerous but lightly armed and poorly disciplined Muslim armies. They would not run from a battle.

It was not far from Troina, some miles to the west in the valley of the

Cerami River, that the two armies met. The Normans had just over 500 fighting men, only 130 of them knights, to contest the ground against a Muslim combined force numbering in the thousands, even tens of thousands if the chroniclers are to be believed. The same chroniclers also ascribe to Roger a stirring speech on the eve of battle, calling on his men to trust in God's help and their just cause. Roger did not, however, leave success entirely in divine hands; he carefully chose the terrain on which his men would fight. They would make their stand at the top of an open slope, giving them adequate room for their cavalry while forcing their opponents to ford a stream and charge uphill, and providing a quick route back to the fortress of Troina in the event of defeat.

For three days the armies faced each other without engaging, but on the fourth day the Normans incited the Muslims into action. After a raid on the village of Cerami was repulsed by Serlo's 30 knights, the main Muslim attack fell on the Norman vanguard led by Roger. The attacks were fended off time and again, the Normans keeping their formations and Serlo leading countercharges from the flanks. The battle lasted most of the day, with neither side making a breakthrough, but the effort of making repeated unsuccessful uphill charges against the Norman position slowly sapped the strength and morale of the Muslims. Then, toward evening, the Muslims broke off, retired; the withdrawal turned into a retreat, and from that into a rout as the Normans aggressively seized the opening. By nightfall, the Muslim camp and its booty were in Norman hands.

The scope of the victory at Cerami was astounding. Not only had a small Norman force driven off a much larger army; it had defeated it entirely. The Muslims never regrouped; they lost all cohesion, and on the following day the Normans were able to hunt down the scattered groups of their demoralized foes virtually unopposed. So astonishing, indeed, was the victory that it soon took on miraculous qualities: many participants swore to having seen a ghostly knight on a white charger, the banner of whose lance bore the cross, and soon Saint George was associated in the Normans' imagination with the victory.

The fruits of the victory, divinely achieved or not, were most definitely of this world. The booty and the ransoms were huge, the Norman losses few, and the winners were rich men. Their cause had also gained a lasting victory, for the destruction of the combined Muslim armies, African and Sicilian alike, had guaranteed the Normans a permanent footing in eastern Sicily. The Sicilians of course were by no means broken, and still controlled three quarters of the island including the solidly Muslim south and west; the Normans could not yet profit territorially from their victory. But never again would their previous gains in the Val Demone be at risk, and from that day on the Muslim rulers of the island would be the ones who had to react defensively to the more dynamic if still outnumbered invaders.

Roger had nominally won the battle for his brother the duke, but he was not going to let the absent duke take the glory. For months, it seems, he had seen that his future was to be in Sicily, and he wanted to make his own mark in the world. So it was on his own that he, the Count of Mileto, sent word of his victory to the new Pope Alexander, along with the story of Saint George's reputed role in the victory and a gift of four captured camels to astonish the good bishops at the Lateran. The gesture was a great success; Pope Alexander badly needed friends and undoubtedly was glad to have this sign of support from an ascending young power. The pope, in response, sent Roger a papal banner to sanctify his future actions against the Muslims, and offered blanket absolution to soldiers fighting the Muslims in Sicily. Slowly but surely, the conquest of Sicily was taking on the nature of a religious war, a sort of pre-crusade, even though the main Crusading movement would not begin for another thirty-five years.

In strategic terms, the Norman advances in southern Italy and Sicily had sped up a change in the Mediterranean balance of power that would help make the later Crusades possible. Muslim domination of the central Mediterranean had already weakened over the past generations; raids into southern Italy had virtually ceased, while Genoa and Pisa had closed down the corsair bases in Sardinia. Now, with the Normans controlling both sides of the Straits of Messina, Muslim sway had been broken. A Sicily once again in Christian hands could even be envisaged, and with it the expansion of Christian trade into the Mediterranean on a grand scale.

The enterprising leaders and merchants of Pisa were not slow to see the possible benefits to them of Roger's victory at Cerami, and the possibility it gave for attacking Muslim naval activity in the great port of Palermo. The Pisans quickly sent a fleet to the area, and a mission to Roger at Troina, proposing a joint attack on Palermo. The proposal may have been tempting, as the Normans as yet had no naval capability to match that of the Pisans, but Roger knew that his army was too small to conduct a land operation successfully against the strongly defended metropolis. He may also have distrusted the Pisans, whose reputation for selfish action matched that of the Normans. In any event, he declined. The Pisan fleet, frustrated, tried their own hand at a raid on Palermo, and succeeded in breaking the chain that defended the harbor as well as in capturing a few vessels. While a propaganda victory for the Pisans, the raid was scarcely a significant setback for the rulers and merchants of the Sicilian capital.

Roger had indeed been prudent in choosing not to attack such a formidably defended site with his small force. Palermo, the metropolis of the region, had a population of over a quarter of a million and was richer than any Mediterranean city other than Constantinople or Cairo. So large that it could boast 500 mosques and even 150 butchers, the sprawling city and its suburbs had five quarters, two of them fortified: the commercial town and its port, and the official city with its arsenal and naval basin. The coastal plain surrounding the city, on which over half the population lived, was lush with gardens and farms, easily defended on the landward side by the range of rough mountains now called the Conca d'Oro. It would take a major army to capture the city, or even to approach it.

It was still worth it, the Hauteville brothers decided, to make an effort at testing the city's defenses; perhaps, if they were lucky, they might capture it. Robert had informed his brother that he believed that he had things well enough in hand in Apulia to be able to bring a substantial army with him into Sicily the following year, in 1064. Although it turned out that he was mistaken about the situation in Apulia, as revolt broke out there once again the moment his back was turned, he did indeed bring 500 knights and double that number of fighting men into Sicily in early summer. Combined with Roger's men, this made the largest Norman army yet to come to Sicily, and the two brothers decided to at least try a reconnaissance in force toward Palermo. Their passage was unopposed through Cefalu and other towns along the north coastal route, which came to be known as the "Via Francigena" or Frankish route because of the number of times they used it for raiding. But, once encamped in the hills of the Conca d'Oro, they found more difficult opponents. Palermo's defenders were persistent, and the Norman army could make few gains in the rough terrain. Worse yet, they had camped in a dreadful place, a hillside that turned out to be infested with tarantulas, whose venomous bites were almost more demoralizing than the attacks of the defenders.

Despite their difficulties, the Norman force maintained the pressure on Palermo for three months. But their attack never amounted to a serious siege, as their numbers were inadequate and the absence of a naval force to close the harbor left the defenders well supplied. While some booty had been accumulated from pillaging, the expedition was making no progress and the Apulian troops were looking homeward. Robert in particular was anxious to cut the effort short, since the rebellion in Apulia had begun to take on serious proportions indeed, and his presence there was increasingly essential. Reluctantly, the effort was abandoned. But a valuable lesson was learned. Next time, the brothers would bring a larger force, and a navy, to do the job properly.

Frustrated at Palermo and preoccupied with his problems in Apulia, Guiscard withdrew with his army to the south of the island, where he succeeded in capturing only the insignificant town of Bugamo near Agrigento. In his anger, he deported its population to Scribla in Calabria before returning to Italy to deal with his rebellious barons. Roger was left in command in Sicily, a situation that he found to his liking but which was nonetheless frustrating for his ambitions. His forces, never more than a few hundred knights, were too few to allow him to challenge the Sicilian rulers or their major towns. He had learned, however, to control his impetuousness, and saw that he would have to limit himself to tactics of attrition until his elder brother could once again muster the greater resources of Norman Italy and bring a major army to the island. It would be a long, if not uneventful, wait, as events in Italy kept Guiscard occupied there for the next seven years.

Rebellion

T he failed attack on Palermo having put an embarrassing end to the
brothers' initial drive into Sicily, Robert returned to Apulia to deal
with his ever-rebellious barons. His Sicilian expedition had achieved
little, on the face of it, but nonetheless the brothers had made progress. The
Hauteville base in Sicily was strong. In four years, Roger and Robert had
won great victories at Castrogiovanni and Cerami, had established a reputation for winning, and had gained a solid foothold on the island. Normans
were firmly in control of the Val Demone, while the regions of Catania and
Syracuse to the south remained in moderately friendly hands, those of the
successors of Ibn Timnah. Roger and his small band of knights were poised
to expand their borders as luck allowed, and to fatten their treasury through
the raiding and pillaging at which they excelled. Lacking men and wealth,
however, Roger would have to put aside ideas of attacking Palermo or other
major cities until Robert could once again lead an army from Italy.

In Apulia, Robert faced a long and painful struggle against his rebellious barons. The rebels had crucial support from the Byzantines, who
hoped to use dissension within the Norman ranks to weaken the upstart
duke and bring about a Byzantine resurgence in Italy. From Durazzo on
the Albanian coast, Perenos had been able to draw on the ample treasury
of the empire to stir the disgruntled barons into revolt, but he could spare
no troops to send to their assistance. The atmosphere in Constantinople
remained hostile to the military, and available forces were badly needed
in Anatolia to face an imminent invasion by the Seljuk Turks. The Byzantines had hoped to draw the western empire and the antipope into their
anti–Norman scheme, but that had collapsed with the defeat of Honorius.
The western empire, under the still minor Henry IV, would nonetheless
lend its political support to the rebellion.

Guiscard could expect no outside help. Alexander II now held his seat as pope thanks to Norman power, but he was still faced with the implacable hostility of the empire even after the deposition of the antipope Honorius. Alexander was too weak to help his Norman allies with little more than political gestures—his granting of a green light to William of Normandy to invade England can be seen in this context. And perhaps, in fact, he may not have been all that eager to help Guiscard with his internal problems in any case; distrust of the Normans remained high in Rome even though the necessity of alliance with them was recognized. Better to see Guiscard distracted by a revolt of his barons, it was probably reasoned, than to have him free to follow his expansionist ambitions. Gisulf of Salerno, being cautious, had offered no help to the rebels, but neither had he proffered any to Guiscard. The growing coolness between the two men probably ruled out any help from Salerno, even had Robert been prepared to ask for it on the basis of the marriage alliance that theoretically joined them. Richard of Aversa, too, was unlikely to lend aid to Guiscard; he had ambitions in the Campania to pursue, and no desire to help his rival.

The rebels included a number of the largest landholders in Apulia. Some of those lords held major, well-fortified towns, while others were relatively secure in hilltop strongholds; but all had built up substantial local power. What they sought was to regain that autonomy that the original Norman pact at Melfi had promised them, to return to the more egalitarian circumstances of the early days in Apulia. Resentful of Hauteville pretensions to demand their service as vassals, the barons had watched Guiscard's rise to duke, and the subsequent expansion of his holdings and ambitions, with misgiving. And even though revolt in the eleventh century rarely needed a pretext other than self-interest, the Apulian barons were able to cite Guiscard's seizure of the succession from Count Humphrey's sons Abelard and Herman as plausible cause for their action.

Abelard was the nominal leader of the revolt, and his supporters included others of Guiscard's kin. A nephew, Robert of Montescaglioso, was among the original group, as was Ami of Giovinazzo, nephew of Guiscard's relative Pierre of Trani whose family had consistently challenged the Hauteville brothers' leadership. Also involved were Roger Touboeuf, inheritor of the lands of that powerful knight who had killed the herald's horse a generation earlier, and Jocelyn of Molfetta, the knight who had earned Robert's enmity by restraining him during his altercation with Humphrey. As the revolt continued, other barons such as Pierre II of Trani joined in, while others took sides by refusing Robert's demands for military service, as was the case with another nephew, Geoffrey of Conversano.

The revolt began with seizure of Matera from the Hautevilles, and extensive raiding and pillaging of Hauteville lands. Moreover, the Byzantine authorities showed signs of a new activism: the energetic mercenary who had led the Byzantine army two years earlier, Abul Kare, had just been appointed *katapan*, and had arrived to take over command of the troops in Bari, Lecce, and the other enclaves still in Greek hands. The Byzantine commune of Bari, for some years at peace with the Normans, was impelled by the revolt to break its treaty and give support to the resurgent Byzantine cause.

Robert was in a hard place. He had stayed too long before Palermo to nip the revolt in the bud, and even after his return from Sicily he was tied down for some months in Calabria, where he had found he had to put down a completely unrelated revolt by the town of Aiello. When Robert finally returned to Apulia in 1065, the rebel barons largely retreated to their strongholds, in effect challenging him to winkle them out, one by one. Ending the revolt, in the circumstances, could involve a costly and time-consuming series of sieges, with uncertain prospects for success. Although the chroniclers give us few details of the period, it appears that Guiscard held a very weak hand: even his loyal barons were not entirely dependable in a fight against their Norman colleagues, and his brother Mauger was no longer available for command (and was possibly even dead). One reassuring presence, at least, was his wife Sichelgaita, who stayed by his side during this troubled period and undoubtedly shared with him the courage and determination with which she, too, was well endowed.

Characteristically, Guiscard took decisive and strategic action. He decided to attack the Byzantines, whom he saw at the root of his problem, rather than to try to reduce the baronial strongholds. And he would attack them where they least expected it, in their Illyrian territories across the Adriatic. Calling on the Calabrian cities to provide ships and sailors, Guiscard quickly raised a makeshift fleet, with which he planned to attack Perenos in his headquarters of Durazzo. To command the fleet he enlisted his distant nephew Geoffrey of Taranto, cousin to the rebel Ami but a knight who had proven his enthusiasm for fighting the Greeks by his recent captures of Otranto, Mottola, and Taranto.

For once, Robert's reach had exceeded his grasp. The Durazzo expedition failed. Not only that, but its failure allowed the Byzantine admiral, one Mabrikas, to bring a substantial force to Bari in 1066 that included units of the elite Varangian Guard. In short order, Brindisi and Taranto fell to Abul Kare and the Byzantine forces, while Castellaneta and Conversano were handed over by dissident barons. Abul Kare, however, apparently did not have the manpower to extend his conquests, and the war gradually reached a virtual stalemate.

What might have been a long and costly struggle was suddenly reversed in Guiscard's favor by events in Constantinople. In the spring of 1067, Basileus Constantine died. His neglect of the military had weakened the state, even as the Seljuk Turks continued their relentless advance from the plains of Asia into the Anatolian heartland of the empire. His death had only compounded the damage, by leaving the imperial government in the shaky hands of his widow. Byzantium's plight was eased somewhat when the soldierly Romanus Diogenes succeeded to the purple some six months later by marrying the empress, and embarked on a campaign to strengthen the empire against the Seljuk menace. But the prolonged period of confusion in Constantinople, added to the imminence of the Seljuk danger, had robbed the Italian expedition of its remaining momentum, and perhaps of its very purpose. Byzantine aid to the rebels dried up. Within months, Robert had moved back on the offensive against his opponents, and he began to reduce them one by one. The last major baron to fall was Geoffrey, who had earlier refused to provide his feudal obligations, and had even turned over Conversano to the enemy. When he surrendered his stronghold of Montepeloso, near Bari, at the beginning of 1068, the revolt effectively collapsed. To make Robert's victory more complete, the year also saw the death of two of his principal Byzantine opponents, Mabrikas and Argyrus.

Guiscard had survived, through perseverance, audacity and more than a bit of good luck. The disloyal barons trembled in anticipation of his retribution, knowing that he preferred to be feared over being loved. He could be a cruel man, and he had good reason to be vindictive against vassals who had rejected his authority and given his enemy an almost fatal opening. But he was also a realist, and one who reportedly did not take opposition personally. His sudden victory over the barons had finally left him free to pursue more far-reaching goals, ones for which he needed their support or, at a minimum, their acquiescence. As a result, his justice was easy; only Jocelyn and Roger Touboeuf were stripped of their possessions, the former immediately fleeing to exile in Constantinople. The others, even Abelard whose presence would inevitably provide a pretext for further sedition, were relieved of a few of their properties but otherwise left free. Once they had renewed their oaths of fealty, they could return to their castles, free to mull over why they had lost what had seemed so close to their grasp.

In Sicily, meanwhile, Roger had been making limited progress. With Palermo, the interior, and the west solidly in Muslim hands, the populations hostile, and the emirs capable of putting large armies into the field, he had sought few confrontations. He built up strength through raids and pillaging expeditions, and occasionally had the manpower to force a town to pay tribute. Progress, undoubtedly, was frustratingly slow for the ambitious youngest son of Tancred. But the slow pace of events may have hidden the trend, which remained in favor of the invaders. By mid-decade, Norman bands were able to raid throughout the island with relative impunity, and their presence, their demands, and the necessity of paying them off became an accepted part of the Sicilian scene, one which would play a role in softening up the populations for eventual Norman rule. Even so, Sicily was unlikely to fall to attrition tactics of this nature as readily as had the more thinly defended Calabria. Only major victories, with significant psychological impact, could break the strong Muslim resistance.

Fortunately for the Normans, their opponents were too involved in their own continuing feuds to mount a successful counteroffensive; in fact, they actively avoided any large scale engagements. The Berbers from Tunisia and the native Arab Sicilians had fallen out soon after their defeat at Cerami, and they began a struggle for supremacy under the banners, respectively, of Ayoub and Ibn Hawwas. In 1067, the two Muslim armies met in a fierce battle in which the last of the old *qaids* was killed. While the death of Ibn Hawwas should have given the victory to the Tunisian faction, it was by no means secure. The Berbers faced increasing popular unrest from the Sicilians, whom they had come to help but wound up ruling. Ayoub, looking desperately for a way to consolidate his shaky position as ruler, and for once unchecked by an armed opposition faction, decided that his best tactic would be to move against the troublesome and hated Normans. He sought a battlefield victory against the invaders, hoping it would restore his fortunes.

Ayoub's march out of Palermo in the summer of 1068, at the head of a great army, the largest the Muslims had put in the field against the Normans in five years, caught the Normans unprepared. Roger and his knights had been engaged in one of their regular raids into the mountains behind Palermo, where previous experience had led them not to expect heavy opposition, much less an attack by a major army. Nonetheless, they decided to hold their ground and accept the challenge. We may even assume that they welcomed the opportunity — battle was more noble than raiding, and after a half dozen years in Sicily they had developed confidence that they could defeat the Muslims handily. Roger's speech of encouragement to his knights before the battle, as relayed by the chroniclers, seems almost routine: We've done it before, we can do it again, particularly since God is on our side, he more or less said.

This time, there was no divine intervention reported on the Christians' behalf, but the result was the same as it had been at Cerami — a crushing Norman victory over a larger force. To rub in his victory to the citizens of Palermo, even faster than the few Muslims who escaped could do so, Roger improvised a new form of psychological warfare. He sent back to the city, via the carrier pigeons that had accompanied the Muslim army, messages written with the blood of the Muslim dead.

That the Norman victory had taken place at Menzel al Emir, or Missilmeri, which is just ten miles southeast of Palermo, made it all the more crushing to the morale of the defenders.[1] It meant that Palermo itself was no longer immune from attack, and presaged that the Normans were likely to prevail over the long run. For the Zirid faction, the defeat also meant the end of their aspirations to rule Sicily. Their ambitions crushed, Ayoub and Ali returned to the relative security of their father's pirating capital of Mahdia. Nor did any Muslim leader of stature emerge to take their place. So great, in effect, was the resulting dissension and disorganization among the Muslims that Roger was able, for the first time in years, to leave front line command to others.

The situation in Sicily had ripened for the Hautevilles. After the battle of Menzel el Emir, it was evident that the Normans held the initiative and could return to the attack at a time of their own choosing. The great and rich capital of Palermo, and with it inevitably control over the rest of Sicily, was within Norman reach. But the city would not fall without a prepared siege and a good fight, and the embarrassing expedition of 1064 had shown that a navy to cut off supplies would be essential.

Robert's success in Apulia, followed shortly by Roger's victory, put the initiative back in the Hauteville brothers' hands. Robert, however, had decided that he could not afford another expedition to Sicily until he had secured his hold in Italy. His attempted expedition against Durazzo had shown Guiscard that Norman gains in Italy could best be protected by eliminating the remaining Byzantine footholds on the peninsula, or even forcing the imperial forces across the Adriatic Sea onto the defensive. Militarily, depriving the Byzantines of their Italian footholds would help preserve Norman occupation of the Apulian coastal cities, some of which had changed hands repeatedly over the previous ten years. Politically, depriving the Byzantines of their presence in Italy would make it more difficult for their spies and envoys to remain in permanent political contact with his restless barons and the Lombard population, whose loyalties were uncertain. Finally, a campaign against the Byzantines would be popular among all the Normans, and Robert needed support. The barons owed him a limited amount of military service, but Robert knew that Norman cupidity would be his biggest ally in raising an army: were not the wealth of the Greek cities, the possibilities for booty, and his own liberality in the division of spoils, all well enough known to rally his colleagues?

Bari, the ancient capital and still the principal Byzantine city of Italy, was the prize, but its strong walls, armed militia, and Byzantine garrison would not make it an easy one to capture. Situated on a peninsula projecting into the Adriatic, the city could be easily resupplied or relieved from the sea. A successful siege demanded a major effort, bigger than anything the Normans had attempted to date, including a serious naval blockade of the harbor to close the siege. Robert was ready. He called upon his vassals to provide their troops and the port cities ships and sailors, and he began to assemble the mercenaries, siege engines, and other elements of the huge undertaking.

Notes

1. Almost 800 years later, Missilmeri once again witnessed history when the Italian patriot Garibaldi joined there with Sicilian revolutionaries in order to mount their successful attack on Palermo.

Victory

The siege of Bari began in the heat of summer in 1068, some fifteen months after the death of Emperor Constantine had dried up the rebels' support. Once he had put down the rebels, Guiscard had moved methodically onto the offensive. First, he had advanced a seemingly preposterous claim to inherit the property of the deceased governor Argyrus, which, when it was refused, became his legal justification for attacking. He had then sent a small vanguard of troops to Bari to test the defenses. The citizens of the town at first mocked the Norman troops, looking on them as little more than members of one of the raids that had troubled, but never truly threatened them, for the previous twenty-five years. But their tone changed sharply when the main body of the army, with its enormous siege engines, began to show up. It changed yet again when the various units of the Norman navy showed up and deployed in a concerted pattern that belied their eclectic appearance. Roger and his engineers had determined to seal off the sea approaches to the city with a continuous line of ships fixed in position about the entire peninsula, and connected to each other by heavy chains.

The citizens of Bari, recognizing that this time they were faced with a determined attacker — one who was prepared to spend the time and wealth necessary to break their opposition — swallowed their pride and asked Constantinople for a relief expedition. Luckily for them, their emissary got through the Norman lines. The authorities in Constantinople, even though heavily preoccupied with preparations for the campaign that their new Basileus intended to launch against the Turks, all the same found that they could not ignore the pleas from their last major foothold in Italy. A sizeable fleet with food, arms, and new military leaders was prepared for the relief of the besieged citizens.

The Greek fleet arrived off Bari early in the new year, was intercepted by Norman vessels, and lost twelve of its precious cargo ships in the ensuing engagement. Even then, to the relief of the citizens and the great consternation of the Normans, the fleet succeeded in breaking through the necklace of blockading ships, and delivered the great bulk of its supplies. With their staying power thus increased many times, the citizens redoubled their efforts to frustrate the attackers. The siege dragged on throughout the year and the next year, with little progress made by either side. The Norman army was unable to breach or even do serious harm to the massive city walls, and their siege engines were routinely destroyed or put out of action by the tenacious defenders. Over two years of dreary and dangerous siege warfare sapped the hopes of glory and spoils that had inspired the Norman army at the outset, and Guiscard's usual ability to motivate troops under his command was put to its greatest test. He attempted to raise morale by a lightning raid on Brindisi, the only other city in Italy remaining in Byzantine hands. The effort, unfortunately, backfired when the expeditionary force was ambushed and defeated by the Greeks, and Robert was forced to swallow his frustration.

Guiscard's readiness to share the hardships of life in the field with his troops was a significant element of his leadership, and helped maintain the army's spirit. At the beginning of the third year of the siege, however, it almost cost him his life. The Byzantine military leaders, recognizing that it was Guiscard's will that was keeping the Norman army at their necks, decided to have him assassinated. They suborned a Norman soldier, who agreed to do the job for a substantial reward and had little difficulty in penetrating the Norman camp at night. Nor, he subsequently reported, did he have trouble approaching Guiscard's virtually undefended quarters, which consisted of a simple hut made of branches. He had launched his lance at the duke's head, and then slipped away. What he wasn't able to report was that he had not hit Guiscard. The duke, it so happened, had lowered his head at the critical moment, either from tiredness or a hacking cough (the chroniclers' versions differ), and the lance had flown by harmlessly. All the same, it was a close call, resulting in tightened security for the duke and construction of a small stone command post for his use.

As the stalemate moved well into its third year, the prospect of another hard winter prompted both parties to look for a way to break through. Guiscard sent to Sicily for Roger, who arrived with only a few knights, but did bring a number of ships from Messina, and, even better, his spirit of enterprise and winning reputation. More importantly, Guiscard's political efforts to weaken the city's defenses from within had begun to bear fruit.

His agents had for some time kept him in contact with, and provided support to, a pro–Norman faction in Bari led by a citizen called Argyrizzos. Many of the non–Greek citizens of the town had become proponents of a negotiated settlement, thanks in part to Guiscard's money, which Argyrizzos had used to make discreet but generous distributions of food and supplies. The city's leaders, on the other hand, remained resolutely opposed to negotiations, and trusted in the city's unbreached defenses. But they saw that dramatic measures were needed to raise morale before supplies began to run out, or the internal opposition could reach a critical mass. They decided to send a new, and this time more desperate, appeal to Constantinople for relief and reinforcements.

The court in Constantinople, still preoccupied with its immediate Turk menace, nevertheless determined once again to help the defenders. The Norman navy had failed to stop the first fleet, and had allowed a number of blockade runners to escape as well, so there was a reasonable chance that the city could be relieved by sea. A fleet of twenty ships carrying food, arms and additional soldiers was fitted out and set off from Durazzo. In command was a man who had every reason to cause Guiscard harm: Jocelyn, the ex-lord of Molfetta, who had been driven out of Italy after his leading role in the barons' revolt, and who had been received with honor in Constantinople and made ruler of Corinth. His fleet made the short voyage from Durazzo without challenge, while the citizens of Bari, who had been alerted to its impending arrival, eagerly awaited it.

Perhaps the citizens were too eager, for in their efforts to guide the relief fleet to the harbor at night they overdid their signal fires. The Normans, alerted by the unusual activity, had time to prepare their fleet fully, set pickets, and keep a sharp lookout for the Byzantine ships. When they were finally sighted one night, the Norman fleet, under Roger's command, set out to do battle at sea rather than at the blockade line, which had proven vulnerable in the first resupply effort. The battle that followed was furious and confused; the Byzantines were caught unprepared for its scale and were eventually overwhelmed. Even though fighting in the dark of night, the Normans had been able to concentrate their attack on the enemy flagship, which they succeeded in capturing along with its commander. Nine of the relieving ships were sunk in the struggle. Norman losses in this, their first major sea battle, were also heavy, one ship having gone to the bottom with all hands when its 150 heavily armed men rushed to one side and caused it to capsize. But the joy in the Norman camp, on the return of the victors, was great. The embarrassment of their earlier failure to stop the relief fleet was erased, and Bari's defenders had been dealt a severe blow. Robert, who had been worried about his younger brother's safety in the unfamiliar circumstances of a sea battle, rushed to the shore to welcome Roger back in a tearful embrace.

The defeat of the relief fleet was fatal for the defenders' hopes. Without the new supplies, they could not hold out long; the winter had emptied their warehouses as the loss now depleted their morale. More and more voices were heard to argue for a negotiated settlement. When Argyrizzos and his supporters took the opportunity of the growing dissension to seize one of the watchtowers, the Byzantine commander saw that the city's defenses were in danger of being compromised from within, and agreed to parley while he still had a modicum of control.

With the victorious Normans showing remarkable leniency, terms of surrender were rapidly agreed. When Robert, with Roger at his side, rode triumphantly through the streets of their new conquest in April 1071, they did so in a city that had succeeded in retaining many of its traditional privileges. A basis for mutual understanding, as well as a frame of reference for the surrender, had been provided by the reasonably stable treaty relationships that the Normans and the commune of Bari had enjoyed for some years. The Byzantine officials were released and sent packing, only Jocelyn, who was imprisoned for the rest of his life, suffering the full ducal anger. The Bariots were left in possession of their property, including those properties outside the walls that the Norman army had despoiled during the siege. Their local administration was left largely intact, albeit responsible now for collecting taxes on behalf of the Normans rather than the court in Constantinople. In accordance with the Normans' feudal customs, the commune swore fealty to its new duke, and was saddled with new requirements for military service, including the provision of naval forces in times of need. In many ways, the settlement resembled a treaty relationship more than an outright surrender, and the citizens of the defeated city were greatly relieved.

The basis for Robert's leniency was not compassion; that was not in his nature. It was realism and a growing quality of statesmanship. He could no longer rule as a robber baron, or even as a parvenu count or duke. With the acquisitions of Calabria, eastern Sicily, and now the last but most glorious remnant of Byzantine Italy, he was faced with the necessity of governing a major state. And while he was still too much the adventurer knight, the conquering warrior, to have much patience for governance and administration, he was farsighted enough to know that good government would mean less internal unrest and, done right, a smoother collection of taxes to finance his ambitions. His desire to divert as few as possible of his Norman followers from the priority task of conquest encouraged him to adopt a policy of local self-rule for his new subjects. As long as his forces retained overwhelming coercive power, government through the existing local mechanisms provided an opportunity, not a challenge. Generosity to the citizens of Bari, moreover, might even win enough of their support to help maintain a balance against his still fractious barons. This pragmatic approach, later adopted as policy by Roger and his successors, prepared the ground for the flowering of a multi-ethnic state, remarkable for its time, in the following centuries.

But Guiscard also had more short-term considerations in mind when he granted lenient terms to the citizens of Bari. He needed their help, as he had already begun to envision his next strategic step. The time was right, he and Roger decided, to capitalize on their advantage in Sicily by capturing Palermo. His knights were victorious, confident, and eager for new victories that could increase the modest spoils they had enjoyed from Bari. The makeshift navy had proven itself. Bari could, and did, supply new money, ships, and men for this effort against the Muslims, a fight that its good Christian citizens could join without qualm even though it meant helping their recent enemy. Brindisi, too, was soon captured, and its citizens required to join the rest of Roger's subjects in making their contribution to the effort. Rapidly, since neither Robert nor Roger were given to delay when opportunity presented itself, a major army and fleet began to form in Otranto.

The army that was being assembled was no longer a Norman, or even a Frankish, affair, but had taken on a polyglot character, including Greek and Lombard contingents from the Hauteville lands in southern Italy, and mercenaries from various parts of Europe. No units from Salerno or Aversa, however, joined the army; Guiscard's rivals there were probably wishing the expedition no particular luck. Comprising perhaps as many as ten thousand men, the army was the largest yet mustered by the Normans in Italy. The expedition was unusual in another way, as well. For the first time, the Normans had made the naval arm an integral part of their expedition's planning; the 58 fighting ships of the fleet would not only carry out the amphibious operations but would also coordinate a naval blockade with the land force.

The army proceeded by land through Calabria, joining up with the fleet in Reggio. By the end of August, only four months since the victory at Bari, the army, its supplies and its horses were already across the water in Sicily. Rather than proceed directly to Palermo as might have been expected, the two brothers decided on a diversion that would strengthen their rear area. Catania, down the coast from Messina, was ruled by the successors to Ibn Timnah, reasonably friendly to the Normans but still representing a potential threat to their rear once the army moved on to

Palermo. Roger proposed a ruse to capture the city. He would take some of the fleet, claim he was headed to raid Malta, and ask permission for a harbor stop in Catania. The rulers there, he predicted, would agree, and once his fleet was inside the harbor, Catania could be seized with ease. It was not a very honorable plan, but it was an effective one. All went exactly as Roger had expected, and the Normans soon found themselves in possession of a rich and strategically important city at virtually no cost.

With their rear thus secured (and their coffers refilled), the two brothers headed off to Palermo. Roger went with the army overland, through Troina where he could spend a few days with Judith, and Robert by sea, accompanied it seems by his omnipresent wife Sichelgaita. Protection of their rear area would be in the hands of a small army under the command of their brilliant nephew Serlo, who would attack and deflect Muslim relief expeditions as necessary. On the way to Palermo, neither party encountered any obstacles other than the summer sun, and by the end of the month the army had crossed the mountains where the expedition of seven years earlier had had its miserable camp. They took up positions in the gardens east of the city, awaiting the arrival of the fleet and securing their position by capturing a small fort, the Kasr Yahya, at the mouth of the Oreto River.[1] The arrival of Robert and the fleet signaled the beginning of the siege. The army closed around the city to cut it off from the prospect of resupply and to test its defenses, while the navy, abandoning the tactic of a chain of vessels which had been only partially successful at Bari, attempted to deny the harbor to the Muslims through a permanent seaborne watch from their base at the mouth of the Oreto.

The Palermitans had been preparing since their loss at Menzel el Emir for the eventuality that now faced them. They had strengthened the fortifications, walled up some of the gates, improved the sortie points in others, and had laid in supplies for a protracted siege. For months, they fought with courage and determination, repulsing Christian attacks on the walls and drawing the attackers into costly skirmishes outside. But they suffered a major blow in the autumn, when a relief fleet was repulsed in a day-long and hotly fought battle off the port. The defeat of the relief fleet was compounded when the pursuing Norman vessels were able to force their way into the harbor and destroy the remnants of the Sicilian navy before the horrified eyes of the citizens of the town. The loss of their fleet meant that the Palermitans could expect no relief from the sea, while the effectiveness of the Norman siege lines gave them little hope for resupply from the land side, either. They would have to try to break the Norman stranglehold. The fate of their city, and most likely of the rest of Sicily, seemed likely to be determined by a single battle.

It was Robert, anxious to break the stalemate and avoid another long siege, who attacked. In early January, he launched an all-out assault on the larger of the two walled and fortified areas of the city, the Kasr or Fortress, which contained the principal markets, houses, mosques, and population. The Palermitans did not let the attackers hammer at the walls, but instead counterattacked and forced a pitched battle outside the gates. In fierce fighting, the citizens almost overwhelmed the attacking infantry with their numbers, courage, and desperation. Luckily for the Normans, however, there was room for their cavalry to operate, and their charges succeeded in stopping, and then breaking, the Muslim troops. The Palermitans retreated, seeking the safety of their city's strong walls. Most never found the safety they sought. Their own commanders, who feared that the Christian army would be able to force their way past the opened gates much as the Norman navy had done at the port, closed the gates in the faces of their doomed soldiers. The sacrifice of their soldiers outside the walls, though, allowed the remaining defenders to hold the walls and gates of the Kasr, and over the next several hours they courageously repulsed every Norman attempt to storm or scale the defenses.

As the struggle raged around the walls of the Kasr, Robert looked for another point of attack. Judging that the lower fortified section of the city, which was called the Khalisa and contained the administrative offices, the arsenal, and the Emir's palace, might have been stripped of some of its defenders, he determined to try his hand there. Leaving Roger in charge of the battle, he and several hundred picked troops opened a surprise second front with a scaling ladder assault on the Khalisa's walls. It was a fortuitous choice; the lower town had been left only lightly defended. The Norman party was soon within its walls and in control. Their success enraged the defenders of the Kasr, who once again made a sortie in force to try to drive the Normans out of the lower town. The close combat raged well into the night, and when the fighting subsided the outcome remained mixed: the Muslims still held the upper town, the Christians the lower.

While not defeated, Palermo's defenders had few if any prospects of victory after the deadly day's fighting. They had lost too many men, the capture of the Khalisa had cost them their armory and treasury, and the chances of a relief army or navy getting through were nonexistent. While the Kasr could still be defended for a good period of time, the likely outcome was already clear. Better to sue for peace while they still had some bargaining leverage, the municipal council decided. The next morning, a delegation of notables agreed to discuss terms of surrender with the Normans.

As he had done at Bari, Robert allowed generous terms. His leniency was truly remarkable in an age when towns resisting seizure were often sacked, their citizens killed or sold into slavery. Muslim Palermo, captured in a time of growing religious fervor, had risked even worse. The Christian army had been inflamed by the anti–Muslim rhetoric of the campaign, a long and bloody siege, and a desire for vengeance after over 250 years of murderous Arab sea raids against Christian communities. Zeal for holy war had begun to take root amongst the Franks, a fanaticism that would culminate 27 years later when the soldiers of the First Crusade waded through the blood of their defeated foes in Jerusalem.

In the prevailing mood, Guiscard's generosity to the defeated Palermitans did not sit well with all his followers. Some just wanted booty, but others were truly offended by his tolerance. Guiscard, of course, was by no means without choler, and he had shown streaks of cruelty in the past. But he was, above all, a calculating man, and he saw that leniency in the circumstances would have practical advantages. He saw into the future of the state he was winning, and in it a need to govern a predominantly Muslim population with minimum force. Moreover, he calculated, Palermo's merchants and craftsmen represented a goose that could lay many golden eggs for his benefit if treated right. The army might resent his generosity, but it could be assuaged, and he was burdened with no great rival lords to contest his wishes.

Guiscard agreed to allow municipal self-government under the old laws, including the free practice of the Muslim faith and the continuation of Islamic law for Muslim subjects. No looting, beyond that which had already taken place in the lower town, would be permitted, and the lives and property of the citizens would be respected. In return, Robert demanded the municipality's fealty, payment of an annual tribute, the return of the ancient basilica to the Christians, and the building and garrisoning of a Norman fort which would enforce his rule over the city. He also would leave his personal representative in the city, who would oversee the government in his name, and — as a preview of the happy eclecticism which would mark Norman rule in future — the ducal official would hold the Arab title of emir. The citizens of Palermo, expecting much, much worse, were delighted with the terms, and showered their new duke with presents in token of their gratitude and to win his favor.

In allowing the Muslims to practice their religion and law, Robert was not only being politic, he was also following the Islamic tradition, which permitted subjected communities to practice their faith under Muslim rule. Robert was once again being practical, above all in judging how best to govern a multi-ethnic and potentially hostile population. The wisdom of his policy was soon proven when the governors of the Val Mazara, a

solidly Muslim area in the southwest corner of the island, decided voluntarily to put their cities and properties under Norman domination on the
terms offered Palermo, rather than face eventual conquest.

Robert and Roger entered Palermo in triumph on January 10, 1072,
nine months after their victory in Bari. To mark the occasion, a grand
thanksgiving mass was held in the hastily re-consecrated church of Santa
Maria, led by the bishop of the small but enthusiastic Greek rite community of the city. Amidst the color and pageantry of the mass, Roger and
Robert had time to consider how kindly fortune had dealt with them over
the past year. The capture of Bari, and now Palermo, had put them within
easy reach of fulfilling their dreams at Melfi just over twelve years earlier:
the dukedom of Apulia, Calabria and Sicily was now a fleshed-out and
powerful reality. The Hautevilles had become the key strategic figures of
the entire region: they had spearheaded a revival of the Latin Church in
southern Italy, and returned Sicily to the faith after centuries of Muslim
rule. Although their days of cattle thieving and petty extortion in Calabria
were still a present memory, they had risen to join the ranks of the most
powerful and richest men in Italy.

It remained for the two brothers to settle matters between themselves.
The circumstances had changed so much since their earlier fights over
property in Calabria, however, that they were able to reach a settlement
with relative ease. Robert was to be recognized as the lord of Sicily, an
integral part of his greater dukedom. But Roger was to have a virtual free
hand to rule in Sicily in the duke's name. This was the kind of autonomy
that he had always been seeking, and it gave him opportunity to exercise
his talents, greater than his brother's, as a ruler. The duke would hold as
his own fiefs only Palermo, half of Messina and the Val Demone. The rest
of the island was at Roger's disposition, including those areas that still
remained to be wrested from the Muslims; Roger also retained his share
of the joint properties in Calabria. Roger intended to pass on some of his
land to his two principal lieutenants in Sicily, including his nephew Serlo.
Sadly for the two brothers, however, their heroic and beloved nephew met
his death that very summer, ambushed and outnumbered by a band of
Muslim cavalry who, rumor had it, ate his heart after killing him so that
they could partake of some of his bravery.

Robert and Roger's arrangements assured that Sicily, from the very
beginning of its return to the European polity, was governed as a single
political entity. While introducing feudal concepts of government to the
island, neither Robert nor Roger would countenance the creation of many
small fiefdoms, held in chains of fealty descending from the duke. They
had seen enough of independent barons in Apulia, and wanted to create

no centers of power that could diminish their authority. Limiting both the number of large fiefs that they created and the number of vassals dependent upon them, they continued to hold most of their vast estates, as well as the major cities, directly, granting only a few large fiefs to noble families. They were, however, generous in their donations of land to the Church, both Latin and Greek, as gifts to those institutions not only magnified the Hauteville fame but posed no political challenge. (Their habit, however, of naming their own candidates to head these establishments, without consultation with Rome, soon led them into conflict with a reforming Church determined to assert its authority.)

Robert lingered in Palermo into the late summer. Perhaps he and Sichelgaita were simply seduced by the pleasures of the place, the luxury of the life to which they were now exposed, or the honors heaped upon him by his colleagues and the obsequious Palermitan notables. Or perhaps he enjoyed setting up his new administration for the island and building the castles that would dominate the city in his name. Or perhaps he was just tired; he was now in his middle fifties and had led a life largely in the saddle for most of those years; the chance to rest must have been welcome. But, given his normally restless nature, his long stay in Palermo seems unusual, and doubly so when seen against the fact that some of his barons in Apulia were once again in revolt. In fact, they had begun their revolt the previous autumn, when the siege of Palermo was still new, and yet he had not yet made any decisive move against them. It was not until a full year later, in the autumn of 1072, that Guiscard left the pleasures of his great victory in Sicily to face, once again, the politics and struggle of Italy and Apulia.

Notes

1. After the fall of Palermo, the castle was dedicated to St. John by Roger, who also founded a church there dedicated to the saint. Subsequently the complex became part of a leper colony, hence its modern name of San Giovanni dei Lebbrosi.

The Duke and the Pope

The venerable abbey of Monte Cassino was the scene of a remarkable conclave in October 1071. In the presence of Pope Alexander and an unparalleled gathering of southern Italy's rulers, including no less than forty-eight bishops, Abbot Desiderius presided over the rededication of his rebuilt abbey church.[1] The splendor and pageantry of the dedication spectacle, the importance of the guests, the opulence of the arrangements, all had been designed by Desiderius to make a point: that the abbey was strong; it was of value to all, and it had many friends and protectors. Just as the church itself had been rebuilt, Abbot Desiderius wished to create a sound political environment in southern Italy, one in which the abbey and its widespread and rich lands would be protected from the kinds of depredations that had been visited upon it earlier by the likes of Pandulf and the Norman adventurers. His long efforts at conciliation and mediation had begun to pay off, at least as well as possible amongst such ambitious and predatory men as the rulers of the time. The dedication gathering, indeed, witnessed the lords of the sword vie with each other to show their devotion to the abbey, and to pledge their support.

Conspicuous by their absence at the gathering were the Hauteville brothers. It was unavoidable. Robert and Roger were, at the moment, before Palermo, ratcheting up the siege on a prize that would soon be theirs. Not that the good abbott and his domains in fact had much to fear from the brothers, since their energies and ambitions were clearly centered elsewhere for the moment. Desiderius had concluded moreover that Robert was not an evil man, and — now that he was rich, powerful and beyond the petty avarice of his brigand days — might even be of service to the Church. Had not Robert shown both a great largess in his giving, as well as a winning humility of spirit, during a visit he had paid to the abbey some four years earlier? At that time, he had impressed the abbot and the monks by attentively touring the buildings and the hospital, praying as well as eating with the monks, even asking that they pray for his sins, but, above all, by showering lavish gifts on the establishment and its members.

The two brothers' absence from the ceremonies at Monte Cassino proved to have its cost. At the banquets, in the halls, in walks about the abbey, their enemies consulted, agreed, and put into motion a conspiracy against the Hautevilles.

Few, indeed, were the lords present at Monte Cassino who wished well to the sons of Tancred. Robert's successes during the twelve years since Pope Nicholas had made him duke at Melfi had been so great as to stir the envy of many colleagues who were resentful of his luck and talents, afraid of his ambitions, or both. Rarely beaten in battle, quick and decisive in action, adept in the uses of intelligence and ruse, Robert had defeated both Byzantines and Muslims and amassed lands without match in the region. Clearly, the conspirators reasoned, he needed to be taken down a notch. They planned to make the simmering discontent of Guiscard's Apulian barons, beaten in their earlier revolt but not at all subdued, the vehicle for his embarrassment.

This time, the Byzantines could provide no help to the potential rebels. The eastern empire was in grave danger. On the Anatolian field of Manzikert, the Seljuk Turks in 1071 had crushed a great Byzantine army, led by the Basileus himself.[2] As a result of this historic defeat, the empire would henceforth be permanently on the defensive in its very heartland, distracted from serious thoughts of regaining influence or power in its lost Italian provinces. Constantinople had ceased to be a factor in Italy; it had sent no one to help dedicate the church at Monte Cassino, and even the Greek Patriarch had less and less of a role to play in supervising the remaining Greek rite congregations. As if to cap off the empire's reduced state, the new Basileus, Michael VII, was weak and ineffectual. Putting aside the pride of his predecessors who wore the purple, he sought aid from the papacy and even hoped — unwisely, it turned out — to neutralize Guiscard's potential for trouble by the risky diplomacy of offering him an imperial wedding alliance.

The main instigator of the conspiracy against the Hautevilles appears to have been Richard of Capua. He and Robert Guiscard had come a long way since the days, 25 years before, when they had arrived in Italy as young knights errant. They were now great lords, arguably the most powerful in southern Italy. Richard's seat at Aversa had always caused him to focus on Lombard princely politics and relations with the papacy and Monte Cassino; his troops had put two popes on their thrones, and his rise to ruler of Capua had made him a wealthy prince and the strongest one in the Campania. He and Robert were related, as he had married Tancred's daughter Fressenda. And yet a rivalry persisted between him and Robert; their lieutenants competed to seize lands in the Abruzzi, and Robert's vast territorial gains in southern Apulia, Calabria, and in Sicily must have been troublesome to the ruler of Capua. Richard had promised Robert that he would send troops for the siege of Palermo, but had not done so, and it appears that Fressenda's death at about this time had dissolved one of the few bonds between the two rivals.[3] Richard was probably concerned that Robert, whose ultimate victory in Sicily was now foreseeable (and moreover delegated to his brother Roger), would look to the Campania for future additions to his land. The prospect could not have been comfortable. Far better, in Richard's view, would be to keep Guiscard tied down by fomenting disorder in his own lands.

Gisulf of Salerno was also a supporter of Richard's plan. His wedding alliance with Guiscard had not worked out as he had hoped. Sichelgaita had identified more with the interests of her powerful Norman husband than with the Lombard family in which she had been raised, and Gisulf's dream of reviving the fortunes of his ancient princely house seemed farfetched as long as the Hautevilles continued their rise to power. As it had turned out, he was locked in a long struggle with the commune of Amalfi just to regain control of that city-state. He, too, badly needed to keep the Hautevilles on the defensive.

In that respect, Gisulf's interests matched those of the papacy. Pope Alexander and his advisor Hildebrand had worried, once their Norman allies had removed the antipope Honorius from the scene, whether such allies could be loyal ones. They worried, too, whether Pope Nicholas, when he had recognized Norman title to their existing landholdings, had abandoned the only effective leverage the papacy had held over those ambitious knights. Rather than becoming good vassals, the Normans had instead continued to infringe on papal lands in the Abruzzi and elsewhere, the pope even having to excommunicate William of the Principata for a time to get him to reverse some of his seizures. In the circumstances, the papacy looked for ways to put the Normans on the defensive, or to inflame the rivalry between the two major leaders, Richard of Capua and Robert Guiscard, so as to weaken them both.

It took only a little prodding to get the disaffected Apulian barons to resume their revolt, which they did while Robert was besieging Palermo in early 1072. Abelard and Herman, Humphrey's two sons, once again provided the kernel and rationale for a revolt; they were rejoined by Ami of Giovenazzo, Pierre of Trani and Robert Areng, as well as others. Working in consort with their external supporters, they had sweeping early successes. Abelard and Ami made devastating raids against Robert's properties in Calabria, while Herman did the same in Apulia, and Gisulf used the Salernitan fleet to ravage the coasts of Calabria. Richard of Capua even seized the town of Cannae, adding it to the list of baronial strongholds already in revolt. The rebellion also gained the sympathy of many Lombard and Greek communes, most of which as yet had no loyalty to their new Norman rulers. But the revolt peaked early; few new towns joined the revolt outright, and the situation began to stabilize, allowing Guiscard to spend the summer, as we have seen, in uncharacteristic inactivity in Sicily.

When Robert eventually did return in the autumn, he lost no time. Landing in Apulia because of the rebel activities in Calabria, he proceeded immediately to Melfi and called an assembly of his barons. There, he demanded the military service that his vassals owed him, and rallied the major number of his barons to his side even though Pierre of Trani tried to stir them up. His campaign began in January and was over in less than four months, the major breakthrough coming in February when Guy of Sorrento, Gisulf's uncle, captured Trani for Guiscard and with it two of the major rebels, Pierre and Herman. Richard of Capua and Gisulf soon withdrew from what was obviously a losing effort, and most of the remaining rebel strongholds were reduced one by one.

Robert, always in a hurry, had forced the surrender of the town of Cisternino, a fief of Pierre of Trani, by a crude but effective act of intimidation. When the townsmen refused to surrender, Guiscard had his prisoner Pierre tied to a wicker framework, which he then wheeled out at the head of the troops as they advanced on the town's walls. Not wanting to fire on their humiliated and piteous lord, the citizens promptly ended their resistance, and Guiscard gained possession of the town without a fight. In fact, one gets the impression that the rebellion was put down without much bloodshed; the campaign was primarily one of movement and threat of siege rather than fierce fighting.

The rebellion was suppressed. Guiscard had, once again, proven himself to be effective as a leader of men, as field commander, and as statesman. He exacted little retribution; the humiliated Pierre was forced to give up his major city of Trani, but was allowed to keep his other extensive castles and estates. The remaining rebels were ignored rather than crushed; Abelard and Robert Areng were even tolerated as holdouts in their mountain strongholds for well over two more years. Robert's leniency was politic. But the spark of rebellion had not yet been extinguished, and would flare up yet again.

And then, suddenly, in his new town of Trani, Robert Guiscard was laid low by illness. The nature of his affliction is unclear, and it may have been connected in some way with his unusual stay in Palermo over the summer, but what is clear from the chronicles is that his life was feared for. As he lingered near death, his family and his barons were faced with an unavoidable crisis: the question of his successor. No longer would the successor be chosen by a vote of the Norman barons of Apulia. The duchy and its vastly expanded territories had become a Hauteville fief, to be passed by Norman custom within the family. And yet there was no clear family successor, and Robert had made no provision for the eventuality. Bohemund, Robert's son by his first wife, Alberada, was of an age to succeed, and had inherited from his father both an imposing physique and many abilities as a leader and mighty warrior. And yet Bohemund could not succeed; the dissolution of his mother's marriage had made him legally a bastard, and even though a special dispensation might have been obtained from the Church to make him eligible, Robert had never requested one. In spite of the affection and trust he placed in his eldest son, he could not make him his heir. To do so would damage his relations with Sichelgaita, whose support was essential both on a personal level, and because she and her sons gave him legitimacy amongst his Lombard subjects, including a potential claim on the throne of Salerno. Unfortunately Sichelgaita's first son, Roger, was still a child, not ready to rule an unstable state still in the process of formation.

Sichelgaita, never the withdrawing chatelaine, was determined to fight for the interests of her son. This woman, who had stood and fought resolutely by the side of her husband for fourteen years, now stood in his place as he lay insensible. She called for an assembly of the barons, where she convinced them through force of her personality that Roger, a youth of unknown capabilities who displayed indications of a weak character, nonetheless had the stuff to make a future duke under her guardianship. Her husband's vassals soon acquiesced, and swore loyalty to Roger, only the absent Abelard objecting. The barons may have been swayed by Sichelgaita's arguments, or they may simply have been willing to see a less overwhelming duke succeed as their lord; we do not know. We do know that Bohemund, with no one to champion him and perhaps not even present at the assembly, had to accept the decision, though he did so with reservations that would emerge later.

Among the letters that were sent to Sichelgaita, as virtual regent during Robert's illness, was one from the newly elected pope: Gregory VII by title, none other than the longtime papal advisor Hildebrand. Pope Alexander had died, and his powerful archdeacon had been obliged to step out from his advisory role and assume the papal throne, the power of which he had virtually exercised for years. Hildebrand was truly a remarkable man. Small, ugly, and poorly born, he had dominated the papal Curia for much of the past twenty years by the force of his personality and the strength of his convictions. His central aim was to establish the primacy of the Latin Church in both ecclesiastical and lay matters, with the pope as supreme and unquestioned leader of the Church. He had already established the principle of papal election. Now he was determined to push the program of Church reforms with a kind of muscular obstinacy, demanding celibacy from the clergy and an end to ecclesiastical appointments by secular rulers, as means to his great goal of forming a Church independent of the emperor or any secular lord. In his papacy, a theory of armed Christian action took root, which would flower a generation later in the Crusades. His ambitions were as great as his personality was combative; he would claim supremacy for the Church in all of the lands claimed in the spurious Donation of Constantine, and would do so with an unparalleled degree of bluster and impetuousness.

Pope Gregory's letter to Sichelgaita, however, showed a surprising degree of conciliation. His attitude to the Normans had always been suspicious at best; their continual depredations against Church property and insistence on appointing their own men to Church positions had incensed him. Guiscard, in particular, had shown himself to be too supple in his political and religious behavior to merit the confidence of this rigid and moralistic pope. And yet, Gregory had to admit, the Normans had shown themselves ready to take militant action in the name of the faith, and had opened up vast areas to the Latin Church. They might be harnessed, as Desiderius had long argued, and moreover the opportunity might now have come through the succession of the unformed, pious, and half–Lombard young Roger as duke. The pope's letter, therefore, was sincere in its purpose, even if insincere in its words. Professing his love and admiration for the (presumably) deceased Duke Robert, the pope flattered his widow, and offered to confirm the child Roger as successor in lands his father had conquered. As an act of conciliation, the letter was well-conceived even if somewhat risible in its phrasing. Robert Guiscard must have found it interesting reading, for by the time it arrived he had quite recovered from his illness.

Robert was eager to pick up the new pope's olive branch. There would be complications, of course, but Guiscard hoped to benefit from Gregory's professed amiability, without actually changing his own behavior. He did nothing, for example, to rein in the activities of his trusted brother Geoffrey of the Capitanata and his nephew Robert of Loritello, who were continuing to expand into lands claimed by the pope in the Abruzzi.[4] Guiscard doubtless hoped to disarm Gregory's complaints on that score with the diplomatic evasions at which he had become adept, and to secure a formal reinvestiture from Gregory of the lands he had conquered since Melfi. Accordingly, Robert wrote a conciliating letter in response to the pope's, thanking him for his good wishes and informing the dignitaries at Rome of his good health.

While Gregory may have been less than overjoyed at Robert's unexpected return to the living, both parties sought Abbot Desiderius's good offices to set up a meeting. The meeting, however, never took place. The chroniclers tell that it was planned for Benevento in the heat of August, but that the protocol and security arrangements fell apart under the conflicting demands of the two proud and suspicious principals. One suspects that more was at play. Perhaps the matter of the Abruzzi could not be glossed over, perhaps Desiderius gave up his thankless task of mediation, or perhaps the pope had simply been playing a double game once he learned that Robert had not died.

Whatever the reason for the failure of conciliation, Pope Gregory left Benevento in September for Capua, where he reversed the tables by confirming Richard in possession of his lands and entering into an alliance with him. The main purpose may have been simply to excite the rivalry between Richard and Robert, and in this the pact proved successful, although as it turned out, not to the pope's benefit. Gregory also entered into a similar agreement with Landulf, the prince of Benevento. Coupled with the papacy's already strong relations with Gisulf of Salerno, this meant that the pope had formally created an alliance with all the old Lombard principalities, evidently aimed at resisting any expansion by the Duke of Apulia.

The pope's new alliance, however, served more as a goad to Robert than a restraint. Soon, his forces were in the field to harass and harm the pope and his allies. His main effort was against Capua, where he began raids into the heart of the Garigliano valley, took advantage of a family feud in the Teano region to take sides and seize some castles there, and resupplied his forces through Naples—with which he had formed an alliance of his own, directed at Capua. Roger also provided support, while Monte Cassino's silence was bought by lavish gifts. In the Abruzzi, Robert took no new action, but it was already clear that neither the pope nor Landulf had sufficient power or clear authority to stop the Norman expansion there. Both emperor and pope claimed to be overlords of the numerous small *gastaldts* who ruled there as virtually autonomous remnants of the old Duchy of Spoleto. But neither could give them much more than moral support, and as a result those small counties, and even some of the Church properties in the region, had been falling to various Norman knights for over a dozen years. Robert controlled few of the marauding knights; indeed one of the major ones had for some time been Richard of Capua. Now, following the failure of the talks at Benevento, Robert showed even less inclination to restrain his own family members from their expansion into lands which he, in any event, claimed to be outside papal protection.

Against Salerno, Robert at first took no direct action. After all, his brother William in his County of Principata had been a sufficient thorn in Gisulf's side for many years, during which he had torn away great parts of the Prince's traditional lands. Suddenly, however, Robert was given a golden opportunity to do his opponent additional harm. The opportunity arose from Gisulf's long struggle to gain control of Amalfi. In the fall of 1073, the Duke of Amalfi died and the commune, suffering from years of Gisulf's raids on their shipping and his encirclement from the land, looked for a strong lord to protect their city against their avaricious and vindictive neighbor. They had first offered to place themselves in the hands of the pope, but he had declined because of his alliance with Gisulf. The commune determined to look elsewhere, but ruled out Richard of Capua as too strong and too close for comfort. They turned instead to the strongest of Gisulf's enemies, Robert Guiscard, who, moreover, had the new advantage of being in a position to assure them access to the trade of Sicily. Robert was quick to agree, as becoming lord of Amalfi and its rich trade would provide great benefits. For the moment, however, he could not provide the beleaguered city with the protection that his new lordship entailed. He was still tied down in Apulia, and unable to provide more than limited support, a small garrison force of Norman troops and a few ineffectual naval units. The Amalfitans nonetheless proved themselves quite capable of holding on for two more years, and Robert would wait to take up their cause actively until he was ready to use it against Salerno itself.

Gregory's alliance diplomacy against the bold and lucky Hautevilles had backfired. His was a character of determined purpose, however, and a setback only made him try harder. If his local allies had proven ineffectual in stopping Guiscard, then he would find support elsewhere. Correspondence with the weak Basileus Michael in Constantinople had given him the germ of an idea, which he tried to nourish into an alliance. Michael, fearful of the strength of the victorious Turks, had asked the pope to organize help from the Christians of the West, an idea that appealed, in spite of its outlandishness, to Gregory's concept of muscular Christianity. The pope, surely, also saw a way to turn the idea to his own benefit. He began to canvass among friendly rulers for support, and soon had promises of troops from Burgundy, Tuscany, Pisa, Capua, Salerno, and Benevento. His plan was to march a large army through southern Italy, sailing to the relief of Constantinople from Bari and, not coincidentally, using the muscle of his transiting army to scare the renegade Duke of Apulia into submission. Seeking potential contributors to his coalition, he wrote:

> "We also hope that out of this will arise the possibility of another advantage, for, once the Normans are constrained to make peace, we can pass on to Constantinople to aid the Christians who are continually afflicted by the attacks of the Saracens and pray for aid from our hand. In fact, against those rebellious Normans, we already have more than enough warriors on our side...."[5]

To emphasize his determination, Gregory also used his spiritual powers; he had Robert (and Robert of Loritello too, for good measure) excommunicated. But in the end, the pope's scheme proved an illusion. The expedition began to gather in June 1074 in northern Italy, with the Pisans having agreed to supply the naval arm. When they learned, however, that the coalition also included Gisulf of Salerno, whose ships had been preying mercilessly on Pisan commerce for years, and whom they considered to be a man "without pity, who has condemned those of our city to be drowned at sea," they balked. The Pisans dropped out, and with this first thread pulled from the pope's delicate fabric, the whole web began to unravel.[6] The alliance broke up before the army ever left Viterbo.

The threat of the crusading army marching through his territories had at least prompted Robert to try to conciliate the pope. He had even gone, hat in hand, to Benevento to try to arrange a meeting. It had not worked out, but Guiscard realized that he still had incentive, even after the threat was lifted, to come to better terms with the pontiff. The thought of lifting his excommunication may have played a role in the decision, though probably a minor one. Robert was a pious man, and he must have been inconvenienced and saddened by the limitations the papal excommunication placed on his lifestyle. But rulers in those days learned to live with such fulminations, and Robert's reasons for seeking an understanding with the pope were above all practical ones. He had already made his point with his raids into Capua; he had shown he could neither be ignored nor easily punished. But he had no demands against the papacy or animosity to Gregory, and in fact had refused to become involved in an attempted anti-papal scheme that the Roman families had asked him to join.

For much of the next year, the situation remained unchanged, in spite of Robert's tentative efforts at opening a dialogue, or his offer to cease his raids if Gisulf did likewise towards Amalfi. Robert also maintained a correspondence with Gisulf, but it did not lead to an easing of tensions any more than did his contact with the pope. In an intemperate letter, Gisulf had even suggested insultingly to Robert that he owed service to Salerno as its vassal. Before long, the gulf between the two brothers-in-law had become too deep for diplomacy to resolve. On the other hand, such was not necessarily the case in Robert's relations with the pope. Admittedly, Gregory had renewed his excommunication against Robert, but that could be overcome. What was more significant was that Gregory was increasingly under stress from events to the north, and thus potentially in need of Norman support. Gregory's conflict with the emperor-designate, Henry, King of the Germans, had in fact begun to escalate into an epic struggle for supremacy, one that would change many political calculations.

Notes

1. Of the church built by Desiderius, virtually nothing remains. The abbey was extensively damaged in an earthquake in 1349, and then largely redesigned and rebuilt in the seventeenth century. Much of it was destroyed once again during World War II. The post-war reconstruction recreated the abbey in its Baroque style of the eighteenth century. An idea of the church built by Desiderius can possibly be had from a visit to Sant' Angelo in Formis, near Capua, also built by the abbot.

2. One of the cavalry commanders for the Byzantines at Manzikert, the Norman mercenary Roussel de Bailleul, deserted the Basileus in his hour of need. As a result, Constantinople refused to hire any further Normans, considering them both too ambitious and too untrustworthy. Instead, the Byzantines began actively to recruit Saxon warriors, exiles from England where they had been defeated and made landless as a result of the Norman invasion led by William the Conqueror. Robert would meet these fiercely anti–Norman fighters in due course.

3. Loud, p. 199.

4. The eastern areas of the modern province of Molise represent to a large degree lands claimed in the eleventh century by Benevento, but no longer controlled by the princes of that state. They, and the Abruzzi proper to the north, were commonly called the Abruzzi by the contemporary chroniclers, and will be in this discussion

5. *Gregorio VII Registrum*, no. 46, as cited in Delogu, pp. 98–9.

6. Amatus of Monte Cassino, VII, C. 12, p. 308, as cited in Delogu, p. 100. Amatus, who lost no opportunity to defame Gisulf, is probably not telling the full truth. The coalition was, at best, a shaky proposition, and the Pisans' attitude was only one reason for its failure. Loud, p. 199.

Salerno

The crisis that finally erupted between the pope and the German king would change the entire political landscape. The bellicose Gregory had unleashed the crisis himself, when at the Lenten Synod of 1075 he had announced a rigorous reform program aimed directly at Church practices in Germany, and particularly King Henry's habit of investing high Church officials for consideration received, and without reference to Rome. But headstrong Henry, who depended on these sales of Church offices for a large part of his revenue, was eager and ready to strike back; his hands, moreover, were free as he had just defeated a great conspiracy of his princes. He and his bishops, at a synod in Worms the following year, repudiated their allegiance to Gregory and called for his deposition in the rudest of terms. Gregory in turn responded by excommunicating not only Henry, but all his bishops as well, and excused imperial subjects from allegiance to their king. These steps threw both Church and state in Germany into confusion, and gave the Saxon and other princes a chance to renew their rebellion. Henry was once again placed on the defensive. The two obstinate leaders had thus begun a violent struggle between papacy and empire, one that had been looming for a decade because it was inherent in the reform program, but which now, out in the open, would last for over a hundred years, and would profoundly influence the politics of all Europe.

For Guiscard, the pope's new preoccupation smacked of opportunities for advancing his own interests. The first one came unexpectedly. King Henry, who at the time was planning to bring a German army to Italy to depose the pope in person and achieve his long-delayed coronation as emperor, sounded Robert out early in 1076. Would the duke, his emissaries suggested, be prepared to join in open opposition to the pope if

Henry were, in return, to invest him in his recently conquered lands as an imperial, rather than papal, vassal? Robert studied the proposal carefully, but found it lacking. For one, Henry could guarantee no lasting imperial presence in southern Italy or Sicily to protect his vassals; interventions by previous emperors had been episodic and short-lived, whereas the papacy was already a permanent regional power. It might not be wise, in the circumstances, to give future emperors new grounds to intervene in the region. Secondly, Robert already had legitimacy for the lands he had conquered, in the form of Pope Nicholas' investiture at Melfi. Henry's act could add very little. And, finally, Gregory might make a better offer, and the best option would be to remain as independent as possible from both of the feuding powers until the offers got still better. These considerations, and doubtless others, caused the duke to politely but firmly reject Henry's offer. His response is worth quoting because it seems to show the duke's frame of reference clearly:

> I have taken this land from the dominion of the Greeks with great loss of blood and after suffering great need, poverty, hunger, and misery. And many times Normans have conspired against me trying to persecute and capture me. I withstood the pride of the Saracens as well as hunger and great tribulation on the other side of the sea. So that I might have the assistance of God and so that my lords Saint Peter and Saint Paul…would pray for me, I submitted myself to their vicar, the Pope, along with all the land which I had conquered. And I received them back from the hands of the Pope so that, through the power of God, he would be able to protect me from the malice of the Saracens and vanquish the pride of foreigners…. Because I desired to be subject to God, I was able to conquer it through his grace. I hold from Him the land which you say you want to give to me.[1]

Guiscard's prudence turned out to be wise, for soon Henry, weakened by a new rebellion at home, was forced to bend his knee to the obstinate pope. Appearing as a penitent outside the mountain town of Canossa in midwinter of 1077, the king made a public and humiliating submission before the pope in order to maintain the legitimacy of his rule and the possibility of a papal coronation. But it was more a tactical move on his part than a surrender to Gregory's demands. As soon as he had been absolved by the pontiff, Henry returned to Germany to resume the struggle against his rebellious subjects. He would renew his argument with the pope once he had his own house in order.

At about the same time as his dalliance with Henry's ambassadors, Duke Robert had another proposal from a surprising source, but one that was more readily acceptable because it entailed no cost and a large potential benefit. No less than the Basileus Michael proposed a marriage alliance, offering to marry his eldest son to one of Guiscard and Sichelgaita's numerous daughters (they would eventually have at least seven, in addition to three sons). Michael, disappointed at the failure of the pope's relief effort, still felt himself in need of friends in the West and must have thought that, at a minimum, he could buy Guiscard's neutrality — if not necessarily his support — by the marriage. Guiscard found the proposal seductive from both the personal and practical points of view. To be thus accepted, or at least tolerated, by the haughty power that he had struggled against for years was surely heady stuff. Moreover, he realized that an alliance with the royal house in Constantinople would give his family still more legitimacy and acceptance with his Greek subjects, much as taking on some of the trappings and ritual of his Byzantine predecessors in Italy had done. Even better, the proposed alliance raised the possibility that a grandchild of his could at some time become emperor, or at a minimum would give the Hautevilles an instrument to use in the games of power played in that richest of all capitals, Constantinople. The proposal was worth a daughter. The daughter chosen, Olympiade, soon fond herself in the imperial capital, where she was renamed Helen, and began her training in the intricate politics and ceremony that marked the court of her intended's family.

With his rear thus somewhat secured by his entente with Byzantium, Guiscard could study the developing struggle between the great powers, pope and emperor, to see how it might create openings for a nimble lord to seize. He saw that the new circumstances had made the rivalry between himself and his fellow Norman ruler Richard of Capua pointless; better that they make up their differences and decide together how they might pursue common interests in a period of uncertainty. Richard needed no persuading; indeed he may have reached the logical conclusion even before Robert. The two called upon Abbott Desiderius— always ready to make peace between his bellicose and dangerous neighbors— to help them come to terms, as he had already tried to do the previous year. At that time, his effort had fallen through when Richard had refused to abandon his alliance with the pope. This second time, however, it was not difficult to find terms. Neither, in spite of their long rivalry, had made any permanent gains at the expense of the other, nor had they any significant claims to sort out. And the failure of the pope's military schemes had made Richard's papal alliance less of a threat to Robert. The two proud, competitive, but above all opportunistic leaders rapidly agreed to return the territories they had seized from each other, and to look for common opportunities.

At the same time, Gregory, too, had seen that success in his struggle with Henry would require a new diplomacy, and powerful allies. His effort to incite Robert and Richard against each other had failed; in fact, it had contributed to their reconciliation. The same reasons that had caused Gregory and Pope Nicholas to acknowledge Norman power at Melfi in 1059 were once again coming into play; the papacy was inevitably going to need armed support to prevail, and that inevitably meant the Normans. But Gregory was too proud, too embarrassed by the failure of his recent anti–Guiscard campaign, and not yet in dire enough need to make an open overture to his Norman nemesis. He limited himself for the moment to a very indirect olive branch: in the early spring of 1076, Roger's soldiers about to go on campaign in Sicily were offered a papal absolution. This signal of good wishes to the Hautevilles was also to be accompanied by a hint, which the pope directed his bishop to give, that Robert himself might have the anathema lifted and be welcomed back to the fold. If Robert ever received the indirect suggestion, he apparently found it too little to act on. He had other plans, which included settling accounts with his brother-in-law, who was also the pope's ally, Gisulf of Salerno.

Guiscard was free to move against Salerno because of the pope's current weakness, in addition to the accord he had just reached with Richard of Capua. The days of Norman-Salernitan alliance had died years before with Prince Guaimar. Gisulf's continued siege of Amalfi, even since Robert had become its lord three years earlier, was grounds enough to attack. But Robert, in addition, had not forgotten Gisulf's lack of gratitude for being restored to his throne, his absence at the time of Civitate, or his support of the recent barons' revolt. The two brothers-in-law by now probably despised each other, as evidenced by the manner in which the Norman chroniclers did their best to blacken Gisulf's name through their tales of his cruelty, unreasonableness, and avarice.

By June, Guiscard's forces, with detachments of Lombard, Greek and even Arab troops from Sicily, had surrounded Salerno by land and sea and begun a determined siege aimed at starving the town into submission.

First, both Desiderius and Sichelgaita were enlisted to give mediation a last chance. Both were unsuccessful. According to the admittedly biased chronicles, Gisulf proved entirely unmoved by his sister's pleas for a peaceful settlement, flying into a resentful rage instead. One can scarcely blame the isolated and resentful Prince, no mater how good or evil his character; after all, he was being asked to abdicate in favor of his tormentor's son. Moreover, he may have had good reason to distrust his sister's capacity to be a disinterested mediator. After fifteen years as a Hauteville, he could see, her ties of sympathy for her brother and her natal family had been deeply altered. Moreover, she had an interest in Robert's claim: would not Salerno be hers, and then her son's, if Robert were to seize it?[2]

The failure of overt diplomacy with the Prince did not, however, stop Robert from using covert diplomacy as a weapon to wrest control of the city from Gisulf. His spies had, as was his practice, established communication with citizens within the walls, who were courted as potential supporters and urged to come over. A market was also made available in the Norman camp to those who came out of the town, where supplies were increasingly scarce. As the severe blockade moved into the winter, starvation became common, and eventually the suffering citizens of the city turned against their lord, who reportedly was profiting from the shortages. By mid December, resistance collapsed; Guiscard's troops entered the city and accepted the surrender of the outnumbered and starving garrison. Gisulf and his remaining supporters fled to the citadel, where they held out with a desperate hope for a further five months.

Beaten and bitter, Gisulf had to surrender his rights in the city that his family had long ruled, to the brother-in-law whom he had always resented. Each had recriminations against the other; each complained that the other had not lived up to the obligations of the marriage alliance or their feudal allegiances. Both had reason to complain, but in the predatory world of mixed allegiances and shifting alliances in which they lived, it was force and skill that mattered, and Guiscard had more of both than the defeated Prince. A final scene demonstrates the sort of rancor in which they parted. One of the great relics of the city, a tooth of St. Matthew, had been found missing when the city surrendered, and Robert now demanded from Gisulf that it be turned over. Gisulf apparently complied but Guiscard, suspicious and no stranger to deception himself, demanded that the item be authenticated. When it turned out that the supposed relic had recently been extracted from an unfortunate citizen's mouth, Robert lost patience: either the genuine item, or a tooth from Gisulf's head each day, was his ultimatum. Finally surrendered by Gisulf as a result of this threat, the relic would stay in Salerno.

Guiscard's terms for the surrender of Salerno were similar to those he had negotiated at Bari and Palermo: local officials, justice, and finances remained largely unchanged; most Salernitans and even some of the princely family retained their property. For Gisulf, the terms were harsher, but not punitive. Gisulf and his brothers, Landulf and Guaimar, were allowed to keep their personal effects and considerable wealth, and Gisulf was permitted to depart his native city in style and take up a comfortable exile in Rome. The brothers were obliged, on the other hand, to give up all their estates and castles. Among the properties that thus passed into

Hauteville hands were San Severino, Policastro, and most of the Cilento region. Along with the lands that William had already amassed in his County of the Principata, this made the Hautevilles the major landholders in Salerno, as well as lords of the city and successors to the princely family. Salerno was a crowning addition to Robert's string of successes, a city with a rich history, thriving commerce, and a significant role in Italian politics. Robert decided to make the city the capital of his flourishing duchy.

The gaining of Salerno had been made easier by the neutrality of Richard of Capua, and the time had come for Robert to pay back the favor. Richard had long had his eye on Naples, the natural port of Capua, whose independence and continuing ties to Constantinople had become a bit anachronistic. Richard's army, which had been harassing the city for years, now moved in for a protracted siege, reinforced by a fleet on loan from his new ally, Robert. Their enterprise looked invincible, and gave the two new allies an appetite for further cooperation. Soon their lieutenants in the Abruzzi, Richard's son Jordan,[3] and Robert's nephew Robert of Loritello, had increased the pace of their conquests in that region, the former on the inland plateau and the latter along the coast. As summer moved into autumn and then winter, the two great Norman lords were clearly set to sweep up the remaining pawns left on the chessboard of southern Italy.

Pope Gregory was powerless to stop the Norman advance. His ultimate frustration was the assault by Robert Guiscard, twice excommunicated but still defiant, on the papal city of Benevento in December. Guiscard had laid claim to the city upon the death of the ruler, Gregory's direct vassal Landulf, but his attack was for all intents and purposes an attack on the pride, even the body, of the papacy itself. Gregory was infuriated that Normans were also raiding deep into territory claimed by the papacy, even as far as the Sabine Hills. But his nearest armed allies were in Tuscany; his focus, perforce, had to remain on his struggle with King Henry, and he had no assistance to offer the beleaguered Beneventans or his other vassals. He could only fulminate. Once again, he called on bell, book, and candle to excommunicate Robert, Richard, Jordan of Capua, Robert of Loritello, and many of their supporters. The pope was not sanguine, however, that the new anathema would keep his antagonists in line, any more than the previous ones had. So he also gave a signal of conciliation. While the ban covered many of Robert's knights and bishops, the new terms were eased somewhat, in order that the general population would not be deprived of all Church sacraments.

Abruptly and surprisingly, the situation was reversed. In April 1078, just as a new campaigning season was about to begin, Richard of Capua died, following a short illness and an even shorter reconciliation with the

Church. With his death, the tide turned against the Norman project. Jordan rapidly succeeded his father as ruler, but had neither the qualities nor, at the moment, the opportunity to cut the same figure. As he would hold Capua as a vassal of the pope, Jordan as a new ruler simply could not maintain the aggressive policy that his father had been following, even had he wanted to. The pope would scarcely confirm him in his lands unless he first made his peace with the Church. To assure his investiture, therefore, Jordan had the siege of Naples lifted, held back the detachments in the Abruzzi, and promptly sought Gregory's absolution and lifting of the excommunication.

For Robert, the death of his contemporary, a whilom brigand colleague, perpetually a rival but not an enemy, meant a sudden turn of fortune as well. Their alliance had helped him gain Salerno and had promised much more. Now it was at an end, before it could bear its full fruit. Angered and exposed by Jordan's sudden willingness to placate the pope, Robert was obliged to drop his own siege of Benevento.

Gregory may have been relieved by the removal of the grave threat to Benevento and the remaining papal vassals in the Abruzzi, but he had no intention of remaining passive. He would seek to take further advantage of his sudden good fortune. He visited Capua to bring the force of his personality to bear on the young Prince. There, lifting Jordan's excommunication but dangling his investiture as a prize still to be earned, Gregory succeeded in totally reversing the recent alliance between the Norman leaders. He convinced Jordan to lead an effort to undercut his uncle through still another insurrection of the perpetually disgruntled Apulian barons.

Once again, it was not hard to stir the barons to revolt. The same malcontents as before took the lead: Abelard, Geoffrey of Conversano, Robert of Montescaglioso, Pierre (now of Taranto), Ami of Giovanezzo. Robert had, to some degree, brought the outbreak upon himself by ruling in a manner that his barons saw as high-handed. He had tried to dispossess the heirs of Geoffrey of Taranto, brother to Pierre and Ami, deepening his quarrel with that important landholding family. He had, in some barons' eyes, taken on entirely too much the air of an oriental despot, making unilateral demands rather than living by the feudal system of mutual obligations. Then he had alienated all his barons, in Calabria as well as Apulia, over a family marriage. After the conquest of Salerno, he and Sichelgaita had sought to capitalize on his rising status in the world, negotiating advantageous alliances for the family through marrying their daughters into the great houses of Europe. When the first such marriage had taken place in the spring of 1078 in Apulia, to a son of the Duke of Este, Robert had browbeaten his barons into making lavish bridal gifts to enhance the pageantry and display — a yardstick by which a ruler was measured — of the event. Such gifts were not a common feudal obligation, but Robert had insisted. Feeling consequently ran high among the barons that they had been imposed upon to feed the self-importance and grandeur of their already demanding duke. With that incident adding more fuel to the kindling that was always in place, Jordan was able to inflame the situation with relative ease.

The revolt this time had little outside support, and even Jordan himself took little active role other than igniting the kindling, and then passing money (presumably much of it the pope's) to the rebels. Nevertheless, by late autumn the rebellion had spread to Calabria as well as Apulia. Trani, Bisceglie, Corato, Andria and others towns declared for the rebels or withheld support from Robert, and even Bari joined the rebellion when Argyrizzos, the man who had led the pro–Guiscard faction in that town six years earlier, went over to the rebels and married his daughter to Abelard. But the wave soon crested, and Robert was deliberate but unrelenting in his counterattack, concentrating first on reducing rebel strongholds in Calabria, where he had more loyal barons. By summer, he had effectively regained that province while cutting back on the rebellion's support in Apulia. Jordan, in the meantime, had fallen afoul of Pope Gregory over other maters and had lost enthusiasm for a rebellion that offered him no gain. He accordingly saw that it was time to cut his losses and, following the somewhat flexible political morality of the time, sought to mend fences with the uncle whom he had just betrayed.

Aided as usual by the omnipresent mediator Desiderius, Jordan and Robert eventually reached a truce that left the remaining rebels isolated. One castle after another fell to Robert's forces, and then the towns. He was in a hurry; he even let his formidable Sichelgaita lead a successful siege of Trani at the same time that he invested Taranto. Bari returned to the duke's camp in early 1080 when Argyrizzos changed coats once again, and the rebellion was over. This time, Robert would not be so lenient, and his terms for surrender were harsher. Many of the barons lost much of their property, while Abelard and Herman were obliged to flee to exile in Constantinople, Argyrizzos to Illyria. In reapportioning the land confiscated from the rebels, Guiscard rewarded only his most loyal vassals, with the result that his hold over Apulia was greatly strengthened. With control and the revenue of the major Apulian cities — Bari, Trani, Taranto, Otranto, and Brindisi — added to his holdings in Calabria and Sicily, he had become the wealthiest, as well as the most powerful, ruler in the region.

The pope, nevertheless, had won a partial victory, since the revolt that he had fostered had kept Guiscard tied up for almost two years even though it had done him no major harm. The pope, on the other hand, had not been able to profit from the time gained. In fact, he was, if anything, worse off, for in the north, his prospects were frightening. King Henry had, by the middle of 1080, prevailed in the civil war in Germany. He had emerged determined to settle accounts with Gregory, and gain the imperial coronation that had so long been denied him. In a flurry of mutual excommunications, the emperor-designate and the pope fought for the support of other powers, with Henry having gained somewhat of an edge when he induced the powerful archbishop of Ravenna into insubordination. Not only had the archbishop withdrawn his numerous Italian dioceses from the authority of the papacy, he had also allowed himself to be nominated as a new, imperial pope, designated to crown Henry as emperor in Rome as soon as Henry could raise an army that would force his way into the holy city. It appeared that the imperial invasion of Italy, threatened for the past four years, was finally to become a reality.

Pope Gregory had no allies in Italy capable of stopping an invasion if it materialized; he could only hope to hold Rome and somehow deny Henry a victory. Jordan of Capua had proven himself unreliable as an ally. To Gregory's chagrin, the only ruler who was in a position to change the balance in his favor was the very man whom he had been trying to cut back for over twenty-five years, Robert Guiscard, Duke of Apulia. Gregory realized that he would finally need to accept the reality that his colleague Pope Nicholas had acknowledged at Melfi: that Norman energy and power would be more useful if harnessed somewhat to papal policy than if constantly in conflict with it. It would cost, he knew it; the Normans were above all demanding. But he needed them, and had almost no other option. He called on Desiderius to negotiate a lifting of the excommunication and a mutually agreeable arrangement with Robert.

At Ceprano, in June 1080, Robert Guiscard pledged his obedience and fealty to the pope. The statuesque and fearsome duke and the small but morally powerful pope had sparred and fought for years but had finally realized that their separate interests might best be served by making common cause. The terms for the momentous event had been negotiated by Desiderius and, on the face of it, represented a victory for neither lord. Robert swore support and loyalty to the pope, in return for which:

> I Gregory invest you, Duke Robert, in the lands which were conceded to you by my saintly predecessors Nicholas and Alexander. As for the lands that you hold improperly, such as Salerno, Amalfi, and part of the March of Fermo, for now I shall be patient, confiding in almighty God and your goodness that you will in future comport yourself in a manner appropriate to the honor of God and St Peter...[4]

In short, the duke was confirmed in some but not all of his territories. Apulia, Calabria and Sicily, promised to him by Nicholas, were his without dispute. But his more recent conquests—Amalfi, Salerno, and the March of Fermo in the Abruzzi—were left in limbo: Robert was not invested with those lands, but neither did the pope contest his possession of them. The matter would be decided by time, and, in that dimension, Guiscard had the clear advantage of possession.

The winner at Ceprano was clearly the duke. He had gained papal recognition, however grudging, of his expanded duchy, and the road ahead represented opportunity. The pope, had he been able to look into the future, would have seen that the agreement had created an alliance that would give historical support to the papacy. But for the moment, Gregory could only hope that the new accord would give him some leverage against King Henry, provided he could get the necessary help from his powerful but undependable new vassal.

Notes

1. Amatus of Monte Cassino, VII, C. 27, p. 321, as cited in Wolf, p. 111.

2. Marriage alliances provided useful extra channels of communication when the two involved families were at odds, a situation common in view of the competition and conflict between clans that dominated aristocratic culture at the time. But, generally speaking, wives were expected to support the interests of their marriage, rather than natal, families. Robert had good experience of this fact: his sister Fressenda was loyal to her husband, Richard of Aversa, throughout the long competition between the two Counts, while another sister had raised two sons, Robert and Geoffrey, who were regularly to be found among the ranks of the rebel Apulian barons.

3. Jordan was doubly related to Robert, both nephew and brother-in-law. His mother was Robert's sister Fressenda, and he had married a sister of Sichelgaita.

4. *Gregorio VII Registrum* no. 16, as cited in Delogu, p. 109.

Carrying War to the Enemy

O ver a quarter century three popes, reluctantly, had come to the same conclusion: that it would be better to recognize, and try to guide, the growing Norman power in the south of Italy than to see it directed against their interests. Leo in 1053, Nicholas in 1059, and now Gregory in 1080, had each been obliged by the force of circumstances to confirm the Normans as vassals in the territories they had conquered. Each time, the extent of those territories had increased, as had the need of the papacy for Norman military help.

Pope Gregory, at Ceprano, had agreed to an alliance with the Normans, whom he had so long distrusted, only because he needed them, desperately, to counterbalance the military force that King Henry, finally victorious over the Saxons, was threatening to bring against the papacy. The pope's only other major supporter in Italy, Duchess Matilda of Tuscany, could not spare enough troops to do more than guarantee the pontiff's safety in still friendly Rome. But Henry was threatening to invade with a considerable force, aiming finally to obtain his coronation and an end to the papacy's interference, as he saw it, in the affairs of the German church. Only the Normans— Jordan of Capua but particularly Robert Guiscard — could defend the pope and the reform movement (however tenuous Norman support for the reforms may in fact have been). It is scarcely surprising, therefore, that rumors began to circulate that summer that Gregory was planning to reward Guiscard by crowning him, rather than Henry, as emperor if he drove off the German threat.

Whatever the truth of those rumors may have been, Guiscard was not interested in such a farfetched scheme. He saw little advantage in getting involved in the complications of north European politics, much less as the pope's creature. Ever ambitious and alert to opportunity, he wanted to keep his freedom of action. He was helped toward that objective by Henry himself, who suddenly handed him an excellent card to play. The king had renewed his courtship of Robert, urging him to desert the pope's cause in return for investiture as imperial vassal in the March of Fermo, in the Abruzzi, plus offering a marriage alliance with the royal house — one of the available Hauteville daughters to King Henry's son Conrad. However Guiscard, once again preferring to be a vassal of the militarily weak pope rather than giving the powerful emperor-designate cause to meddle in his activities, declined the new offer. He was, at the same time, careful to inform Pope Gregory of Henry's offer (as well, of course, as his refusal), thereby gaining not only credit for loyalty, but also additional leverage over the increasingly anxious pontiff.

Even more importantly, Guiscard had more immediate plans, closer to hand. Although the pope had refused to confirm him as lord of Amalfi, Salerno, or in the March of Fermo, the ambiguous formula reached at Ceprano meant in reality that his possession of those lands had been recognized, as no one's vassal. Robert intended to push forward, to reinforce and expand his domain by controlling more of the Abruzzi, and he considered that he needed neither the pope's acquiescence nor the emperor's license to continue his piecemeal advance. But even that would wait. For the present, he had still grander aspirations, well beyond Italy, and had even gotten Pope Gregory to bless them at Ceprano. Guiscard was planning to attack Byzantium itself.

Strategy as well as his always restless ambition had propelled Guiscard toward this new venture. His ambition was fueled by a mixture of admiration, envy and greed. Over the years, he and his fellow Normans had been powerfully affected by the rich culture, the administrative capabilities, the luxury, and the wealth of the empire from which they had stolen their lands. Almost twenty years of rule in heavily Hellenized Calabria had subtly affected Robert, to the degree that his initial interest in and appetite for Byzantium's riches had grown into emulation of Byzantine ways. Such emulation, indeed, was politically useful, since adopting elements of eastern panoply and ritual was helping the Normans appear as the inheritors of Byzantium; it increased their legitimacy among their new subjects. Robert had even gone so far as to copy imperial motives into his own seals and otherwise present himself as the successor to the emperor; he used the title "*dux imperator*" and on major occasions wore copies of the imperial robes of state.

Almost as if to justify this presumption of his, Robert had, since 1071, received a series of tentative approaches from successive emperors in Constantinople. Seeking because of their military weakness to bring their powerful neighbor into their diplomatic circle of influence, the emperors had suggested marriage alliances between the upstart Hautevilles and the imperial family. This was indeed heady stuff for a son of Tancred, the simple knight from Hauteville. By the terms of the marriage agreement that had finally been concluded with Basileus Michael in 1074, Robert had been promised the title of "*nobelissimus,*" only a step below that of Caesar, and would be entitled to wear the imperial purple. Even more enticingly, he could envisage that a descendant of his might some day sit on the throne in Constantinople.

However seductive the ideas of marriage ties with the rulers of Byzantium might be, they promised future benefit at best. For the present, the two states were still enemies. Byzantine agents and diplomacy were constantly at work to challenge Norman occupation of the lost Italian provinces. From Illyria, across the narrow Adriatic Sea, Byzantine governors were only too happy to offer asylum to Robert's opponents, such as his troublesome nephews Abelard and Herman, or to finance and encourage any potentially seditious barons in Apulia.

Duke Robert's proposed strategy was typically bold. The current weakness of Byzantium made it opportune to secure his hold in Italy by carrying the war into the empire and destabilizing his old enemies. Robert had been fighting the Byzantines since his arrival in Italy, and had defeated their armies often enough to be scornful of their military qualities. He had attacked the empire once before and been unsuccessful, but that had been merely a tactic to put them on the defensive. This time, he saw a chance to defeat his enemies, gain plunder, perhaps new lands, maybe even a throne. His newly developed naval power enabled him to take a major force across the sea, and to fight his old enemies in their own lands. The prospects were good, because the empire was in crisis; it had lost almost all of Anatolia to the Seljuks, and a new Basileus was faced with a chain of insurrections in his own military. Robert, sensing a moment of opportunity, began preparations for an invasion.

Guiscard also had a politically correct pretext to attack. Basileus Michael had recently been deposed, and the wedding alliance he had negotiated with the Hautevilles had been dishonored. The new emperor had packed off Robert's daughter Helen to a convent, where she was being held as a pawn for a future move on the diplomatic chessboard. Robert must have been disappointed at the failure of the proposed marriage alliance; it had promised much. But he knew, all the same, that Constantinople's politics were an uncertain thing: that Helen might never have sat on the throne, or given birth to a claimant to the throne even in the best of circumstances. Her status as virtual hostage, in fact, could even replace her intended marriage as a means to his ends. So he demanded that her rights, and his, under the old agreement be honored — even though the intended groom, Constantine, was as out of favor as his deposed father. When these demands were ignored or rejected, as the wily Guiscard had no doubt expected they would be, he demanded the release of his daughter, and began his preparations to invade if his demands were not met.

Guiscard embellished his pretext for intervention, in addition, by a somewhat transparent but useful fiction: he claimed that the deposed Michael had somehow escaped to Italy from his exile to a monastery. The purported Michael, by most accounts a wandering monk who had been drafted for the occasion, became a permanent attachment to Guiscard's court, where he was treated with the deference due to a former emperor and advanced as the living justification for the coming expedition. Guiscard had even gotten poor Pope Gregory, at Ceprano, to support the claims of the counterfeit Basileus.

Preparations for the invasion of Illyria had, by the early spring of 1081, reached a climax. Robert had been able to raise a very substantial force because, for the first time in years, he had neither internal nor external threats to arm against. Roger, at the same time, was slowly but successfully subduing the remaining Muslim opposition in Sicily, and neither needed nor wanted Robert's help on the island. Jordan of Capua, for the moment joined with Robert as an ally of the pope, was potentially trouble, but nowhere near the man his father had been; Robert doubtless felt he could readily take care of the young man if the need arose. The possibility that King Henry would invade, and his own duty to defend the pope in that event, was an unfortunate cloud on the duke's horizon, but it could be treated as a distant threat. For the moment, Guiscard had the pope's concurrence for the expedition, indeed his assistance, in the form of a letter of support addressed to the bishops of southern Italy.

He raised an exceptionally large force, consonant with his new power and wealth. It included contingents from his vassals but also many mercenaries: Muslims from Sicily, Greeks, Lombards, and adventurers from all over. In truth, the hired hands would be needed, because Robert's vassals had shown themselves to be grudging supporters of an expedition that would, most likely, benefit Guiscard more than themselves. Nor did the taxes that the duke raised to pay for the expedition, or the hostages he took to assure the good behavior of his troublesome barons, increase the popularity of his effort. The mustering of the invasion force had consequently been almost a two-year affair. Ships had been mustered from his coastal cities, and still more hired from the Adriatic state of Ragusa; the naval contingent numbered a full 150 boats. Figures for the army, as usual, vary, but it was a force of over 1,000 knights, Normans and others who formed the nucleus, supported by as many as 20,000 soldiers and auxiliaries, siege engines, horses and supplies.

Duke Robert, still strong and magnificent at 64, was optimistic and an inspiration as usual to the gathering troops. His first son, the even more physically imposing Bohemund, was to be the second in command, and to lead the advance guard of the army into Illyria. Sichelgaita, often clad in armor like her husband, was with the army and a constant presence by Robert's side, presumably as liaison to their son Roger, who was to be left in charge in Italy.[1] All was ready, or almost so. And then, before the expedition could set sail, the political ground began to shift.

Suddenly, the situation in Constantinople had changed. The latest emperor had been overthrown in his turn, by the talented and energetic general Alexius Comnenus. Alexius had been friendly with the deposed Emperor Michael, and was, it was rumored, inclined to negotiate with Robert over his demands. In fact, an envoy whom Guiscard had sent to Constantinople over the winter had returned to Italy with a recommendation that Robert postpone his invasion in light of the changing situation, and the fact that Helen's intended, Constantine, was likely to be restored to the purple as Alexius' co-ruler. This was not news, however, that Robert wanted to listen to. His rage at hearing the advice of the envoy, an unfortunate Count Radulf, was reportedly monumental. He would not be deterred. He had invested too much in the expedition at that point to pull back, and to delay might allow Alexius to remove his pretext for invasion by returning Helen to her family, or exposing the false Michael.[2] As Princess Anna Comnena wrote succinctly and dismissively a half century later,

> That man Robert, who from a most inconspicuous beginning had grown most conspicuous and amassed great power, now desired to become Roman Emperor, and with this object sought plausible pretexts for ill-will and war against the Romans.[3]

In Italy, the situation was also changing. King Henry had finally begun his invasion, causing the pope to send messages of alarm, requesting that Robert come immediately to his aid. Robert could not ignore the pope's pleas for help, but he had no intention of calling off his expedition so readily. He made a short trip to Tivoli, where he offered the pope a contingent of troops under his son and regent Roger Borsa, and reassured the pontiff that he would not fail him in the event of real need. But he refused to call off his expedition. As it happened, Robert's judgment proved correct; Henry had come south with too few troops to do more than occupy the suburbs of Rome, as he did several months later. When the city proved loyal to the pope, Henry withdrew and no relief army was needed.

The Illyrian expedition indeed had already begun. The advance guard under Bohemund had left in April, rapidly capturing the port of Valona across the sea from Otranto, a situation that would provide an excellent bridgehead for the main army. The main force set sail in late May, joining with Bohemund's contingent, and the combined force soon captured the island of Corfu, to the south of Valona. With the sea thus secured against a relief fleet coming from Constantinople, the invasion force was able to consolidate — the entire army did not cross until mid June because of storms — and then proceed northward up the coast to Guiscard's initial goal, the capital city of Durazzo.[4] It would take a serious siege to capture the town, which enjoyed a strong position on a high peninsula guarded by marshes on the land side. But Robert's intelligence services were, as usual, aware of the enemy's weaknesses, which in this case turned out to be the will of the city's military commander, one George Monomachus. An appointee of the deposed emperor, Monomachus did not know how he stood with the new order in Constantinople, and had begun to negotiate with Robert's envoys in an effort to save his own neck. It looked for a moment as if the city might fall to the Norman army without a fight.

Any optimism on this score was soon shown to be misplaced. The new Basileus, the Normans rapidly found out, was an adversary of a quality they had not seen for over a generation. Small, dark and unprepossessing, Alexius was the nephew of a previous emperor, one of the country's best generals from a family of distinguished military leaders, and a man of shrewd and tenacious purpose. He, too, could act fast. In the present danger, he had taken two immediate steps to defend Durazzo. The first was to send a talented soldier, George Paleologus, to replace the wavering commander, Monomachus, and to harden the city's defenses. The second was to appeal to the Venetians, the preeminent Adriatic naval power, for help in countering the Norman naval advantage. The Venetians knew they held a strong hand in those negotiations and drove a hard bargain, gaining unprecedented trade concessions in Constantinople in return for sending their battle-trained fleet to sea.

The Venetian navy appeared off Durazzo just in time, only days after the Norman army had arrived to invest the town. A fiercely fought naval engagement several days later demonstrated how great was the Venetian tactical superiority at sea. The Norman fleet was badly mauled, and from then on was obliged to limit its operations. The encirclement of Durazzo was incomplete. With the Venetian navy reinforcing the city's defenses as well as hindering the Normans' resupply efforts, and Paleologus energizing the Greek army, whatever advantage the Normans had had by their well-timed arrival had been lost. The city's morale was maintained by the promise of a relief army, and the siege settled into a sort of stalemate, punctuated by fierce but indecisive engagements. The Normans could neither cut off the city nor breach the walls, since their siege engines, transported at such great effort from Italy, repeatedly proved ineffective against Paleologus' determination and ingenuity in devising counter mechanisms.

The stalemate was broken in mid October, when Emperor Alexius arrived at the head of the long-promised relief army. Paleologus was able to join him at his camp outside the city, where a hasty war council was held. In the council, Paleologus argued for reinforcing the city and driving the Normans off through attrition. Disease in their camp, their supply problems, and the coming winter, he argued, would break the Norman siege in time, and more surely than a battle. He may have been right. Morale in the Norman camp was not high, and Robert had had little success to show his army, camped as it was on a hostile and unhealthy shore and trying to maintain a costly siege against a tenacious and now heavily reinforced enemy. But Alexius, too, had his problems; he could not count on the loyalty of his hastily recruited army over a long siege, and there was clamor in the capital for an immediate and decisive victory from the new emperor. Like Robert Guiscard, he was a man used to victory in battle, confident in his abilities, and capable of inspiring his troops to great effort. He chose to fight.

Robert drew up his army north of the city, its right wing with its motley assortment of mercenary detachments anchored against the sea where it could not be outflanked, and Bohemund on his left, inland of his own central detachment. In an effort to inspire a determined stand, moreover, he had burned the army's boats and deployed it with a river to its back. The Byzantine army that formed ranks on the plain to attack the Normans encompassed a disparate collection of allied and mercenary troops cobbled together from a military still reeling from the disaster at Manzikert and repeated military insurrections. But it also contained elements of the empire's elite units, the Bucellarion Guard and the imperial bodyguard of Varangians. The Varangians, in particular, were highly motivated. Now heavily manned by Anglo-Saxons driven from their native England by the Norman invaders there, they sought revenge in the coming fight for their fifteen years of exile.

As it was, in their eagerness to engage, the Varangians determined the course of the battle. Their initial attack, on the Norman right, was devastating. Against the onslaught of the Anglo-Saxons wielding their huge two-handed axes, the Norman right wing, foot, and for once even the cavalry, collapsed.

A rout was narrowly avoided, partly because the river blocked the retreat of the Norman auxiliaries, but due also to the valiant efforts of heroic Sichelgaita. Fully armed and brandishing a spear, if Anna Comnena is to be believed, the warrior Duchess left her position by her husband's side and rode toward the action, urging the fleeing soldiers to stand firm and shaming them, by word and example, to rally. Her efforts were rewarded, as the line stiffened once again and the Varangians, their charge finally exhausted, now found themselves in an exposed position well in advance of the Byzantine center. Meanwhile Bohemund, on the left, had seen relatively light action because an effort by the Bucellarion Guard to outflank him had been blocked by the river. He was able to send cavalry to the Norman right wing, where they fell on the now exposed Varangians and cut them down wholesale.

The battle was turned. A sortie from the city by Paleologus was beaten off, and now some of Alexius' allies, notably the Serbians and Turks, began to desert the field. As the imperial army slowly, and then rapidly, dissolved, only the Varangians continued to hold their ground. The brave remnant of the proud but reckless detachment finally retreated to a small chapel, where they were burned to death by the now victorious Norman army. Alexius and George Paleologus, who had been cut off from his command when his sortie failed, were forced to flee among the remnants of the army, the emperor, according to his daughter Anna, barely escaping capture.

For the Byzantines, the defeat was humiliating, but not fatal. The Norman army, admittedly, was able to follow up its victory with relative ease. Marching along the great Roman Via Egnatia, the invaders had occupied most of Illyria by spring, even securing the surrender of the important fortress town of Kastoria in Macedonia. But Durazzo had succeeded in holding out until late February, falling in the end through the treachery of its foreign inhabitants rather than by assault. The Venetians continued to control the sea, harassing Norman communications and resupply efforts. After the fall of Kastoria, moreover, the Norman army had begun to lose its momentum and suffer from supply problems, disease, and attrition from the long field campaign.

The tenacious Alexius was determined to hold on and to confound his Norman opponent. Guiscard, for the first time, had met his match.

Notes

1. Roger, not to be confused with Robert's brother, was generally known as Roger Borsa, because of a habit he allegedly had of fiddling continually with his money-purse, or *borsa*.

2. Poor Helen, so long a hostage to fate and the politics of her family, was finally released by Emperor Alexius, after the death of her father and mother. She never married, and ended her days as a guest at Roger's court in Sicily.

3. Anna Comnena, Book I, p. 31. Princess Anna, the daughter of Emperor Alexius, was later married to the same prince Constantine who had been intended for Helen Hauteville. Her memoirs, which are essentially an encomium to her father, display both admiration and disdain for the Hautevilles, Robert and Bohemund, who would bedevil her father's illustrious career.

4. Durres, in modern Albania.

The Pope's Savior

Alexius, his army defeated by the invading Normans, still could count on the great wealth and the space of the Byzantine empire for his defense. He had to resort to exceptional measures—levying heavy taxes and even unprecedented confiscations of Church property—to pay the costs of raising a new army and conducting an active diplomacy, but in the end they paid off. Before long, he had managed to consolidate his authority and stabilize the situation in Constantinople. Against Guiscard, diplomacy and subversion proved to be his most effective weapons, creating much trouble for the duke in his Italian rear area. From the moment of the Norman landing, indeed, Alexius had resorted to those most faithful of Byzantium's weapons—money and intrigue—to undercut the Norman expeditionary force and to line up allies. It was expensive. He had sent King Henry the lavish gift of 144,000 gold pieces, in addition to precious relics and costly silks, to firm up their anti–Norman collaboration. In addition, he promised another 200,000 gold pieces should the king invade southern Italy and threaten the Hautevilles on their home ground. Alexius' envoys also tried to induce the unstable young Jordan of Capua to break with the pope and come over to the side of the two emperors. In Rome, Byzantine agents worked in conjunction with Henry's men, carefully disbursing gold to weaken support for the pope in his own city. Alexius' agents had also been busy among the fractious Norman barons in Apulia, urging them with promises and money to rise once again in revolt against Guiscard.

Whether as a result of Byzantine money and activism or not, the situation in Italy had become threatening for Guiscard and Pope Gregory by the spring of 1082. In Apulia, the barons—Geoffrey of Conversano, Abelard, and Herman once again at their head—had risen in revolt and soon

Cannae, Oria, Bari, Troia, Ascoli and even Melfi had declared for them. The regent, Roger Borsa, showed little ability to control the situation. To the north, Henry had rejoined the imperial army in Italy, prompting Jordan finally to abandon his alliance with the pope and bring Capua over to what was beginning to look like the winning side. Gregory, increasingly anxious, called for Guiscard to return to Italy to save the papacy. This time, the duke had good reason to share the pontiff's fear, although for a different reason — his main interest was to stop Henry from bringing his army into the south, where he could join forces with Jordan and the rebel barons, and create havoc in Apulia. To forestall such a possibility, perform his duty to the pope, and deal with the rebels in Apulia, Robert realized that he had to leave the expeditionary army in Bohemund's hands and return to Italy.

Guiscard landed at Otranto in April and, after picking up some of the regiments he had left behind with Roger, marched quickly to Rome. There, he found that the citizens had once again maintained their loyalty to the pope, and had successfully driven off the relatively weak imperial force. Henry was for the moment not a threat; in fact, he had taken his army north, where he was busy ravaging the lands of Matilda of Tuscany.

With the situation in Rome apparently in hand for the moment, Robert moved to straighten out affairs yet again with his rebellious barons. Returning quickly to Apulia, he began the process of prying the rebels, once more, out of their various strongholds. There are few details of his campaign, but it was not easy. Not until the summer of the following year was the final rebel town, Cannae, taken from Count Herman and his men. Even then, it had taken some help from the duke's brother Roger, who led several detachments from Sicily to help put down the revolt. After the revolt had been squelched, the two brothers decided to punish Jordan for his change of coat by raiding into Capuan territory. But soon Roger was called back to Sicily in turn to face a crisis of his own there, and the campaign in Capua had to be abandoned. Robert paused, consolidated his forces in Apulia, and studied his next move carefully. Events, both in Rome and Illyria, were moving in unfavorable directions.

In Rome, Henry's troops had finally managed to force their way into the city in early June. With imperial detachments pouring into the city and fighting the papal troops around Saint Peter's, Pope Gregory had fled to a sanctuary in the well-fortified and provisioned Castel Sant' Angelo. Since his partisans still controlled the left bank of the Tiber, an uneasy military stalemate soon ensued in the city. The tension of the situation had eased somewhat by winter, when Henry withdrew the major part of his army because of disease in the city. The Romans tried to mediate between the two sides but Gregory, self-righteous and obstinate as ever, refused to bend. No, he insisted, he would not crown Henry as emperor, not until he repeated the oaths he had been obliged to make five years earlier at Canosa. Gregory would, he let it be known, remain firmly ensconced in his fortress, awaiting vindication from Heaven and military salvation from his ally Robert Guiscard.

Neither the Almighty nor Guiscard, however, seemed to be in a hurry. The duke, for his part, needed time to raise a force large enough to master the situation in Rome (the major part of his army was still in Illyria), and perhaps was not overly eager to risk a pitched battle with Henry in any event. Pope Gregory, he reckoned, was in no immediate physical danger, and could be left waiting.

The news from Illyria was also troubling. Bohemund, who resembled his father so much in terms of audacity, bravery, temper, and physical appearance, had not proven himself to be his father's match in generalship. He had, to be sure, won military engagements at Ioannina and Arta since he had assumed the command, and his forces controlled most of Thessaly and Macedonia in addition to Illyria. But he led an increasingly unhappy army, faced with supply, morale, and pay problems, and a six-month, unsuccessful siege of Larissa had not improved matters. Then, in the spring of 1083, Bohemund had suffered a stinging defeat at the hands of Alexius, who had effectively used deception to lure the Normans into attacking a decoy force. In the ensuing battle, the Norman supply train, with all the captured booty, had been seized by the Byzantines. The blow was fatal to what remained of the expedition's morale, and by the time the army had fallen back on Kastoria later that summer, it was in the process of disintegration. If the situation in Illyria was to be saved, it appeared, Robert would need to lead a relief expedition, and earlier rather than later.

Robert, mustering his army in Apulia, hesitated. Ambition led him toward Illyria, duty toward Rome. For months, throughout the fall and winter, he built up his forces but watched the situation with an unusual passivity, waiting to see how he should move when the campaigning season began in spring. He sent the pope 30,000 gold pieces to help him hold out, but no troops.

In the end, the decision on what action to take was made for Robert by the Romans. Tired of the stalemate in their city, tired perhaps of papal obstinacy in response to all their efforts at mediation, and probably softened up by imperial money, most of the notables who had remained loyal to Gregory for the previous three years suddenly decided to desert him. They informed King Henry that they would surrender the city to him.

The king finally had his triumph. His troops controlled the city; and

Pope Gregory was forced to remain holed up impotently in the Castel Sant' Angelo. In the space of a few weeks, the antipope, Clement, was installed in the Lateran, a group of tame bishops duly deposed Gregory and consecrated Clement, and on Easter day in late March 1084, Henry was finally crowned emperor — even if not by Pope Gregory.

Robert, on hearing of the pope's setback in Rome, finally moved into action. He sensed that Henry's victory, if allowed to stand unchallenged, would ruin not only Gregory but also threaten the whole Hauteville enterprise: his enemies would flock to the imperial banner and pick the duchy to pieces. He may have been too late to stop the imperial coronation, but it was still not too late to render it pointless. Guiscard assembled his army for the march to Rome. By May, they were on the road: more than 1000 armed knights, tens of thousands in the overall force. (The chroniclers speak of an army over 35,000 strong, probably a modest rather than a great exaggeration.) As Robert had intended, his force was so superior to that of the newly crowned emperor that Henry prudently departed the city of his recent triumph in haste, slipping out of town only three days before the Norman army reached the outskirts.

The Romans, who had given over their city to Henry only to see him desert them a few months later, were justifiably terrified of the new army camped outside their gates. The Normans had a well-deserved reputation for indiscriminate pillaging, and moreover were accompanied by sinister contingents of heathen Muslims from Sicily, Greeks, and others from whom the Romans could expect little compassion. The citizens had reason, too, to fear the retribution that a victorious Gregory and his remaining adherents in the city might have in mind for them in light of the support they had given to the now departed emperor. In a welter of indecision, they kept the city's gates closed for three days, but did not take the precaution of manning them thoroughly, so that when Robert finally led a night attack against the defenses on the night of May 27, the outer defenses fell after only a short fight. Once the Norman army had entered the city, however, resistance to it stiffened, and in the fight to gain the Castel Sant' Angelo the whole quarter of the city across the river was consumed by fire.

Robert Guiscard and his troops soon liberated Pope Gregory from his fortress, and bore him in triumph to the Lateran. There, they renewed their homage to him as their spiritual lord — carefully avoiding the unresolved questions of temporal allegiance. The alliance between the papacy and the Normans was still, after all, a matter of necessity for one and advantage for the other, rather than a mutual commitment. But it would grow and mature, and the rescue of Gregory marked the birth of a reality that would shape the destiny of southern Italy for centuries to come.

For Robert, the rescue of the pope was also his own triumph, and the vindication of his career. Just over thirty years earlier, he had assisted in the defeat of a pope at Civitate. Since then, he had been seen — with reason — as a predator on papal patrimony and the nemesis of several pontiffs. But with the expedition to Rome, all that had changed; he had emerged as the savior of the reform papacy and the pope's strong right arm. At a great thanksgiving mass held to mark the occasion, Gregory and Robert may have contemplated the changes that had taken place in the relationship between Church and Normans since that day at Civitate when they had fought on opposite sides. One suspects that Robert, always the man of realism as opposed to Gregory's man of principle, would have been the more likely of the two to see the ironies of the situation.

Unfortunately, the triumph was marred by disaster. Robert had not kept tight control over his army in the city, and the soldiers soon began their customary looting. To Robert, Rome was a city which had resisted capture and was therefore subject to the hard rules of warfare at the time; he had no reason to show the leniency he had shown at Bari and Palermo to those whom he expected to be his own future subjects. Before long, the situation got wholly out of hand. The great wealth of the city — even after four years of warfare — seemed to spur the soldiers, particularly the Muslim contingents, into a frenzy of pillage, murder, rape, and other atrocities. On the third day of terror, the citizens finally rose up against the occupiers. Soon the streets became scenes for guerilla warfare which, combined with the ongoing sack of houses and churches, resulted in total chaos. Large quarters of the city were burned to the ground. Nothing was spared: ancient monuments, churches, homes, palaces were either looted or burned or both. From the Coliseum to the Lateran, scarcely a building stood, and other parts of the city were almost as badly damaged. Robert, to his discredit in modern eyes, did nothing to hold the situation in check. Indeed, once it had become an insurrection there was little reason for him to do so (he was almost captured by irate citizens at one point, saved only by the quick action of his son Roger). Even Gregory, it must be admitted, never showed remorse about the tragic consequences of his liberation by the Norman army. Whether the Romans had deserved it or not, the sack and burning of Rome was the worst disaster to befall that unhappy city for centuries. For the Normans, it was a black mark on the more positive reputation that Robert had been trying to build.

The sack of Rome had more immediate consequences for Pope Gregory. Even though he had been freed from his fortress and the pressures of Henry's army, he was no longer free to live safely in the Lateran, or to perform services at Saint Peter's. Such was the hatred and resentment among the Romans that Gregory could remain in the city only under the constant protection of Robert's army. Yet the duke, his task in Rome completed and his ambitions in Illyria still beckoning, had no interest either in staying in Rome or in leaving a large body of troops behind. The pope, reluctantly, realized that he would have to accompany the departing Norman army. There, he would be an honored appendage, but an appendage for all that, in the train of the man he had more than once tried to destroy.

Toward the end of July, the pontiff and his rescuer left Rome, both for the last time. Perhaps to provide some comfort to a pope driven so ingloriously from his seat of office, the party first spent some time at the great abbey of Monte Cassino, and following that in the papal city of Benevento, before proceeding to Robert's new capital. In Salerno, Gregory was installed in quarters befitting his position, and attempted to conduct the business of the Holy See. If he ever dwelled on his humiliation, or considered the possible parallels between his situation and that of the unlucky Pope Leo after Civitate, he did not let it show; in his outward demeanor he remained sure of his cause, proud of his victory over Henry, determined in his course of reform. It little mattered to Gregory that the false pope, Clement, now sat in the Lateran, and had become undisputed Bishop of Rome. Gregory continued to be convinced that his course was right, and that history would vindicate him. And so, indeed, it largely has.

That winter, pope and duke together participated in magnificent ceremonies reconsecrating the cathedral of Saint Matthew at Salerno. Robert was undoubtedly proud at the additional honor the pope's presence gave to the event. Salerno was the jewel of his possessions, and he aspired to rule in his new capital as legitimate heir of the Lombard ruling house. To boost his credibility among the populace, he had totally rebuilt the cathedral since his takeover of the city some eight years earlier, endowing it with inscriptions celebrating his victory over Basileus Michael. Pope Gregory's presence added still more luster to the occasion.

The ceremony, however, was to be the last great event shared by these two leaders. In May 1085, Gregory died. The pope was buried not in Rome, where even his corpse was no longer welcome, but in the Salerno cathedral. His tomb is still there, honored in a monument of the "damned Normans," a monument, at that, built to glorify the very man whom Gregory had vilified, and against whom he had so long struggled.

Duke Robert was not present at the great pope's burial. He had already embarked on a new expedition to Illyria.

Terror of the World

T he banner of the Hautevilles had never flown higher. Robert Guiscard, the knight adventurer who once had squabbled with his younger brother Roger for control of a few wretched castles and towns in Calabria, now was the most powerful ruler in southern Italy. The excommunicate had transmuted into the savior and protector of the reform papacy, the nemesis of the two emperors. Hauteville armies, principally Robert's and Roger's, dominated the region, even to carrying the struggle into the territory of the enemy and occupying Byzantium's homeland in Illyria and Macedonia. Wealth to finance Hauteville ambitions flowed generously into the treasury at Salerno from the bounteous agriculture of Sicily and the oriental trade of Palermo, Amalfi, and Bari, as well as from revenues from the extensive family holdings in Apulia, Calabria, Abruzzi, and the Campania. Against such power and wealth, those principalities in Sicily and southern Italy that had not yet succumbed to the Hautevilles could only seek to buy time, and hope that the upstarts would somehow fail.

Of Tancred's sons, William, Drogo, Humphrey, Geoffrey, Mauger, and the second William, were all dead, their past achievements vital to the family's success. Robert and Roger had gathered in the fruit of their brothers' labor to establish a dynasty that would have lasting significance. It had been, above all, a collective effort. Rivalry and hot-blooded competition between the brothers there indeed had been, but it had been overcome when needed. Robert and Roger had long ago grown beyond their early rivalry and had learned, once the pressure of need was removed, to share power effectively. The future looked bright.

A second generation of young Hauteville knights, ones who had never known the hardscrabble kind of existence that their uncles and fathers had overcome, had already shown some of the family mettle. Robert was a stern patriarch who kept his family together through fear as much as love, and by and large he and Roger succeeded in retaining the loyalty of their kin. One nephew, Abelard, had unfortunately been driven into revolt and exile, while one of Roger's sons had led a short rebellion, and nephews such as Geoffrey of Conversano had participated in the revolts against Robert, but most of the younger generation had remained true to the Hauteville family interest. What the eight brothers had created, Robert and Roger planned to increase again, and pass on to their blood.

Before long, all of Sicily would fall to the Hautevilles, or to be more accurate, to Roger. Robert never returned to the island after the Palermo campaign, a situation that Roger found entirely to his liking. Necessity tied the two brothers together, and Roger was required both by family solidarity and by his oaths of fealty to provide his brother the duke with the service expected from a vassal, but he was always happier when able to act independently. Robert's preoccupations with Italian and Byzantine affairs meant, for Roger, that he was able to govern the Hauteville lands in Sicily and Calabria virtually autonomously, while gradually extending his personal control over the remainder of the island. Always short of men, he was rarely able to expand by outright conquest. But Roger had learned patience since his impetuous early days, and was prepared to win by wearing his opponents out. As usual with the Normans, his strategy was based on fortifying those places already under his control, and using pillaging raids and other forms of harassment to keep his enemies off balance and on the defensive. Major castles were built at Mazara, after its surrender in 1072, and at Adrano and Paterno, to protect the Norman lines of communication around the Mount Etna massif. He also encouraged the strengthening of Christian institutions on the island, both native Greek rite and the Latins whom he encouraged to set up in Sicily, as a bulwark of the new order.

In addition, Roger had begun a farsighted policy aimed at gaining the acceptance of the Muslim communities, which comprised over eighty percent of the island's inhabitants. Like his brother a pragmatic man, Roger was willing to employ crusading rhetoric in order to motivate the campaign to retake Sicily for Christianity, but his real concern was for the reality of power and control. By offering liberal terms to those towns that surrendered, leaving much of the local administration — particularly tax collection — in the hands of the natives, offering Muslims freedom to practice their religion, and enlisting qualified Muslims into his administration as well as the military, he laid the foundations in the short tem for domestic peace, and in the long term, for the remarkably tolerant, multicultural approach that would characterize Norman rule of the island.

Fortunately, the remaining Muslim leaders on the island remained divided, and unable to mount a coordinated offensive against the expanding Normans. The Zirid Emir of Mahdia, Tamim, made one last effort in 1074 to harm the Normans by sending a naval expedition to Calabria, where they ravaged the coast and plundered Nicotera, carrying away into slavery many inhabitants of the town. A second raid the following year, against Mazara in Sicily, was almost successful; the town was captured but the Norman garrison was able to hold out in the citadel until relieved. Following that check, Tamim rethought his involvement in Sicily. What his sons Ayoub and Ali had briefly held had been lost, at great cost, and he no longer had the power to push the Christian invaders off the island. Moreover, war in Tunisia had deprived Mahdia of much of its hinterland and the pirate city-state needed access to the wheat of Sicily to feed its citizens. In 1075, Tamim and Roger negotiated a truce that ended Mahdia's support to Sicily's emirs. The remaining Zirid troops withdrew from the island and, in return, Roger promised to supply Mahdia with its food needs—a highly lucrative trade that would soon link the interests of the two states as firmly as they previously had been opposed.

One Sicilian leader, however, remained adamant in spite of the Zirid sellout. In Syracuse, Emir Ibn al Ward (known to the chroniclers as Bernavert) was determined to oppose the invaders, and for ten years remained a thorn in their side. Roger, too weak to take on the well-fortified city, stuck to his strategy of attrition, bypassing Syracuse until he could reasonably take it on. The first city that fell to the Normans after Palermo was Trapani, in the west, which fell in 1077 by a ruse rather than attack. The Norman commander was Roger's bastard son Jordan who, according to the chronicles, obliged the citizens of the town to surrender when he succeeded in capturing all their livestock. The easy surrender can also be explained in political terms. In light of Roger's policy of leniency toward cities that yielded, the citizens may simply have been unwilling to undergo the hardships of a siege which, with the loss of their foodstuffs, they could not win and for which they would be punished. Two years later, a six-month land and sea siege of Taormina led to its surrender. The fall of that fortress, which had been considered impregnable by the Muslims until faced with the reality of the Norman's capabilities in deploying siege engines and closing off all access, led to further surrenders. Soon, all the island north of a line between Catania and Agrigento was under effective Norman control.

Ibn al Ward found the chance to strike back. Roger's attention had been diverted to Italy, where he had been called in order to help Roger Borsa take up the regency during Guiscard's first expedition to Illyria. In

Roger's absence, the Emir recaptured Catania. Although Jordan rapidly seized the city back, the Emir was enheartened by his temporary success and awaited an opportunity to do further harm. Once again, Roger's absence gave the Muslim an opportunity. In 1084, Roger was needed in Apulia to help Robert put down the latest revolt of his barons, following which he had to deal with a short revolt by his own son. Ibn al Ward sent a fleet that ravaged the Calabrian coast, pillaging Nicotera, Reggio and — the crowning insult to the Normans — abducting nuns from a Calabrian monastery and depositing them in the Emir's harems. Normans tempers were inflamed; the incident threatened to set of a religious war that Roger, anxious to gain the acceptance of his Muslim subjects, could not afford.

Ibn al Ward had miscalculated. His act had elevated him in Roger's eyes from a nuisance to a danger that had to be eliminated. Roger was temporarily distracted by the events surrounding the death of his brother and the beginning of the civil war between Roger Borsa and Bohemund, but he was determined to make a decisive attack against Syracuse. The army and fleet that he began to gather would be the largest force he had raised since the siege of Taormina. It took most of six months, but in the early summer of 1086,[1] he was ready. The fleet sailed from Messina, and several days later joined with the army under Jordan, just north of Syracuse. Following a daring reconnaissance that disclosed the size and disposition of the Muslim fleet, the Normans decided to attack by sea rather than try a siege. The battle was fought in the same waters off Syracuse where the Athenian fleet had been destroyed almost a millennium and a half earlier. A newer weapon, the crossbow, decided the day. The Muslims, seeing that the Norman crossbows could cause crippling casualties at long range, decided to close in for hand-to-hand fighting, and almost prevailed in the ensuing melee. But in the confusion, Ibn al Ward tried to board an enemy ship in haste, fell overboard, and was promptly sucked down by his armor. The death of their valiant and charismatic leader, the last emir capable of inspiring serious resistance to the Normans, took the spirit from the Syracusans. Their fleet broke off the engagement and tried to flee, but most of the ships were captured at sea. The remaining galleys eventually yielded to the Norman army, which had in the meantime appeared before the walls of the city. The city still fought on, but the Normans were practiced in siege warfare and there was no hope of relief. In October the citizens, deserted by their fleeing leaders, accepted Roger's terms.

With the fall of Syracuse and Ibn al Ward, the surrender of the rest of Sicily was a matter only of time. It had been twenty-five years since the first raid on Messina, and another five years would pass before the last Muslim rulers surrendered. But the conquest was virtually over.

Roger, unlike his elder brother, had projects beyond the act of conquest. He was drawn to issues of governance, and had a vision of the state he needed to build. He had recognized that he could not successfully rule by traditional Norman methods over lands populated by a majority of Muslims and Greeks. The different customs, faiths, and laws could not be overridden, nor could they be ignored. New institutions or approaches would be needed to reconcile, bypass, or soften the differences. He began with a principle that had governed Muslim rule: that the different communities would be free to worship in their own faiths, and adhere to their own law for private matters, as long as they accepted the rule of their duke and his law on matters of state. The Latin Church would, of course, have primacy and would be a pillar of the state; its institutions would, as much as possible, be put in the hands of loyal Normans, Franks or Lombards. Latin dioceses and monasteries would be set up throughout Sicily. But Greek settlers from Calabria were also encouraged, to help boost the Christian population, while in Rogers' Calabrian lands the Greek rite dioceses continued to serve their populations. Another principle was that local administrative mechanisms, particularly the Muslim tax regime in Sicily, which was very thorough, would be left in place as much as possible. Doing so would both co-opt the local leaders into the state, and spare the few available Normans for other duties. A third principle governed relations between members of the governing aristocracy, and doubtless was inspired in reaction to the feudal chaos of Apulia: there would be no large fiefs, meaning no powerful and autonomous barons. Feudal rights over land in Sicily, and also to some degree in Calabria, would remain in the hands of Duke Robert, Count Roger, and other loyal members of the family, to the greatest extent possible. Only religious establishments—both Latin and Greek—would be granted extensive independent holdings. These main principles, presumably put in place with Robert's consent, would over time enable the Norman regime in Sicily and Calabria to evolve into a unique model in early medieval Europe.

Roger's successes, in battle and in statecraft, were troubled by one shortfall: in 1085 he was approaching 55 years of age and still had no appropriate heir. His beloved Judith had died in 1080, mother of four daughters but no sons. He had remarried Eremberga of Mortain, with whom the family grew to seven daughters but only two sons one of whom had died while the other, Geoffrey, suffered from leprosy. Roger did have a son of whom he was very fond and proud, Jordan, but he could not, legally, be a potential successor since he was the outcome of a liaison with a concubine.[2] Jordan had, in fact, gone out in revolt against his father in 1082 (the only one of Tancred's grandsons to do so), and at the time had caused his father considerable anxiety. Roger had put down the revolt with a combination of guile and ruthlessness—he at first gave signals of clemency to the conspirators, but then arrested Jordan's colleagues and had their eyes put out and their lands confiscated. Jordan, who had been subjected to a period of anxiety before being pardoned and returned to his father's grace, had since distinguished himself at Syracuse. He had the necessary qualities of leadership, but, like Roger's nephew Serlo, he would die young — carried away by fever at Syracuse, in 1092.

Even as Roger was beginning his preparations for the attack on Syracuse, Robert Guiscard had returned to Illyria to take up the gauntlet again against Byzantium. Once again a major army had been raised and equipped, a fleet — even larger than the first one — procured. But this time the expedition would face an emperor who was sure on his throne, a Venetian fleet that was determined to block any Norman effort to control the choke points of the Adriatic Sea, and a Byzantine army that was ready as well as confident from recent successes.

The Norman gains of the previous expedition had, in fact, almost completely been lost since Guiscard had left for Italy. After its defeat at Larissa, the army had begun to disintegrate. Bohemund had not been able to hold on to Kastoria, and had been obliged to return to Italy in an attempt to raise more men and money. No sooner had he gone, however, than large numbers of knights and soldiers, short of pay, supplies and hope, had deserted in response to the enticing rewards offered by the Byzantines. The army had no choice but to fall back to the coast which they had left some two years earlier, after the battle at Durazzo, with so much hope. Even Durazzo was denied them; a Venetian fleet and Byzantine bribes had succeeded in recapturing the city, and also the island of Corfu. It was at Valona, then, the site of the original beachhead some three years earlier, that Duke Robert and his reinforcements joined up with the beaten and demoralized remnants of his first invasion force.

In retrospect, Robert's enthusiasm for renewing the Illyrian adventure is hard to explain. His pretext for intervention in Byzantine affairs by now was threadbare, the imperial government was united behind a dynamic and successful Alexius Comnenus, and the expeditionary army was a patchwork thing after the disappointment of the first campaign. Yet the man's optimism, his ambition, and his restlessness drove him forward, even if his objectives were less than clear. It may be that he thought an external adventure was the way to occupy and control his restless barons, and indeed the booty from the first expedition had been good. But it was surely the challenge, even in his late sixties, that impelled him. The enterprise, the pride, and the energy that had fueled Robert Hauteville's remarkable career to date would not let him leave unavenged the one major military check that he had suffered. He was, according to his enemies, a "firm upholder of his own designs, and would never willingly give up anything he had once planned."[3]

Whether eager to renew his glory or just pursuing a grudge, Robert had typically chosen adventure over the messy work of ruling. There was much still to be done in Italy in the way of the difficult work of consolidating his rule and building institutions, but that was not the kind of activity which the duke liked. While he had moved his capital to Salerno, which had its own venerable governmental traditions, his base in Apulia and Calabria was still a political and administrative hodge-podge. Governing Apulia, it is fair to say, would never be easy; the major barons had too much land, too much power, and too little fealty to any Hauteville to be tractable. Even the tenants of Robert's own lands had gone occasionally into revolt. Robert, to put it simply, was unprepared to reduce his prerogatives or make political compromises with his vassals as long as he thought he could beat them in battle.

The province continued to prosper in spite of its political instability: trade flourished,[4] the population was growing, and new Norman and Lombard settlements were being established, supported by the strong economic and political bulwark created by an expanding Latin Church. As long as he could successfully demand the military service and taxes that were due, Robert was prepared to put off state-building. He was confident enough about affairs in Italy, in any case, that when he embarked from Otranto, he had left behind no regent. All three of his sons joined him on the Illyrian campaign: Bohemund, whose talents as a military leader would be needed, Guy, because his history of previous contacts with Constantinople made him suspect and best kept under observation, and Roger Borsa, who needed seasoning as a military leader.

Duke Robert's ability to motivate his armies, and his positiveness, were quickly put to the test. Shortly after the army and the fleet were marshaled at Valona, they were attacked by a large fleet of Greek and Venetian ships. The Norman navy responded to the challenge, and fought — but all the same lost — two fierce battles over the space of three days. The Venetian commanders, confident they had won total victory, then made the mistake of sending some of their ships back to Venice to announce the good news, and beginning to overhaul and repair the others. But they had counted out Guiscard before he was ready. Rallying the remnants of his manhandled fleet, he inspired them to attack the Venetians and Greeks. Falling on their unexpecting enemy, the Norman fleet reversed the situation: the allied fleet was destroyed. Thousands of Venetian soldiers and sailors drowned when their ships, unballasted during the overhaul and consequently top-heavy, capsized in the fighting. Once again, Guiscard had proved his talent as a military leader, revived the spirits of his men, and emerged victorious from a desperate situation. The victory allowed the force to move to Corfu, and to recapture it once the Byzantine fleet had been driven from the sea.

Winter quarters in Corfu, however, were a disaster. The weather was severe, but the real damage came from an illness, probably typhoid, which swept through the Norman camp. Thousands died, including 500 knights, and those who were spared were so weakened as to be useless for hard duty for months. Even the strapping Bohemund was infected, though he survived and was sent off to Italy to recuperate. When spring finally came, the badly weakened army was in no state to begin a campaign on the mainland. Robert decided to take a step at a time, and occupy the island of Cephalonia. In early summer, he sent Roger Borsa ahead to seize the place, following himself several weeks later. But once at sea, Robert fell ill of the disease that had so ravaged his army, and by the time his ship reached Cephalonia, he was already at death's door. Put ashore at the nearest harbor, he weakened rapidly as his seventy-year-old body gave in to the disease. On July 17, 1085, only two months after Pope Gregory, and accompanied by only one from his family, the loyal Sichelgaita, Robert of Hauteville, known as Guiscard, Duke of Apulia, Calabria, and Sicily, died.

Robert's mortal remains still had one more adventure, a macabre one, to live through. The ship on which Sichelgaita transported his body back to Italy was caught in a fierce storm off Otranto, and the coffin washed overboard. When it was eventually recovered, the body was found to be in such bad condition as to require immediate embalming, after which it was taken to the family burial spot at Santissima Trinita in Venosa. There, Robert's body was buried in the abbey next those of his brothers, who had paved the way for him to establish his greatness. Robert's monument — long since destroyed — carried a boastful epitaph which the contemporary chronicler William of Malmesbury tells us began, "Here lies the Guiscard, terror of the world...."[5]

Boasting aside, Guiscard had left an immense legacy. By his talents as a warrior, and a military commander, his strategic vision and his political acumen, but above all by the force of his personality, he had taken the barony his brothers had created and made it into one of the powers of Europe. He had driven the Byzantine rulers out of Italy and the Muslim ones from Sicily, saved the reform papacy, embarrassed emperors of east and west, and permanently changed history by the creation of a new state. The daughter of his last adversary, Anna Comnena, has given us an unforgettable picture of the man — a generous one, perhaps (except for the conclusion), because Robert was dead when she wrote, and no longer a threat to her father the Basileus:

> Now Robert, as rumor insisted and many said, was a most excep-
> tional leader, quick-witted, good-looking, courteous in conversation,
> ready too in repartee, loud-voiced, easily accessible, very tall in
> stature, his hair always close-cut, long-bearded, always anxious to
> maintain the ancient customs of his race. He preserved the perfect
> comeliness of his countenance and figure until the end, and of these
> he was very proud, as his appearance was considered worthy of king-
> ship; he showed respect to all his subordinates, more especially those
> who were well-disposed towards him. On the other hand, he was very
> thrifty and fond of money, very business-like and greedy of gain, and
> in addition to all this, most ambitious; and since he was a slave to
> these desires, he has incurred the serious censure of mankind.[6]

In his time, he was a model for others. Even William the Conqueror, the chroniclers tell us, found inspiration in the valor and the exploits of his Norman counterpart of the south. As the Norman enterprise in Italy went from success to success, later chroniclers added luster to the image of the man; he became a paragon of virtue, a model for the aspiring young knight, a hero beloved for his success. The reality was less: he was a hard man in a hard time, and that accounted for much of his success. Yet the contemporary records agree that he could also be an extraordinarily affable man, one who knew how to lighten the moment, inspire his friends, and disarm his opponents. His life was one long, and successful, adventure, yet a creative one. The state that he had done so much to bring into existence would last, amidst drama and tragedy, for almost eight centuries.

Notes

1. There is some debate about the date of this campaign, as well as the campaigns against Agrigento and Castrogiovanni. I have followed Loud.
2. There were other illegitimate sons as well, as Roger had several long-term
mistresses and a number of shorter-term affairs.
3. Anna Comnena, Book VI, p. 144.
4. Norman rule in Bari and Amalfi was ultimately harmful to those cities'
trade. Once they lost their Byzantine ties, they were put into direct competition
with Venice, which took advantage of its greater political and military leverage in
Constantinople to gradually freeze them out of the trade that had made them
wealthy.
5. Norwich, p. 247. The full epitaph read, "Here lies the Guiscard, terror of
the world. By his hand, he whom the Germans, the Ligurians and even Rome itself

called King was driven from the City. From his wrath neither the Parthians nor the Arabs, nor even the forces of Macedon, could save Alexius, whose only hope lay in flight; while for Venice, neither flight nor the protection of the ocean was of any avail."

6. Anna Comnena, Book VI, p. 150.

The Quest for Glory

uiscard's death thrust Sichelgaita, once again, into the fight for succession, as it had twelve years previously when Robert had fallen ill. At that time, she had seen to it that Robert endorsed their son Roger Borsa as his successor.[1] The duke's confidence in his son, however, never appears to have been very great, and with good reason. Roger Borsa was a good-hearted, competent fellow, but wholly lacking in the kind of leadership abilities needed to hold together the still unformed and fractious state that was the duchy. His brother Guy, an even weaker character, was not even a factor in the succession, but their half-brother Bohemund, the only son who approximated his father in characteristics, abilities, and ambition, definitely was. Everyone expected him to make a lunge for power, and it was said that he had formed an alliance with Jordan of Capua to achieve it.

To counter Bohemund's ambitions—the poor man himself was still recuperating in Bari—Sichelgaita worked assiduously to promote Roger Borsa's right to the succession. He had already been acclaimed as ruler in Corfu by the army, but that scarcely mattered as the army had dissolved in unseemly haste after Guiscard's death. What did matter was the support of the Apulian barons, and that Sichelgaita gradually obtained through persuasion, or a judicious gift or promise when it could be useful. The barons, presumably, found it fairly easy to accept Roger Borsa, since for the majority of them a weak duke was preferable to a strong one—and Bohemund looked as if he could be as tough with them as his father had been. What assured the succession for Roger Borsa, however, was support from his uncle and namesake, the Count of Sicily. Count Roger had mixed motives for supporting his nephew, but his support was decisive. Thus it was that in September, with Robert's body freshly laid in the tomb at

184

Venosa, Roger Borsa received the oaths of fealty from his Apulian barons. Shortly thereafter his uncle, fresh from his victory at Syracuse, swore fealty for his possessions in Calabria and Sicily.

Roger Borsa was duke, but he still had to defend his right to the duchy against Bohemund. Their feud would last for ten years, and began almost immediately. Bohemund struck in Hauteville-controlled land in the heel of Italy, where there were few other barons to obstruct him, and where the towns were only lightly defended. Within weeks, he had moved from his seat at Taranto to seize Oria and Otranto, facing Roger with a fait accompli. Roger had neither troops nor allies, and most probably not the will, to fight his half-brother, and had little choice but to meet Bohemund's terms. In a meeting at the family shrine at Venosa, Roger yielded to his imperious brother. He agreed that Taranto, Oria, Otranto, Brindisi, Gallipoli, and the territories between would be granted to Bohemund as Prince of Taranto, only nominally as vassal to the duke. Roger may have gained some small consolation for his defeat by the knowledge that Bohemund had thereby inherited the job of controlling a difficult new vassal of his own, their ever-rebellious cousin Geoffrey of Conversano.

Bohemund was not the only relative to take advantage of Roger Borsa's weak position. Count Roger also exacted a price for his support. His price was the revocation of the fifty-fifty deal he and Robert had stuck many years earlier in Calabria; Roger Borsa agreed to surrender the duke's share of all the castles and towns they had held jointly. The deal set a precedent for further such arrangements, through which Roger Borsa periodically gave away segments of his father's patrimony to his uncle, in return for the latter's continued support. Over time, the nominal vassal Roger expanded his power and control over lands previously held by the duke, and further earned the title by which he soon became known: the Great Count.

After the fall of Syracuse, Count Roger had moved rapidly to eliminate the remaining areas of Muslim rule on the island. Not strong enough to attack the last great stronghold at Castrogiovanni, he moved against Agrigento, whose territories he had been raiding for years. In the spring of 1087, his army settled in for a siege of the town on its ancient acropolis. So low had the state of Muslim morale fallen that, by July, the town surrendered. In a stroke of luck, Roger found that among the prisoners were ones he could exploit politically: the wife and children of the Emir of Castrogiovanni, Ibn Hamud.

Some months later, Roger appeared before Castrogiovanni with a body of knights and invited the Emir to a parley. The Emir held a weak hand in the subsequent negotiations. He could force the Normans to mount an expensive siege, and hold out in the fortress; the small Norman army available could not storm it without high losses. But his supplies would inevitably run out, and there were no other Muslim forces on the island or in Mahdia who could come to relieve the town. Resistance would only buy time, at an unknown cost, and one of the potential costs could even be the Emir's own family. On the other hand, he could not simply yield without a struggle; his pride and his standing required it. Fortunately, Roger had learned well the subtleties of diplomacy in Sicily, and soon the parties at the parley had come up with a piece of theater that would meet the requirements of the situation.

Not long thereafter, the Emir and a sizeable body of his troops and advisors left Castrogiovanni on an expedition, by a route that led them through a narrow defile. In the defile, surprise! They were suddenly ambushed by a much larger body of Norman knights, who cut off their retreat and threatened them with annihilation. Resistance evidently being futile, Ibn Hamud prudently yielded to the superior Norman force. Surrender of the now leaderless town soon followed. By this cleverly devised charade, the great hilltop fortress that had repelled the early Norman attacks, and stood seemingly unassailable ever since, fell with scarcely a casualty on either side. The remaining Muslim towns, Butera and Noto, could offer no resistance and fell with ease in the coming years, while Ibn Hamud retired in luxury, with his family, to an estate in Calabria provided by Count Roger.

By 1091, all of Sicily was finally under Norman rule. Roger even went on the offensive overseas. He sent his fleet to Malta, crushing the corsairs who had disrupted his trade and threatened Sicily's coastlines. The raid not only gained great booty and resulted in the freeing of hundreds of Christian captives, but also marked another step in the opening up of the central Mediterranean to European shipping.

The conquest of Sicily had taken almost thirty years, and had been helped by dissension as well as incompetence in the ranks of the defenders. In the end, though, it was the result of the persistence, military fortitude, and political skill of a small number of Norman knights led by Roger, now virtual ruler of an island of immense wealth.

While Count Roger was consolidating his hold on Sicily and Calabria, Duke Roger Borsa was making a mess of his rule in Apulia and Salerno. The truce with Bohemund lasted little more than a year, and soon the two half-brothers were engaged in a low-grade but damaging civil war across the duchy's Italian territories. Roger was no match for Bohemund, who succeeded in annexing Bari to his principality in 1090, and also gained the loyalty or support of most of the barons in Apulia, from Melfi south. Duke

Roger was gradually losing control of his base in Apulia, and the barons of the Abruzzi were also increasingly independent. Even Robert of Loritello, one of Roger Borsa's main supporters, ran his county with little or no deference to Salerno. At the same time, Roger was also ceding more of his patrimony to his uncle Roger — the duke's share of the revenues of Palermo, for example, having been yielded in return for assistance against Bohemund's attacks.

Unfortunately, Roger Borsa's fecklessness in protecting his duchy was not redeemed by political successes elsewhere. He intervened inconsistently in papal politics, which had become hopelessly convoluted following the death of Pope Gregory. The reformers, looking anxiously for a successor to Gregory who could mount an effective opposition to Emperor Henry's creature, the antipope Clement, could find common ground only in the nomination of Desiderius, the abbot of Monte Cassino, who had done so much to reconcile the papacy with the Normans. Desiderius was eventually elected against his will. The poor man knew he was not cut out for the ruthless cut and thrust of the politics of the day; he much preferred the contemplative life of abbot, interrupted only by missions of conciliation to his obstreperous neighbors. But elected he was, as Victor III. Roger Borsa, demonstrating to all that he did not have his father's gift for backing a winner, opposed the new pope's election for inconsequential reasons. The Norman military expedition that assured the new pope's safe consecration in turbulent Rome was, as a result, led by Jordan of Capua, with Roger Borsa reduce to the role of a decidedly secondary actor.

Victor unfortunately turned out to be both an ineffectual and an ephemeral pope, dying shortly after his elevation. The struggle was rejoined. The pro-reform cardinals elected still another pope, Urban II, in a Rome that continued to be largely controlled by Emperor Henry's partisans. Urban, a man of zeal like Gregory but blessed with more political finesse, looked to Count Roger of Sicily for the Norman support necessary to assure his elevation to the seat of Saint Peter; he simply ignored Roger Borsa because of his record of inconsistency. Count Roger succeeded in getting his warring nephews to accept a truce, and soon yet another Norman expedition to Rome installed Urban in the Lateran long enough to be consecrated (although his seat there proved to be only temporary). Roger Borsa, upstaged this time by his uncle, played a supporting role once again and gained little or no credit with the new pope.

Roger Borsa's most historic contribution to the duchy, indeed, turned out to be almost accidental. It presaged the absorption of Capua. Roger's relations with Jordan of Capua had never been good, as the latter had tended to side with Bohemund during the long civil war, even though he had never taken up arms. Jordan had died in 1090, at which point the Lombard citizens of the principality rose up against the Dregnot family and refused to accept Jordan's son Richard as their ruler. Richard, nonetheless, continued to harbor hopes that he could regain the principality his grandfather had striven for so long, and when he reached his majority in 1097 he appealed to his fellow Normans, Roger the count and Roger the duke. They agreed to help, but only on terms that would be costly to the Dregnots and lucrative to the Hautevilles in the long run. Count Roger asked that Richard abandon all his claims on Naples, while Duke Roger demanded that Richard, if restored to power in Capua, hold the principality as a vassal to the Duke of Apulia. Richard, who really had little choice, agreed to the terms. With their help, Capua was forced to surrender after a short siege in the summer of 1098. Richard was soon reinstated on the princely throne, but his concessions had created a mortgage on his possession. It only awaited a duke of Apulia more ruthless than Roger Borsa to turn suzerainty over Capua into actual rule over the principality. The Hauteville line would indeed produce leaders of that caliber.

A second stroke of luck ended the calamitous civil war and removed the greatest threat to the integrity of the duchy. Roger Borsa, however, had little to do with the happy development: his great rival Bohemund suddenly determined to leave Italy in order to find his fortune and glory elsewhere. Bohemund, who had had the bad luck to be declared illegitimate simply to serve his father's political goals, had struggled all his life for the respect that he felt was due him as Robert's firstborn. He bitterly resented having to play second fiddle to his hapless half-brother, and being kept in check by his uncle. He had inherited all of his father's restless ambition, and many of his talents as warrior and diplomat, but neither his patience nor his subtlety. Even his status as Prince of Taranto, vassal to his brother, would always be a half-loaf. Bohemund aspired to a greater status. The chance to gain it came with the declaration of a crusade to free the holy city of Jerusalem from Muslim rule.

The crusading movement had been gathering momentum for some time. The great abbey of Cluny in France, mother of the reform movement and sponsor of the great pilgrimage to Compostella in modern northwest Spain, had given strong support to the Christian princes of that region since the beginning of the century. As those princes struggled to expand their territories at the expense of the their Muslim neighbors, their struggle had increasingly taken on a religious tone, with the abbots of Cluny urging the Christian princes of the north to aid their brothers in Spain. In the same spirit, Pope Nicholas II had sanctioned the Norman invasion and reconquest of Muslim Sicily, though he did not actually characterize it as a holy war. But later Pope Alexander II had gone a step farther, when he offered indulgence to all those who fought for the Cross in Spain, and made a similar offer to the Normans in Sicily following their great victory at Cerami. Pope Gregory, that most zealous warrior for the Church, had joyously fostered the idea of holy war, and had made it still more attractive to restless knights: he had ruled that Christians were free to enjoy any lands they conquered from the infidel.

The new pope, Urban II, was a follower of Gregory and a believer in the same sort of muscular Christianity, but he was also a much more effective diplomat and statesman. Forced to spend the first years of his papacy as an exile from Rome, which was still controlled by Emperor Henry's partisans, he had been obliged to rely on Norman support but prudently sought to reach beyond such selfish partners. He tried to build support wherever he could, even encouraging reconciliation with Constantinople through correspondence with Alexius, who asked for assistance against the Turks. By 1094, Urban had won over many Spanish and Frankish princes; he even had some support in Germany where he had encouraged a revolt by Henry's son. Then, in a masterful political move that isolated Henry and his antipope, and assured Urban's moral leadership of the Church and of western Europe, Urban reached beyond the princes and preached a great crusade to the Holy Land.

Urban's impassioned crusading appeal was made at Clermont in France, in November 1095, before a great throng that included emissaries from Basileus Alexius. The pope's call to mobilize the energies of the West, to save Christianity in the East and the holy sites at Jerusalem from the Turks, was met with an instant and enthusiastic response. Religious enthusiasm, desire for adventure, and greed for fame and gain spread rapidly throughout the knightly class, and within months many of the best knights and princes of Europe had flocked to the Cross and begun the trip to Constantinople. The enthusiasm of the crusading knights transiting Apulia in the autumn of 1096, and the possibilities in the orient which suddenly seemed open to men of enterprise, convinced the restless Bohemund to take the Cross as well. Joining him were no less than five other grandsons of Tancred of Hauteville. There were also two great grandsons, one of whom, a new young Tancred, would bring great fame to the old patriarch's name.

Bohemund, a renowned fighter with a cohort of seasoned men, proved an invaluable addition to the Christian army, indeed he became one of the great heroes of the First Crusade. More experienced in the east than his fellows, speaking Greek and familiar with the fighting capacities of the Muslims, the Prince of Taranto emerged as a natural leader. His courage and military skills were proven in the great battles of Dorylaeum and Antioch, and the glory of his and Tancred's exploits were celebrated by the chronicles and ballad singers for centuries. But he did not go on to Jerusalem with the army. Instead, he took advantage of the victory at Antioch to take possession of that wealthy and strategic principality for himself. The illegitimate son had finally won the independence, magnificence and renown that he had sought, and established a dynasty that lasted for two centuries. But his own reign was short. He defied both Turks and Byzantines, but a battle lost to the Turks of the upper Euphrates in 1101 cost him his freedom. He was forced to spend the next three years as a prisoner before he could be ransomed, at a crippling cost to the Antiochenes. He then returned to Italy to raise money and a new army to save Antioch. Unwisely, he decided to carry the war to his old enemies the Byzantines, and invaded Illyria once again, "like a thunderbolt":

> Bohemund took after his father in all things: in audacity, bodily strength, bravery and untamable temper; for he was of exactly the same stamp as his father, and a living model of the latter's character.[2]

Once again, Bohemund was beaten in Illyria. Returning a last time to Apulia he died, a broken man, in 1111. The most romantic and the most tragic of Tancred's progeny, Bohemund had lit up the history of his times like a meteor, but perished like one, lacking the cold constancy of his father and uncle.

Robert had died in Illyria; Bohemund's spirit was crushed in the land of the Turks. Italy had grown too small for these adventure-loving scions of Tancred. Not for them were the daily nuisances of governing, the small satisfactions of feud or private warfare. Once the conquest of southern Italy was largely complete, they saw little glory to be won in its consolidation or the establishment of order and justice. The ambition that had driven Guiscard to become the most successful military adventurer of his age also drove his son, and caused them both to reach for glory until the quest finally destroyed them. They undoubtedly would not have had it otherwise.

Notes

1. Sichelgaita's championship of her son's cause was so notable that it may have prompted the accusations, by the later Anglo-Norman chroniclers Ordericus Vitalis and William of Malmsbury, that she secretly had Robert poisoned. The charges have generally been dismissed as fabrications. Norwich, p. 250.

2. Anna Comnena, Book I, p. 37.

The End of the Beginning

The crusading fervor that had gripped so many of his fellow rulers may have moved Count Roger, but it did not motivate him. He was now over 65, and no longer had the zest for adventure that had marked his brother Robert to his last day. Roger had become a builder, finding his priority in promoting the security and prosperity of the lands he had already conquered. A holy war was, to the contrary, something to be avoided. He needed above all to maintain the religious harmony that allowed his lands to prosper. He ruled an island that was predominantly Muslim, he was resettling Muslims in depopulated parts of Calabria, and he relied on Muslim military units to flesh out his armies. Peace with his Muslim neighbors was also beneficial, now that the grain trade with Mahdia and the other states of North Africa had become an important source of revenue. Roger consequently had every reason to keep the profitable truce with the Zirids, and to encourage them and the other North African states to remain neutral in the struggle raging between Christianity and Islam in the Levant.[1]

Roger's concern for the sensibilities of his Muslim subjects and neighbors was not simply a matter of policy, but also one of respect. He found that he had assumed rule of a state with a rich and inventive culture and tradition, one that could, in the proper circumstances, flourish side by side with Latin and even Greek traditions to the mutual benefit of all. Whether by conscious design or out of convenience, a cultural and official eclecticism took root that would mark Norman rule for centuries. The toleration and justice of Roger's mixed administration, in turn, gave opportunity for a revival of the ancient Arab arts and sciences, even as the Norman administration was also promoting the establishment of Latin dioceses and monasteries, and establishing new Greek rite monasteries.

While the Great Count's rule in Sicily and Calabria may have been tolerant and inclusive in its application (at least vastly more so than was the norm in an intolerant era), its direction was very centralized. Roger kept court, most often in his original Sicilian stronghold at Troina or in Mileto in Calabria, and his court was the unquestioned center of power. In the polyglot court, Oriental and Lombard concepts of absolutism and regal display began to take hold, a trend that conveniently served Roger's purpose of strengthening central rule. He also saw to it that no centers of influence that could compete with the court were given an opportunity to develop, by granting major fiefs only to loyal members of the extended family, or to Church foundations that owed him their loyalty. Roger's policies encouraged coexistence, but not the integration, of the three cultures, and were designed always with an eye to assuring control by the small Norman ruling class. For example, while local administrations were largely left in place under Norman supervision, local initiative (outside of the arts and trade) was discouraged. New Norman and Lombard settlements were established and fortified, even as Muslim towns were stripped of their defensive walls, the Muslim populations increasingly tied to the land, and the communes of Palermo and other cities suppressed.[2] Roger also sought dispersion of power and diversification of population through a variety of methods, some of them harsh, such as the forced resettlement of some villagers in Calabria. Others were more subtle, such as granting religious foundations based in one province properties in another.

By the turn of the century, Roger had succeeded in laying the foundations of a secure, stable, and prosperous regime. Trade flourished, the arts were reviving, new settlements were returning the land to productivity, the currency was sound, and the administration, untidy as it may have been, was effective and the ruler both respected and feared. The Crusades, which Roger had avoided, would prove to be a huge blessing. With the sea around it largely free of Arab corsairs, Sicily became a great entrepot for the crusading enterprise. The trade of Europe and the Levant flowed through the Straits of Messina and into the cities of Calabria and Sicily, where Arab and Greek merchants made their fortunes, and the tax collectors took their share to assure that the Count's coffers were also kept full. Sicily and Calabria were made as rich or richer than they had ever been, and Roger and his descendants found they had done much better by staying at home than they ever could have by joining the crusading adventurers.

Roger's good fortune increased when a long-simmering dispute with Pope Urban was settled to his entire satisfaction. Over the years, Roger's establishment of new Latin dioceses and monasteries in Sicily had been gratifying to successive popes. But, at the same time, they were more than annoyed at Roger's proclivity to appoint bishops and abbots with only the slightest consultation — had not simony been at the root of the papacy's struggle with the emperors for all those years? Pope Urban also distrusted Roger's sponsorship of Greek rite monasteries, as well as his tolerance of Muslim practices, and had tried to impress upon Roger his duties as a loyal vassal of the Church. Roger, for his part, had met the pope's complaints with promises of loyalty to papal authority, but had more or less continued to act as he wished. The pope needed Norman support too much to bring the matter to a head, but a crisis, nonetheless, occurred in 1098 that obliged the two rulers to come to agreement over the issue. Urban reluctantly had to acknowledge Roger's stronger position, and the services he had rendered the Church, and as a consequence agreed to hand him a victory that formally authorized him and his heirs to exercise the powers of papal legate. Roger was to be, in effect, the head of the Church in his own territories, a distinction at the time given to no other ruler.

Roger had still another source of satisfaction: he finally had a legitimate heir. When his second wife died in 1089, he had quickly remarried, to the Italian Adelaide del Vasto. In 1093, and again two years later, Adelaide presented the proud Count with two heirs: Simon and Roger.

The Great Count lived his last years in comfort, knowing that he had established a strong and prosperous state, and that his young sons were likely to succeed him without challenge. He died peacefully in the June of 1101. He had come to Italy, a young man of 26 seeking his fortune, some 44 years earlier. His elder brothers had opened the way for him, but they had not made it easy. To establish his position in the world, he had had to fight both his enemies and on occasion his brother Robert. On both counts, he had succeeded brilliantly. His military victories were the stuff of legend, and he had finally had his way with his brother as well. In the latter years, he had sheathed his sword to become a wise and foresighted ruler, creating the basic framework of a government that would be one of the marvels of the dawning century. The youngest of Tancred's sons had died the last, having gathered in the harvest of his brothers' work. Considered one of the foremost rulers of Europe even in his time, he left a legacy that his progeny would burnish till it shone for centuries.

Roger had outlived his brother by fifteen years, but the era had already changed. The great adventures were over, the great conquests achieved. In time Capua, Naples, and even Benevento would come under Norman control, but their loss of independence was gradual and their freedom limited in practice by Norman dominance, even before they yielded. Those new borders of the state that the sons of Tancred founded would last, virtually unchanged, until the great Risorgimento of the nineteenth century united all of Italy into the country that we know today.

It would, in fact, take almost thirty years from Roger's death for the Hauteville state itself to crystallize. The dukedom still was a diverse political creation, divided by Bohemund's revolt and the deal that had been struck by Robert and Roger after the capture of Palermo. Roger's family would have a free hand to govern in Sicily and their share of Calabria, under only the lightest of claims of suzerainty by the Duke of Apulia. Union of the various pieces would not come until later.

Roger was succeeded by his eldest son Simon, who ruled only four years, dying still a minor under the regency of his mother Adelaide. He was in turn succeeded by his brother, the new Count Roger, but as the boy would not reach his majority until 1112, his mother continued as regent. Considering that Adelaide's prime qualification as Roger's third wife had been her presumed fecundity, she proved to be a remarkably competent caretaker — the one possible caveat being the exceptional privileges granted to her family, the Alerami.[3] Adelaide followed the general policies set down by her deceased husband, with one significant exception: she moved the capital to Palermo. In that more oriental, exotic atmosphere, the future counts of Sicily were raised. In a court in which Italian, Arabic, Greek and even Lombard influences mixed and competed with Norman ones for the young ruler's attention, the special nature of twelfth and thirteenth century Norman rule in the south was formed. It was a wholly different world from that of the castle of a minor knight in Normandy, and one has to wonder if old Tancred, had he been alive to meet his grandson, would have understood what had happened.

Apulia, in the meantime, continued under Roger Borsa's indifferent government until his death in 1111; he was succeeded by his son William who, unfortunately, showed little more talent as a ruler. Only the Latin church thrived; Roger had been particularly generous in his gifts to churches and monasteries in both Italy and Normandy, careful to finance works that would redound to the credit of his family.[4] The condition of the duchy, however, even with its share of profits from the crusading trade, deteriorated. William was ever short of money, even giving away his remaining rights in Calabria and Sicily to his nominal vassal Roger of Sicily to pay back a loan. Although Bohemund and his family no longer caused them trouble, the dukes of Apulia still proved incapable of keeping the peace in their land. Private warfare thrived; the economy limped along; the currency was debased. By the time William died in 1127, the duchy had lost the energy and vitality with which Robert had endowed it, and risked sliding into disarray.

Duke William's greatest gift to his duchy was, perhaps, the fact that he left it, and the world, with no heir. Roger II had foreseen the possibility two years previously, inviting William to Messina, where he was persuaded to acknowledge his powerful and rich host as heir to the duchy — in return, it must be admitted, for another substantial loan. On this basis, Roger immediately claimed the succession when his lackluster cousin died. The two parts of the Hauteville domain were not, however, to be brought together as a single political entity without still another struggle. The Apulian barons, perhaps predictably, balked at the prospect of a strong ruler such as Roger had already shown himself to be, and rose in revolt. They were aided by the pope of the time, who was as anxious as the barons not to see Roger become too powerful and was trying, as had popes before him, to play the Prince of Capua off against the Hautevilles. Roger, however, acted decisively. He first secured the submission of Salerno, and then turned on the pope and his allies, the Prince of Capua and the rebellious barons. It took a year for him to gain the upper hand, but thanks to the wealth that allowed him to keep a large army in the field, and his persistence, the opposition gradually crumbled without any major fighting.

In late August 1128, the outmaneuvered pope reluctantly invested Roger II, already Prince of Salerno, with the dukedoms of Apulia, Calabria, and Sicily. The title had first been given to his uncle Robert almost 70 years earlier, when it was more prospective than real; it had been earned over years of hardship and battle. Roger had now inherited a duchy in reality, one with problems but great potential. He still had the Apulian barons to bring into line, but with the wealth and power of Sicily behind him, he would surely prevail. Looking further into the future, he wanted to achieve what his uncle had not succeeded in doing — indeed, Robert had scarcely tried. Roger held the ambition to knit the dukedoms of Apulia, Calabria and Sicily together into a single strong, law abiding and prosperous state. In time, he would succeed. But for the moment he, like any good Hauteville, had even greater ambitions. The thirty-two-year-old duke aspired to be a king.

He first needed to consolidate his rule over the new and unruly counties. Showing a military aptitude that his rebellious vassals had not suspected, Roger gathered another large army in Sicily, returning to Apulia in the spring of the following year with three thousand knights, Muslim auxiliaries and thousands of crossbowmen. Faced with their duke's overwhelming force and display of determination, and as unable to cooperate effectively among themselves as they were rebellious, the dissident barons and cities allowed themselves to be picked off one by one, so that by late summer the rebellion was over. With a few exceptions, Roger pardoned his new vassals and reconfirmed them in their holdings, hoping to tie them to his rule to the greatest extent possible. He wanted, moreover, to dramatize their ties of fealty, which he did by summoning all the lords of Apulia and Calabria —counts, abbots, and bishops— to a great council at Melfi. There, in a great public ceremony that must have made the fractious barons apprehensive for their future, each of them was required to swear his fealty to the new duke. Not only fealty, though, for further commitments were to be required. First, the counts were obliged to swear that they would not countenance lawlessness on their lands, and would surrender all brigands to the duke's justice. Secondly, they were to swear to observe a new ducal edict forbidding all private war; that is, to renounce their time-hallowed and much-exercised right of feud. Together, the oaths spelled out Roger's intent, which was to curb his barons and impose his own truce, as well as justice, on the turbulent land. It was an unprecedented approach in Italy, if not new to Normans: the dukes of Normandy had long imposed their own truce in that county, as had William the Conqueror more recently in England. But in Apulia, the oaths implied the end of a way of life that had persisted since the Normans had first come to Melfi. The barons found, moreover, that Roger was determined to impose his will in the matter, and had the oaths repeated at all suitable occasions during the long years of his reign.

At the end of the year, the ripe Capuan fruit finally fell from the tree. Neither Roger Borsa nor William had tried to enforce the rights of suzerainty they had been granted by Richard II of Capua when he had needed help to gain his throne. Indeed, a strong prince in Capua might have tried to ignore the precedent. But Richard had died, and his successor, Robert, had had the bad judgment to ally himself with the pope and the barons in trying, and then failing, to block Roger's accession to the ducal title. With no allies, and with Capua no longer having any military significance, Robert now found himself vulnerable as a result of his misjudgment. He prudently decided it was better to buy off the new duke rather than face his inevitable hostility. He submitted his principality, voluntarily, to Roger as overlord, and he would in future serve in Capua as Roger's vassal. It was a pathetic submission, if perhaps an inevitable development, but nonetheless an anticlimactic denouement to the generations-long rivalry between the Dregnot and Hauteville families.

The end of Capuan independence left Roger's dukedom as the only locus of power in southern Italy. No longer could pope or emperor hope to play one Norman group against the other; access to Norman support was now only available through Palermo. And once again, the death of a pope had ushered in a crisis in which Norman help would be necessary.

The death of the current pope produced a period of confusion in which two rival popes had been elected, Anacletus and Innocent. While Anacletus and his supporters controlled Rome, Innocent had gradually succeeded in rallying support in France and the north, leading Anacletus to see that his shaky grasp on the seat of Saint Peter might come to an early end. He turned to Roger, and Norman power, to once again save the papacy — or, in this, case, his own claim on it. The duke, as wily as his uncle had been, knew that he could set his own terms. Nothing less than papal confirmation of the power he now held, by making him king, would suffice. He wanted the title, and the consecration that went with it, to help him control his domain, but also so he could speak with an equal voice to the other great rulers of the time. For the desperate Anacletus, it was an acceptable price to pay for Norman support. Roger was already undisputed lord of a land bigger than other kingdoms, one of the richest and most powerful rulers in Europe, and the one, moreover, closest to Rome and most able to protect his hold on the papacy.

Anacletus agreed to Roger's demands. A papal bull was accordingly issued, granting a crown to Roger and his heirs. All of the lands that the dukes of Apulia had held of the Holy See would fall within the kingdom: Apulia, Calabria, and Sicily, plus the Principality of Capua and the "honor" of Naples. In addition, the pope promised the assistance of the papal city of Benevento. The formulation left some matters vague, such as the status of the March of Fermo or even Salerno, in which the popes had never invested the dukes of Apulia; or, for that matter, what the "honor" of Naples implied, as that state was nominally still independent. Roger nonetheless had what he wanted, and was prepared to let the details settle themselves in time; the Hautevilles had found that history for them did not run backwards.[5]

The coronation took place some three months later, on Christmas Day 1130. Roger had used the interim to assure that his principal vassals were consulted, holding a great assembly of his senior nobles and clergy in Salerno to submit to them a proposal for his elevation to their king. Their acclaim, stage managed though it may have been, was nonetheless important in giving his new title the kind of moral and legal sanction that his Norman and Lombard subjects would feel comfortable with. The coronation ceremony itself was magnificent. The duke's vassals, great and small, knights and clerics, had been summoned to Palermo to see him crowned, and it was a vast and colorful assembly that gathered in the metropolis for the occasion. Vying with each other in the festive city to display the grandness of their station by the opulence of their clothes, the magnificence of their trains, or the sumptuousness of their tables, they nonetheless were all eclipsed by the new king. The banquet he gave, on settings of gold, in a hall hung with the richest fabrics, and with servants dressed in silk, was unforgettable to all those who attended. In the ceremony at the cathedral, where Latin rite bishops officiated while Greek rite bishops attended, Roger II was anointed by the pope's special representative and then crowned by none other than Robert of Capua, his senior vassal.

Tancred's progeny had reached the pinnacle of success. William Ironarm's victory over the Emir of Syracuse had begun a series of victories, large and small, through which the Hautevilles had risen from journeyman adventurers to greatness. They had had their share of luck: the shortsightedness of the Lombard rulers that had allowed them to establish themselves, the fatal weakness of the Byzantine state at the crucial time of their early struggles, their amazing victories in battle, the popes' need for support. In addition, the sons of Tancred had proven to be strong leaders, successful soldiers, and in the case of Robert and Roger, farsighted strategists and statesmen. Lesser men could not have matched, or even envisaged, their achievements. The new generation that had taken over might not have their audacity or match their exploits and valor, but in was not necessary. The time of adventure, of expansion and conquest, was over.

The Kingdom of Sicily, Apulia, and Calabria, and the Principate of Capua, in spite of its unwieldy name, would be one of the wonders of the next century, its power providing it respect, and its rulers among the leading men of Europe. The kingdom's central role in the Mediterranean ensured that its commerce expanded, along with its wealth. Learning and the sciences flourished, and great monuments were built. The government was among the most efficient and tolerant of its age, a happy compromise between the various cultural and legal elements of the kingdom. Combining elements of oriental centralized despotism with feudal patterns of obligation and Byzantine administration, it was well adapted to its time and place.[6] The rich, cosmopolitan culture that developed in the kingdom — known as the Regno — distinguished it from much of the rest of Europe, and provided a bridge between east and west, north and south during the period when modern western European thought and civilization was forming. It was a glorious time in the region's history, and in the history of the Mediterranean.

The Hautevilles, however, were not destined to lead the kingdom throughout the period of its greatness. Two kings, both called William, followed Roger II, but, at that point the great vitality of the Hauteville line seems to have deserted it. The second William died in 1190, leaving no legitimate heirs, and was succeeded by a cousin, Tancred of Lecce, who was illegitimate. The valiant Tancred, who was host to Richard the Lion Hearted on his way to the Third Crusade, was not able to hold onto the kingdom. He was driven off the throne by Henry Hohenstauffen, the Holy Roman Emperor, whose claim to the succession stemmed from his marriage to Constance Hauteville, aunt of the last King William. Tancred's defeat after a brief but bloody war marked the end of the Hauteville royal line, and was followed by a purge of the Norman aristocracy in Sicily. German influence became prominent at the court. Norman-Sicilian culture, nonetheless, had a last magnificent expression in the person of Henry's son, Frederick II, the most brilliant ruler of Europe during the first half of the thirteenth century. Frederick was half Norman, raised in Palermo, fluent in the languages of the court — Latin, French, and Arabic — and one of the most learned men of his day as well as one of the most skeptical and arrogant rulers. His genius was very much a product of the extraordinary intellectual and moral climate of his kingdom. Only the court of Norman Sicily, that strange, exotic and remarkably creative hybrid of the Mediterranean, could have fostered the diverse talents that that Emperor Frederick displayed during his long and tempestuous career.

The gap between Tancred of Hauteville and his fifth-generation grandson Emperor Frederick was a huge one. The first was a simple feudal soldier; the second a brilliant precursor of the Renaissance. And yet the connection was there, beyond that of blood. Europe had changed greatly in the two hundred years since Tancred's first sons went south in search of adventure and gain, but what had changed it as much as anything was the opening of the Mediterranean, and with it the opening of the minds of Western men. The Normans, Tancred's sons in the forefront, had played a major role, unwitting or not, in that historical development. They had done so at first for reasons of need and ambition, but gradually as policy. The Mediterranean was a totally different place as a result of their efforts, while the kingdom they founded was the outstanding example for many centuries of a state in which the cultures of the region met in a climate of tolerance and fruitful, indeed brilliant, coexistence.

Notes

1. Roger had also kept aloof from a Pisan raid on Mahdia in 1087, preferring to maintain his truce and trade with that state. In the following century, the Normans would abandon the truce and go to war against the Zirids, capturing Mahdia and other cities along the Tunisian coast and occupying them for several decades.

2. The suppression in Norman lands of communal movements, such as those

that flourished in the rest of Italy from the twelfth century on, has been cited as a reason why the cities of southern Italy and Sicily did not participate in the urban-led flowering of trade, banking and commerce of the late Middle Ages.

3. After she put down the burdens of the regency, Adelaide lived through a short but unhappy episode in the Holy Land as Queen of Jerusalem, wife of Baldwin of Boulogne. She returned to Palermo to live out her days there.

4. The new century marked the Norman apogee in history, a proud period that saw Normans ruling in England, Italy, and the Holy Land, Norman princes contributing to a great expansion of religious building, and those establishments serving as channels for the radiation of Norman art, architecture, and history.

5. In the end, even Norman power could not assure Anacletus his seat, and the schism was not settled by fighting. The extent of Innocent's support proved to be too great for Anacletus to resist effectively, and Innocent emerged as the uncontested pope at the Second Lateran Council in 1139. Pope Innocent was determined to punish Roger for his support of Anacletus, and excommunicated him. In the fighting that ensued during the following year, Roger defeated the papal army, took Pope Innocent prisoner, and forced him to reconfirm the royal title.

6. The Norman regime also left a legacy that, according to many analysts, contributed to the south's falling behind the rest of Italy in subsequent periods. Autocratic rule and large royal and feudal landholdings, as well as the absence of a communal movement, all persisted in the south, where they stifled development of the entrepreneurial capitalism responsible for the great economic expansion of the later Middle Ages and the Renaissance in the north.

Chronology

1017: Norman knights join anti–Byzantine uprising in Apulia, as mercenaries.

1018: Byzantines crush uprising in battle at Cannae. Some Normans remain in Italy as mercenaries with local rulers.

1025: Death of Basileus Basil the Bulgar Slayer; Byzantium enters period of decline.

1029: Rainulf, a Norman knight, awarded a fief at Aversa; it becomes magnet for additional knight-adventurers.

1035: William and Drogo of Hauteville arrive in Italy (approximate).

1038: Byzantines launch campaign into Muslim Sicily. Normans serve as mercenaries.

1041: Norman adventurers join Lombard rebels; seize Melfi from Byzantines. Rebels win battles at Olivento, Montepeloso; begin expansion.

1042: Argyrus selected to lead rebellion, but deserts to Byzantines. Byzantine counter-offensive under Maniakes fails.

1043: Election of William of Hauteville as Count and leader of rebel/Norman forces, as vassal to Guaimar of Salerno. Norman leaders divide Apulia into spheres of influence at Melfi, continue to expand their lands.

1044: Guaimar and William lead raid into Calabria/

1046: William dies; is succeeded as Count of Apulia by his brother Drogo.

1047: Emperor Henry III comes to Italy; invests Drogo as imperial vassal. Robert Hauteville arrives in Italy.

1048: Humphrey Hauteville defeats Byzantines at Tricarico, opens up Calabria to expansion. Robert sent to Scribla in Calabria.

1049: Leo IX elected pope. Holds synod at Melfi; seeks to restrain Norman excesses.

1051: Drogo assassinated; succeeded by Humphrey Hauteville. Pope Leo tries to form anti–Norman alliance.

1052: Guaimar of Salerno assassinated. Normans under Humphrey throw out usurpers, put Guaimar's son Gisulf on throne.

1053: Pope Leo leads punitive army against Normans. Gisulf remains neutral. Pope defeated at Civitate; acknowledges Norman territorial gains in Italy. In Sicily, Kalbite dynasty expires and central government breaks down, while Zirid protectors in Tunisia face invasion and civil war.

1054: Schism with eastern Church. Pope Leo dies and is replaced by Victor II. Geoffrey, Mauger and William Hauteville arrive in Italy. Normans continue expansion in Apulia.

1055: Humphey establishes William on land seized from Salerno, as Count of the Principata.

1056: Emperor Henry III dies; replaced by infant son Henry as King of the Germans.

1057: Humphrey dies; succeeded as Count by Robert. Roger Hauteville arrives; joins Robert on campaign in Calabria. Pope Victor dies; succeeded by Stephen IX, who forms anti–Norman alliance.

1058: Pope Stephen dies; rival popes elected. Richard of Aversa seizes Capua from Lombard ruling house. Roger and William Hauteville rebel against Robert.

1059: Normans under Richard of Capua march on Rome, install Nicholas II as pope; he reforms papal selection process to eliminate imperial role.

Robert and his brothers reconcile; Robert continues to expand lands in Calabria.

Pope holds synod in Melfi; invests Richard in Capua, Robert in Apulia, Calabria and Sicily.

1060: Robert marries Lombard princess, Sichelgaita of Salerno.

Robert and Roger campaign in Calabria; seize Taranto, Brindisi and Reggio.

Byzantines counterattack; besiege Melfi.

1061: Byzantine offensive checked. Robert and Roger invade Sicily; capture Messina.

Pope Nicholas dies, Norman forces assure investiture of Nicholas II over rival.

1062: Robert and Roger fight over division of land and authority.

Zirids send relief army to Sicily. Roger besieged at Troina.

1063: Roger breaks siege; defeats Muslim army at Cerami.

1064: Robert leads army to Sicily; he and Roger besiege Palermo unsuccessfully.

Robert's barons in Apulia revolt.

1066: Barons' revolt continues; Abdul Kare leads Byzantine army into Apulia.

William the Bastard, Duke of Normandy, invades England.

1067: Basileus Constantine dies; Byzantine support for barons' rebellion dries up.

1068: Robert defeats last rebels; begins siege of Bari.

Roger wins battle at Menzel el Amir. Zirid troops leave Sicily.

1071: Bari surrenders. Robert leads army and fleet to besiege Palermo.

Byzantines suffer major defeat by Seljuk Turks, at Manzikert.

1072: Palermo surrenders. Norman barons in Apulia rebel again.
1073: Gregory VII elected pope on death of Alexander.
Robert defeats last rebels; falls gravely ill. He is chosen as protector of Amalfi.
1074: Robert concludes marriage alliance with Byzantium; his daughter Helen to wed son of Basileus Michael.
Pope Gregory attempts to raise army against Normans.
1075: Roger concludes truce with Zirids; begins to trade with African states.
1076: Conflict between papacy and empire heats up over Church reform and authority. Henry faces Saxon revolt and submits to pope at Canosa.
1077: Robert and Richard of Capua form alliance to capitalize on papal-imperial split.
1078: Robert besieges Salerno successfully; expels Gisulf and Lombard ruling house.
Apulian barons engage in short rebellion against Robert.
Richard of Capua dies.
1079: Roger captures Taormina.
1080: Henry defeats Saxon rebels; turns to Italy. Pope Gregory seeks Norman support.
Gregory invests Robert, at Ceprano, in the lands granted by Nicholas and accepts his control of lands seized since then.
1081: Robert and his son Bohemund invade Byzantine province of Illyria.
Alexius Comnenus seizes Byzantine throne; leads army against Norman invasion.
Normans win battle at Durazzo, advance into Macedonia.
1082: Henry invades Italy; besieges Pope Gregory in Rome.
Apulian barons revolt again; Robert returns to Italy to combat rebellion.
1083: Norman army besieges Larissa, but is driven off by Basileus Alexius.
Robert defeats rebels.
1084: Henry has antipope elected in Rome; has himself crowned emperor.
Robert leads army on Rome; lifts siege of Pope Gregory. Rome sacked by Norman army, and Gregory obliged to leave Rome with Robert.
Robert returns to Illyria to resume campaign.
1085: Pope Gregory dies in Salerno.
Robert dies on campaign. His second son Roger Borsa succeeds, and Bohemund goes into revolt.
In Spain, Muslims lose Toledo to emergent state of Castile.
1086: Roger wins naval battle at Syracuse; captures city.
1087: Roger captures Agrigento and Castrogiovanni.
1089: Bohemund and Roger Borsa partition Apulia; Bohemund becomes Prince of Taranto.
1090: Butera and Noto surrender, last Muslim-controlled towns in Sicily.
1097: Bohemund departs on First Crusade. Roger Borsa becomes overlord of Capua.
1101: Roger Hauteville dies, and is succeeded by his son Simon.

Genealogical Table

Sons and Grandsons of Tancred of Hauteville

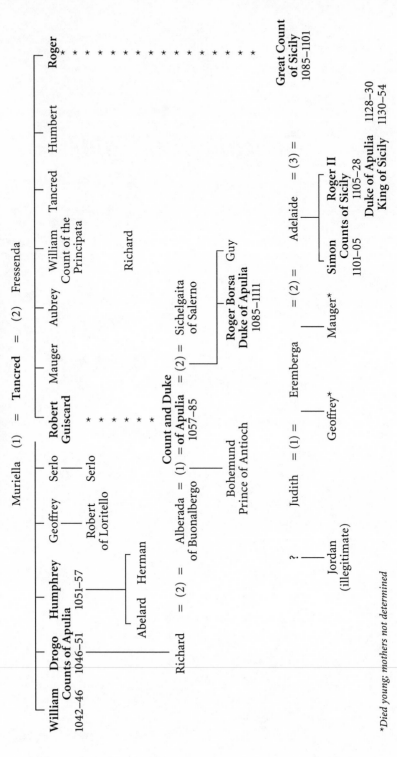

*Died young; mothers not determined

Bibliography

A *note on sources:* The primary original sources on the Normans in Italy are:
- — Amatus of Monte Cassino's *Historia Normanorum*
- — William of Apulia's *Gesta Roberti Wiscardi*
- — Geoffrey Malaterra's *De rebus gestis Rogeri Calabriae et Siciliae, et Roberti Guiscardi ducis fratis euis*
- — Desiderius of Monte Cassino's *Dialogi de Miraculis sancti Benedicti.*
- — Princess Anna Comnena's *Alexiad.*

With the exception of Anna Comnena's, these authors' works remain in the original Latin or early French, and therefore quotes in the text have been drawn from secondary sources. For more information on the primary sources, see note 2 of Chapter III.

Works Consulted

Abulafia, David. *The Two Italies: Economic Relations Between the Norman Kingdom of Sicily and the Northern Communes.* Cambridge, England: Cambridge University Press, 1977.

Amari, Michele. *Storia dei musulmani di Sicilia.* Vols II & III. Catania: Romeo Prampolini, 1935–39.

Aube, Pierre. *Les Empires normands d'orient.* Paris: Perrin, 1991.

Barlow, James W. *The Normans of South Europe.* London: Kegan Paul, Trench & Co., 1886.

Bartlett, Robert. *The Making of Europe.* Princeton, N.J.: Princeton University Press, 1993.

Bouet, Pierre, and François Neveu. *Les Normands en Mediteranée.* Caen: University of Caen Press, 1994.

Brown, H. Allen. *The Normans.* Woodbridge, England: Boydell Press, 1984.

Bunemann, Richard. *Robert Guiskard.* Köln: Bohlau Verlag, 1997.

Cahen, Claude. *Le Régime féodale d'Italie normande.* Paris: Paul Geuthner, 1940.

Capitani, Ovidio. *The Normans in Sicily and Southern Italy.* Oxford, England: The British Academy, 1977.

Cassady, Richard F. *The Norman Achievement.* London: Sidgwick & Jackson Ltd, 1986.

Chalandon, Ferdinand. *Histoire de la domination normande en Italie*. Vol. I. Paris: Alphonse Picard et Fils, 1907.

Comnena, Princess Anna. *The Alexiad*. Translated by Elizabeth Dawes. London: Kegan Paul, Trench, Trubner & Co, 1928.

Contamine, Phillipe. *War in the Middle Ages*. Oxford, England: Blackwell, 1984.

Cowdrey, H.E.J. *The Age of the Abbot Desiderius: Montecassino, the Papacy, and the Normans*. New York: Oxford University Press, 1983.

Crawford, F. Marion. *The Rulers of the South*. Vol II. New York: Macmillan, 1900.

Croce, Benedetto. *History of the Kingdom of Naples*. Chicago: University of Chicago Press, 1970.

Cuozzo, Errico. *Normanni: Nobilità e Cavalleria*. Salerno: Gentile Editore, 1995.

Curtis, Edmund. *Roger of Sicily and the Normans in Lower Italy*. New York: Putnam's, 1912.

D'Alessandro, Vincenzo. *Storiografica e politica nell'Italia normana*. Napoli: Liguori, 1978.

Daniels, Norman. *The Arabs and Medieval Europe*. London: Longmans, 1975.

Decarreaux, Jean. *Normands, papes et moines*. Paris: A & J Picard, 1974.

Delarc, O. *Les Normands en Italie*. Paris: Ernest Laroux, 1883.

Delogu, Paolo. *I Normanni in Italia*. Naples: Edizioni Liguori, 1984.

Deuve, Jean. *L'Epopée des normandes d'Italie*. Conde sur Noireau: Editions Corlet, 1995.

_____. *Les Services secrets normands*. Conde sur Noireau: Editions Corlet, 1990.

D'Onofrio, Mario, editor. *I Normanni*. Venice: Centro Europeo di Studi Normanni, Marsilio Editori, 1994.

Douglas, David C. *The Norman Achievement*. Berkeley: University of California Press, 1969.

Douib, Abdel Majid. "L'Ifriqiya à l'époque Zirid." *Histoire de la Tunisie*. Tunis: Société Tunisienne de la Diffusion, 1978.

Drell, Joanna H. "Cultural syncretism and ethnic identity: The Norman 'conquest' of Southern Italy and Sicily." *Journal of Medieval History*, Vol 25, No. 3, (1999), pp. 187–302.

France, John. *Western Warfare in the Age of the Crusades*. Ithaca, N.Y.: Cornell University Press, 1999.

Gay, Jules. *L'Italie meridionale et l'empire Byzantin*. Vol I. Paris: Fontemoing, 1904.

Gibbon, Edward. *The Decline and Fall of the Roman Empire*. Vol III. New York: Modern Library, 1995.

Guillou, André, and Filippo Burgarella. *L'Italia Bizantina*. Torino: UTET Libreria, 1988.

Hyde, J.K. *Society and Politcs in Medieval Italy*. New York: St. Martin's Press, 1973.

Idriss, Hady Roger. *La Berberie orientale sous les Zirides*. Paris: Institut d'Études Orientales, Faculté des Lettres et Sciences d'Alger, 1962.

Jamison, Evelyn. "The Sicilian Norman Kingdom in the Mind of Anglo-Norman Contemporaries." *British Academy Proceedings*, Vol XXIV (1938).

Kreutz, Barbara M. *Before the Normans: South Italy in the 9th and 10th Centuries*. Philadelphia: University of Pennsylvania Press, 1996.

Loud, G.A. *The Age of Robert Guiscard*. Essex, England: Harlow, Longman Press 2000.

_____. *Church and Society in the Norman Principality of Capua*. Oxford, England: Oxford U Press, 1985.

Macdonald, A.J. *Hildebrand: A Life of Gregory VII.* London: Methuen & Co, 1932.

Manfroni, Camillo. *Storia della marina italiana.* Vol I. Livorno: Academia Navale, 1899.

Martin, Jean-Marie. *Italies normandes.* Paris: Hachette, 1994.

_____. *La Pouille du VI au XII siècle.* Rome: Ecole Française, 1993.

Matthew, Donald. *The Norman Kingdom of Sicily.* Cambridge, England: Cambridge University Press, 1992.

McGeer, Eric. *Sowing the Dragon's Teeth: Byzantine Warfare in the Tenth Century.* Washington D.C.: Dumbarton Oaks, 1995.

Menager, L.R. *Hommes et institutions de l'Italie Normande.* London: Valorum Reprints, 1981.

Norwich, John. *The Other Conquest.* New York: Harper and Row, 1967.

Oman, Sir Charles W. C. *The Art of War in the Middle Ages.* Vol I. London: Methuen, 1924.

Osborne, James van Wyk. *The Greatest Norman Conquest.* New York: E.P. Dutton, 1937.

Runciman, Stephen. *A History of the Crusades.* Vol I. Cambridge, England: Cambridge University Press, 1954.

Schipa, Michelangelo, and Ferdinand Hirsch. *La Langobardia Meridionale.* Rome: Edizione di Storia e Letteratura, 1968.

Takayama, Hiroshi. *Administration of the Norman Kingdom of Sicily.* New York: E.J. Brill, 1993.

Taviani-Carozzi, Huguette. *La Principauté Lombarde de Salerne.* 2 vols. Rome: École Française, 1991.

_____. *La terreur du monde.* Paris, Fayard, 1996.

Verbrugger, J.F. *The Art of Warfare in Western Europe During the Middle Ages.* Amsterdam: North Holland Publishing Co., 1977.

Wickham, Christopher. *Early Medieval Italy: Central Power and Local Society.* Totowa, N.J.: Barnes and Noble, 1981.

Wolf, Kenneth Baxter. *Making History: The Normans and Their Historians in 11th Century Italy.* Philadelphia: University of Pennsylvania Press, 1995.

Index

Abelard (son of Humphrey Hauteville)
83, 123, 125, 141–3, 155–6, 161
Abul Kare 105, 124
Aceranza 50
Adelaide del Vasto (Regent of Sicily)
193–4
Adrano 175
Agrigento 104, 109, 110, 176, 185
Ahmad al Akhal 34–6
Aielo 124
Al Hafs 34
Alberada of Buonalbergo 61, 97, 143
Alexander II (pope) 114–5, 119, 123,
139, 141, 143
Alexius Comnenus (Byzantine
emperor) 61, 163–6, 168, 1769, 189
Ali Ibn Tamim 117
Amalfi 10, 25, 63, 81, 141, 146, 160,
174
Ami of Giovenazzo 123, 141–2, 155
Anacletus II (pope) 197
Andria 156
Anna Comnena 61, 181
Antioch 190
Apulia (description) 40–2
Ardouin 36–40, 43, 44, 51, 69
Argyrizzos 131–2, 156
Argyrus Marianus (Duke of Langobar-
dia) 22, 38, 41, 44, 46–9, 53, 70, 73,
75, 80, 125, 129
Ascetlin of Aceranza 50, 57
Ascoli 40, 50, 169
Atenulf of Benevento 43–4
Aubrey Hauteville 28, 30
Aversa 4, 26, 37, 39, 57, 63, 133
Ayub Ibn Tamim 117, 126–7

Bari 21, 43, 44, 48, 58, 78, 95, 99, 124,
128, 129–33, 137, 156, 169, 174, 186
Basil the Bulgar Slayer (Byzantine
emperor) 10, 22, 34
Benedict X (antipope) 88–90, 94
Benevento 8–10, 24, 56, 66, 69, 72–3,
77, 79, 91, 143, 147, 154–5, 173, 193,
197
Bisceglie 156
Bisignano 60, 82
Bohemund (Prince of Antioch) 97, 143,
163, 165–6, 169–70, 177, 180–1, 184–5,
186–90, 194
Bojoannes, Basil (Byzantine governor)
22, 26, 33
Bojoannes (son of Basil) 43–4
Brindisi 99, 105, 114, 124, 130, 133, 156,
185
Butera 186

Calabria (description) 58–9
Cannae 22, 42, 142, 169
Canosa 150, 170
Caphalonia 181
Capua 10, 22, 24, 26–7, 30, 54–5, 69,
81, 85, 89, 115, 141, 145, 147, 155, 169,
187–9, 193, 196–7
Cariati 99
Castrogiovanni 108–9, 122, 185–6
Catania 108, 122, 133–4, 176–7
Cefalu 120
Ceprano 157, 160
Cerami 118, 122, 126
Cerularius (Patriarch of Constantino-
ple) 73–4, 80
Cisternino 142

Civitate 9, 51, 71, 75, 80, 172
Clement (antipope) 171, 173, 187
Clement II (pope) 54
Cluny Abbey 65, 188
Conrad II (Holy Roman Emperor) 26, 30
Constantine (Byzantine prince) 162–3
Constantine Ducas (Byzantine emperor) 78
Constantine Monomachus (Byzantine emperor) 47, 68, 73–4, 125
Conversano 77
Corato 156
Corfu 164, 179, 181, 184
Cosenza 82
Crusades 119, 136, 144

Desiderius (Abbot of Monte Cassino) 89, 91, 139, 144–5, 151–2, 156–7, 187
Donation of Constantine 11, 73, 93, 144
Drogo Hauteville (Count of Apulia) 28, 30, 35, 39, 50, 53–6, 57, 67, 77, 92
Durazzo 122, 124, 127, 131, 164–6, 179

Eboli 82
Enna see Castrogiovanni
Eremberga of Mortain 178

Fermo 158, 160, 197
Frederick of Lorraine see Stephen IX
Frederick II (Holy Roman Emperor) 199
Fressenda (daughter of Fressenda of Hauteville) 81
Fressenda Hauteville 28, 30

Gaeta 10, 25, 81, 115
Galeria 89–90
Gallipoli 778, 185
Gargano 21, 50, 66, 77
Gauthier (son of Ami) 51, 71, 83
Genoa 33
Geoffrey (son of Roger Hauteville) 178
Geoffrey Hauteville (Count of the Capitanata) 28, 77–8, 82, 91, 95, 99, 144
Geoffrey of Conversano 123, 125, 155, 168, 175, 185
Geoffrey of Taranto 124, 155
Gerace 86, 92, 99, 111–2
Giovinazzo 43
Girard of Buonalbergo 61, 66

Gisulf II (Prince of Salerno) 70–1, 80–2, 96–8, 115, 123, 141–2, 145–8, 152–3
Gregory VII (pope) 68, 88–92, 114, 141, 143–8, 149–52, 154, 156–8, 159–60, 162, 163–73, 187, 189
Guaimar IV (Prince of Salerno) 28, 30, 35, 43–4, 46, 49, 50, 53–5, 63, 67–70, 80
Guiscard see Robert Hauteville
Guy (Duke of Sorrento) 50, 69–70, 81, 98, 115, 142
Guy (son of Robert Hauteville) 180, 184

Harald Hardrada (King of Norway) 35
Helen (daughter of Robert Hauteville) 151, 161, 163
Henry II (Holy Roman Emperor) 13, 54–6, 63, 65–6, 71, 73, 79
Henry III (Holy Roman Emperor) 23, 26
Henry IV (Holy Roman Emperor) 79, 122, 148, 149–50, 157–8, 159–60, 162, 163–4, 168–71, 187, 189
Henry VI Hohestaufen (Holy Roman Emperor) 199
Herman (son of Humphrey Hauteville) 83, 123, 141–2, 156, 161, 168–9
Hildebrand see Gregory VII
Honorius (antipope) 114–5, 122, 141
Humbert (Bishop of Mourmoutiers) 74
Humbert Hauteville 28
Humphey Hauteville (Count of Apulia) 7, 14, 29, 57–8, 69–71, 76–8, 81–3, 92

Ibn al Hawas (Qaid of Agrigento) 103, 108–9, 115, 117, 126
Ibn al Ward 176
Ibn Hamud (Emir of Castrogiovanni) 185
Ibn Timnah (Qaid of Syracuse) 103, 108, 111, 122
Innocent II (pope) 197
Isaac Comnenus (Byzantine emperor) 78, 80

Jerusalem 189–90
Jocelyn de Hareng 77, 123, 125

Jordan (Prince of Capua) 154–6, 157, 159, 162, 168–9, 184, 187–8
Jordan (son of Roger Hauteville) 176–9
Judith of Evreux 110, 115–7, 131, 134, 178

Kastoria 166, 170, 179

Landulf (Prince of Benevento) 79, 145, 154
Larissa 170
Lateran Synod 91, 114
Lavello 40, 57
Lecce 78, 124
Leo IX (pope) 7–9, 12–14, 65–75, 92, 159

Mabrikas (Byzantine admiral) 124–5
Mahdia 127, 176, 186, 191
Maida 85
Malta 134, 186
Maniakes, George (Byzantine general) 36–8, 46–7
Manzikert 140
Martirano 82
Matera 43, 46, 49, 78, 123
Mauger Hauteville (Count of the Capitanata) 28, 77–8, 82, 95, 99, 105, 124
Mazara 137, 175, 176
Melfi 4, 38–42, 50–1, 85–6, 91–2, 105–6, 142, 169, 196
Melo 21–2, 41
Menzel el Emir (Missilmeri) 127
Messina 36, 105–8, 115, 130, 137, 177, 195
Michael VII (Byzantine emperor) 140, 146, 151, 161–3
Milazzo 106
Mileto 86, 104, 106, 110, 111, 192
Minervino 78
Monomachus, George 164
Monoppli 44, 46
Monte Cassino, Abbey 25, 26, 30, 53, 55, 80, 89–90, 91, 139–40, 145, 173
Montemaggiore 42
Montepeloso 43–4, 125
Monte Sant' Angelo 21, 50
Muriella Hauteville 28

Naples 10, 25, 26–7, 145, 154–5, 188, 193, 197

Nardo 78
Nicastro 86, 88, 101
Nicholas II (pope) 89–94, 95, 96, 114, 141, 159, 188
Nicotera 176–7
Noto 186

Olivento 42
Oria 78, 99, 105, 114, 169, 185
Otranto 78, 99, 124, 133, 156, 169, 180, 181, 185

Palermo 109, 119, 122, 125, 126–7, 133–7, 139, 174, 187, 192, 194, 197
Palleologus, George 164–6
Pandulf IV (Prince of Capua) 26–7, 30, 35, 46, 53–6, 57, 89
Paterno 175
Perenos (Duke of Durazzo) 105–6, 122, 124, 196
Peter (Archbishop of Amalfi) 74
Peter of Tyre 60, 100
Pierre of Trani 51, 54, 71, 83, 85, 123
Pierre II of Trani 123, 141–2, 155
Pisa 33, 119, 147
Policastro 81–2, 101, 154

Ragusa 162
Rainulf II (Count of Aversa) 53–4, 57
Rainulf Dregnot (Count of Aversa) 26–8, 30, 50, 53
Rametta 35
Reggio 86, 99, 101, 107, 133, 177
Richard II (Prince of Capua) 188, 196
Richard Dregnot (Count of Aversa and Prince of Capua) 4, 7, 57, 71–2, 81–2, 85, 90, 91–4, 96, 114, 123, 140–2, 145–6, 151–2, 154
Richer (Abbot of Monte Cassino) 89
Robert (Prince of Capua) 196, 198
Robert Areng 141–2
Robert Hauteville, the Guiscard (Duke of Apulia) 4, 7, 57, 59–62, 70, 72, 77–8, 82–4, 85–8, 89, 91–4, 95–101, 105–10, 111–2, 114–5, 120–1, 122–5, 127–8, 129–38, 139–48, 149–58, 159–66, 168–73, 174–5, 178, 179–82, 184, 190
Robert of Grantmesnil 110
Robert of Loritello (Count of the Capitanata) 82, 144, 147, 154, 187

Robert of Montescaglioso 123, 155
Roger II (King of Sicily) 193–8
Roger Borsa (Duke of Apulia) 143–4,
　163, 169, 172, 176–7, 180–1, 184–5,
　186–8, 194
Roger Hauteville (Great Count of
　Sicily) 4, 28, 86–8, 92, 95, 98–9, 100,
　103–4, 105–12, 114–21, 122, 125–7,
　130–2, 139, 140, 152, 162, 169, 174–9,
　184–6, 187, 191
Rollo the Viking 16
Romanus Diogenes (Byzantine
　emperor) 125
Rome 12, 54, 89–90, 94, 114, 157, 164,
　168–73, 187, 197
Rossano 99

Salerno 10, 24, 26, 30, 35, 37, 53, 66,
　71, 80–2, 96–8, 114, 133, 143, 146,
　152–4, 160, 173, 174, 180, 187, 195, 197
San Marco Argentano 60, 82
San Marco d'Alunzio 110
San Severino 154
Sardinia 119
Scalea 87
Sergius (Prince of Naples) 26–7
Serlo (son of Serlo Hauteville) 29, 106,
　117–8, 134, 137
Serlo Hauteville 28–9
Sichelgaita of Salerno 97, 124, 134, 138,
　141, 143, 151, 152, 155–6, 163, 181–2,
　184
Simon (Count of Sicily) 193–4
Siponto 50, 66, 71
Sorrento 30
Squillace 86, 88
Stephen (Byzantine admiral) 36–8, 47
Stephen IX (pope) 71, 74, 79, 80, 82–3,
　86, 90
Syracuse 35, 122, 176–7, 185

Tamim (Zirid Emir of Mahdia) 117,
　176

Tancred (Prince of Galilee) 189
Tancred (son of Tancred Hauteville)
　28, 30
Tancred of Hauteville 4, 28, 30, 193–4,
　198–9
Tancred of Lecce (King of Sicily) 198–9
Taormina 176
Taranto 46, 70, 99, 105, 124, 156, 185
Touboeuf, Hugh 42, 51
Touboeuf, Roger 123, 125
Trani 46, 48, 51, 78, 142–3, 156
Trapani 176
Tricarico 58, 59
Troia 22, 41, 44, 49, 58, 99, 169
Troina 35, 115–7, 118, 134, 182

Urban II (pope) 187, 189, 192–3

Val de Crati 58–9, 82
Val Demone 34, 103, 108–9, 115, 118,
　122, 137
Val Mazara 137
Valona 164, 179–80
Varangian Guard 22, 35, 42, 124, 165–6
Venice 164, 166, 179–80
Venosa 40, 42, 50, 58, 92, 181, 185
Victor II (pope) 79
Victor III (pope) *see* Desiderius

William (Duke of Apulia) 194–5
William I (King of Sicily) 198
William II (King of Sicily) 198
William Hauteville (Count of the Prin-
　cipata) 28, 77, 82, 87, 95, 97–8, 141,
　146
William Hauteville, "Ironarm" (Count
　of Apulia) 28, 30, 35, 37, 39, 43–4,
　49–51, 53, 198
William the Conqueror (Duke of Nor-
　mandy) 20, 123, 182, 196

Zirid Emirate 34, 103, 117, 127, 176, 191
Zoe (Byzantine Empress) 36, 47